WE ANSWER
TO ANOTHER

WE ANSWER TO ANOTHER

Authority, Office, and the Image of God

David T. Koyzis

☙PICKWICK *Publications* • Eugene, Oregon

WE ANSWER TO ANOTHER
Authority, Office, and the Image of God

Copyright © 2014 David T. Koyzis. All rights reserved. Except for brief quotations in critical publications or reviews, no part of this book may be reproduced in any manner without prior written permission from the publisher. Write: Permissions, Wipf and Stock Publishers, 199 W. 8th Ave., Suite 3, Eugene, OR 97401.

The Message. Copyright © 1993, 1994, 1995, 1996, 2000, 2001, 2002. Used by permission of NavPress Publishing Group.

The Holy Bible, New Living Translation. Copyright © 1996, 2004, 2007 by Tyndale House Foundation. Used by permission of Tyndale House Publishers, Inc., Carol Stream, Illinois 60188. All rights reserved.

Revised Standard Version of the Bible, copyright © 1946, 1952, and 1971 the Division of Christian Education of the National Council of the Churches of Christ in the United States of America. Used by permission. All rights reserved.

New Revised Standard Version Bible, copyright 1989, Division of Christian Education of the National Council of the Churches of Christ in the United States of America. Used by permission. All rights reserved.

Pickwick Publications
An Imprint of Wipf and Stock Publishers
199 W. 8th Ave., Suite 3
Eugene, OR 97401

www.wipfandstock.com

ISBN 13: 978-1-62564-045-1

Cataloguing-in-Publication data:

Koyzis, David Theodore

    We answer to another : authority, office, and the image of god / David T. Koyzis.

    viii + 238 pp. ; 23 cm. Includes bibliographical references and indices.

    ISBN 13: 978-1-62564-045-1

    1. Authority—Religious Aspects—Christianity. 2. Christianity and Politics. I. Title.

BR115.P7 K655 2014

Manufactured in the U.S.A.

Contents

Acknowledgements | vii

1. Introduction: Defining The Problem | 1
2. Authority And Power | 17
3. Authority And Autonomy | 59
4. Authority And Legitimacy | 93
5. Office: The Key To Authority | 134
6. The Pluriformity Of Authority | 160
7. Epilogue: Authority And Love | 222

Bibliography | 227
Index | 239

Acknowledgements

MY INTEREST IN AUTHORITY could be said to extend back to the time when, as a small child, I was told to "mind Mommy and Daddy," that is, to obey them. I didn't think much about it at the time, except to note that, if I failed to do so, I could expect to be punished accordingly. But already on a deeper level I intuitively recognized that they bore an office worthy of respect, something reinforced by the Decalogue's command to honor father and mother. A decade or so later, as a young man, I was not so certain that authority should be obeyed, especially if its commands were oppressive or conflicted with Jesus' teachings in the Sermon on the Mount. Another decade passed before I would undertake a study of authority in the course of my dissertation at the University of Notre Dame, focusing on the thought of philosophers Yves R. Simon and Herman Dooyeweerd. Later yet I would become persuaded that authority is very important indeed and that lack of respect for it entails nothing less than a denial of humanity's creation in God's image.

Because I have spent so much time on the subject in recent years, I have been told that I am now an authority on authority. If so, I am the first to admit that I have not become so by myself. In fact, a solid understanding of the place of authority in human life would prevent me making such a claim, because we all in some fashion answer to others who have contributed to making us who we are. In acknowledging the following people, I recognize the God-given authority they possess in their respective fields of endeavor, as exercised in a diversity of offices rooted in their status as divine image-bearers. Accordingly I would like to thank the following people: James W. Skillen, retired president of the Center for Public Justice, Annapolis, Maryland, is someone whom, though never formally a teacher of mine, I have come to regard as something of a mentor. My good friend and emeritus colleague Albert M. Wolters did indeed teach me more than three decades ago, and I have benefitted again and again from conversations with him on precisely the issues I treat in this book.

Anthony O. Simon, son of philosopher Yves R. Simon, was of considerable help to me as I researched my dissertation at the University of Notre Dame in the 1980s, and he has been of further assistance as I wrote this book. Russell D. Kosits is an esteemed colleague, close friend and nearly a brother. Although we are in different fields, our frequent conversations have stimulated my thinking as I have worked through the issues raised by this project. Rob Joustra, Brian Dijkema, Paul Brink, Ed Bosveld, Jane VanStarkenburg Wouda, and Hendrik Vlaar were once students of mine. Not only have conversations with them played a role in shaping the argument of this book, but their continuing loyalty and affection over the years have been personally and professionally gratifying.

My Redeemer University colleagues Harry Van Dyke, Derek Schuurman, James Vanderwoerd, Kevin Flatt, James Rusthoven, Jacob Ellens, Vahagn Asatryan, Kevin VanderMeulen, Elaine Botha, Robert MacLarkey, Wytse van Dijk, John Byl, and Peter Schuurman read partial or complete manuscripts, or provided input in other ways, especially in the context of a monthly faculty discussion group. Shortly before I finished this project, Fr. Victor Lee Austin published what may be the best book in decades on the subject of authority. I gratefully acknowledge his contribution to the ongoing conversation, along with input he kindly gave me on a section of the manuscript. Thanks also go to Harry Antonides (Christian Labour Association of Canada), Darren Walhof (Grand Valley State University), Alex Tuckness (Iowa State University), Gideon Strauss (Max De Pree Center for Leadership), William G. Witt (Trinity School for Ministry), Bruce C. Wearne, Percy Harrison (Eton College, England), Bryan T. McGraw (Wheaton College), and Kathy Vandergrift (Canadian Coalition for the Rights of Children) for their assistance with this project. I thank my wife, Dr. Nancy Calvert-Koyzis, whose keen editorial eye prompted me to abandon some infelicities of expression. I am grateful to Redeemer University College, not only for providing two sabbatical leaves enabling me to start and complete this book, but for providing an exceptional community that has shaped me as a person, scholar, and child of God over more than a quarter of a century. Naturally, although I recognize the authority of these fellow image-bearers of God, I (authoritatively!) assume full responsibility for any defects in this book.

Finally, I would like to express my profound gratitude to my parents, Theodore and Jane Koyzis, who brought me into this world, raised me along with my sisters and brother, and taught us to love God and neighbor with our whole hearts. This book is affectionately dedicated to these two godly exemplars of parental authority.

1

Introduction: Defining the Problem

The Ubiquity of Authority

IT IS MONDAY MORNING. *Michael, a third-year university student, has washed up, dressed himself, and headed out the door. He walks to the cafeteria a quarter of a mile away for breakfast. He joins two friends from his 9 o'clock class at the table, and afterwards they walk together to the building next door where the class will shortly begin. They arrive five minutes early, but are unable to find seats because some of the chairs were removed the previous evening by the drama club. The professor, Dr. Stepanic, asks the three students to bring in more chairs from outside. After class he will phone maintenance to see that the university's policy concerning the removal of furniture is reiterated and enforced. Class begins. Dr. Stepanic reads a short passage from Shakespeare's* King Lear *and begins lecturing on the literary theories of a well-known British scholar. A young woman in the second row raises her hand and asks a question on the assigned reading. Dr. Stepanic asks whether anyone else in the class might be able to address the question. An animated discussion ensues. Near the end of the hour, he tells the students that the class will not be meeting on Wednesday, because he will be away at a conference. In the meantime, they are to keep up with the readings, on which he will give a short quiz when they next meet on Friday.*

After class Michael stops off at the Student Senate office where he usually spends two hours on Monday in his capacity as representative of his residence hall. Here he has two matters to attend to: first, a campus-wide dance planned for Saturday evening; and, second, a petition to be presented to the vice president of facilities-planning requesting that on-campus organizations be given priority over off-campus groups in the rental of rooms outside of class hours. At noon Michael leaves campus to meet a friend at a local fast-food restaurant. He stops at the corner and waits for the walk signal before crossing the street. Because of construction on the street at the north edge of campus, he makes a detour around the block to get to the restaurant, as indicated by the orange signs at the perimeter of the work zone. After lunch he walks to the shoe store where he will be working for the summer. He turns in the form he was asked to fill out when he was hired two weeks earlier. Then he is off to his afternoon classes and studying in between.

At 5 o'clock Michael and a group of his friends play an impromptu game of basketball in the court outside their residence hall. After a quick shower and supper in the cafeteria, Michael phones his parents to let them know that his plans to visit them have been delayed by one week. Although he had originally planned to see them the weekend after the dance, he had volunteered in the meantime to help out at a local food bank that had requested Student Senate's help. His father assures Michael that they understand and will be looking forward to seeing him in three weekends.

In the evening Michael goes to the library to research a paper due in two weeks for his comparative political science class. The topic is Maurice Duverger's theory on the relationship between electoral and party systems in democracies. After spending three hours there, Michael heads back to the residence where he gets into a discussion with his roommate on the relative merits of the New York Mets and the Atlanta Braves. Before retiring, he checks out the baseball scores on the internet and responds to some email. Then off to bed around midnight.

When young people leave the parental home for the first time, they are often struck by the amount of freedom they suddenly have. They can stay up as late as they want. They can set their own schedules. They do not have to be home at a set time for supper, and they are not subject to a parentally-imposed curfew. Even more dramatically, they are being exposed for the first time to new ideas that challenge previous assumptions. The right to think for themselves and to test the intellectual waters is one that young people often find intoxicating. Everything seems possible. The world appears capable of being shaped to conform to these new ideas, and the prospect of making a difference as they stand on the brink of adulthood leaves them breathless with anticipation.

Yet if we look at Michael's day more carefully, we will see that he is not completely free to do as he pleases. At every juncture he comes face-to-face with some form of authority, though he may not immediately recognize it as such. The smooth functioning of his residence depends on a complex of formal and informal rules conditioning life within its walls. Michael himself plays a role in this as representative of his hall in Student Senate. He thus possesses a certain *performative authority*[1] relative to his residence, authorizing him to act on its behalf and to speak for its interests in that body.

Within the classroom, when Dr. Stepanic asks Michael and his friends to bring in the chairs from outside, he is acting within his *authority as the principal coordinator* of the classroom community. To be sure, others bear primary responsibility for ensuring that classrooms are adequately furnished, but in their absence Dr. Stepanic steps in and deals with the matter himself. No one denies his right to do this. As for the course and its subject matter, Dr. Stepanic has the recognized authority to plan its contents and to set the standards to which his students are expected to conform. Much of this is due to his being an authority within the academic discipline he is teaching, as recognized by his possession of the PhD from another university. Yet even having what might be called *epistemic authority*, that is, an authority based on command of a specific field of knowledge, he inevitably appeals to other such authorities, including the British literary scholar. Finally the very conduct of the class depends on the larger university context in which the Senate sets academic standards, the registrar schedules courses, and the staff and administration ensure that everything operates as it should. Most basically, Dr. Stepanic himself, for all his expertise as an epistemic authority in the field of English literature, would have no right to lecture this class apart from the *authoritative office of professor*, which depends on the accreditation of his university.

The subordinate authority of Student Senate is subject to the superior authority of the administration and board of governors. But it does have a certain *performative*, as well as *imperative* authority, enabling it to act to advance and maintain the quality of student life on campus. As Michael heads off campus for lunch, he implicitly acknowledges the authoritative character of pedestrian signals and detour signs, as well as of his future summer employer. His other activities, ranging from the spontaneous basketball game to his time spent in the library, are embedded within a complex pattern of authoritative rules, institutions, relationships, and interactions.

---

1. The taxonomy of authority represented here borrows in part from that of De George, *The Nature and Limits of Authority*, which we shall discuss more fully in chapter 6.

The phone conversation with his parents is noteworthy, because on one interpretation it highlights the freedom Michael now has from his parents' immediate authoritative oversight. However, an equally plausible interpretation would have his parents' increasingly recognizing and respecting Michael's newly acquired *authority* over the direction of his own life. What some might call his *personal freedom* is, as we shall argue below, *one more manifestation of authority*. This is an important point to bear in mind, because it stands in contrast to much of contemporary theory, which posits at least a dialectical tension, if not an outright antagonism between authority and freedom. If Michael's day is characterized by contact with a variety of authoritative agents, one of these agents is, quite simply, Michael himself, who exercises more than one authoritative office and is himself subject to other such offices.

Authority is found everywhere there are human beings, and most visibly insofar as they live together in community. The connection between community and authority would seem evident on one level, although many are loath to accept it. Even the most virtuous and community-minded of people do not cooperate spontaneously and need, at the very least, an overall coordinating authority, if not necessarily one with coercive power. An entrepreneur organizing a bicycle-manufacturing enterprise can hardly depend on its members individually coming up with compatible part sizes, quantity of components, production schedules, and so forth, simply because human beings have limited knowledge and capacities. This is the first and most basic argument for authority. As philosopher Yves R. Simon puts it, authority is needed to choose among equally good alternative means and to determine both form and substance of the common good. Or, to put it in less scholastic terms, authority's communal coordinative function is needed to secure the community's very existence and unity of action.

Yet even to mention authority in conversation is to risk a negative response in many people. It is by no means incidental that, when Simon begins his classic study of authority,[2] he does so by reflecting on the bad reputation it has acquired since the eighteenth century. Americans annually celebrate a rebellion in the 1770s and '80s to secure independence from the authority of the British Parliament and Crown over the thirteen colonies. Britons celebrate the Glorious Revolution of 1688 establishing parliamentary sovereignty against royal authority. And the Dutch look

2. Simon, *General Theory of Authority*. We shall explore Simon's theory as well more fully in chapter 6.

back to the Eighty Years War against Spanish rule. Yet it may be that, more than any other act of rebellion, the French Revolution of 1789 effectively solidified in the western imagination something of the mythology of heroic popular revolt against oppressive authority. So effective was the Revolution in doing this that many are inclined to identify authority *per se* with at least potential oppression, irrespective of what it actually does and how it functions.

At one time it was generally assumed that those defying authority were committing a grave sin imperiling their eternal salvation. They were acting so as to overturn a God-given social and political order, and were little better than common criminals. Nowadays it is often, if not always, assumed that legitimate complaints undergird an insurrection, however violent its effects, and that governmental efforts to quell a rebellion are almost intrinsically repressive.

During a church service near Toronto in early 1994, shortly after the Chiapas revolt broke out in southern Mexico, prayer requests were invited from the front.[3] A parishioner stood up and asked that prayers be offered for the people of Chiapas, that they might receive justice and no longer find it necessary to rise up against the government to advance their cause. The request was duly noted and it was included in the subsequent prayer. What is striking in this incident is that no one in the congregation found such a request at all unusual or out of line. Of course, one would not wish to deny the likelihood of legitimate grievances underlying such an uprising, particularly as it follows upon centuries of oppression of the indigenous peoples of the region. All the same, a few hundred years ago, if a popular revolt broke out against a sitting government, one might have heard a clergyman pray that God would bring down his righteous wrath on the rebels and that the governing authorities, whom he calls to defend justice and punish lawbreakers, might be instruments of that wrath.[4] So thoroughly have attitudes changed that now, if someone were to stand up and request a prayer along these lines, she would at least raise eyebrows and cause discomfort in the pews.

Why have authority and its exercise acquired such a bad name? Simon gives four reasons for this.[5] First, it would seem to stand in conflict

---

3. This episode comes from the author's personal experience.

4. Witness, e.g., the attitude of Martin Luther towards the Peasants' Revolt of 1524–26, which he condemned unequivocally. See Luther, *Against the Robbing and Murdering Hordes of Peasants*.

5. Simon, *General Theory*, 14–20.

with justice. If a government reflexively cracks down on malcontents, it may be guilty of overlooking the justice of their cause. Second, it appears to conflict with the spontaneity and vitality of human life by artificially inhibiting it. How many beneficial inventions might have been stillborn if a government had placed too many constraints on personal innovation? Third, the imposition of authority is reputed to curtail the search for truth, a contention on which John Stuart Mill elaborates at some length in his famous treatise, *On Liberty*.[6] This, of course, raises the epistemological issue of how one apprehends truth. If a government claiming to uphold the entire truth is in error at this basic level, then the imposition of authority at such a point may indeed suppress the truth. Fourth and finally, authority seems often to be connected with human arbitrariness and thus opposed to the universality and stability of law. Other more concrete reasons could be given for this bad reputation, e.g., empirical abuses of authority, ranging from Vietnam and Watergate in the US to the sexual abuse scandals in the Catholic Church, and a plethora of authoritarian and totalitarian régimes in various parts of the globe. Whenever authority is abused, this abuse inevitably reflects poorly on the authoritative office itself and can effectively immobilize the community for which it is responsible.

One might add another objection, which updates Simon's survey into what many label the postmodern era. Marx and his heirs, as well as the more recent deconstructionists, see all authority as little more than self-interested (or, perhaps more accurately, class- or group-interested) domination by one set of people over another. Within this conception, any claim that an authoritative officeholder is acting in the interest of those under her authority cannot be believed. A *hermeneutic of suspicion* must therefore be applied to such claims in an effort to unmask the collective self-interested will behind what is essentially only an exercise of raw power. In this perspective, the classic writings of Plato, Aristotle, Cicero, and Thomas Aquinas are nothing more than the ruminations of those notorious dead, white European males attempting to protect their own material interests against everyone else.

---

6. Mill, *On Liberty*.

Plan of Book

If authority is so intimately connected with our very humanity, then we must begin our discussion by asking what authority is. We shall do this in some detail in chapter 2, initially by distinguishing it from the various capacities or powers at its disposal. There is a complex relationship between power and authority that rules out a facile identification of the two. Yet they cannot be completely separated either and usually tend in some fashion to go together in the real world. The poet not only has the ability, viz., the power, to write poetry but is also authorized to do so under many circumstances. However, if she tries to write a poem while operating heavy machinery in a construction zone during working hours, she can be said to lack the authority to do something she is nevertheless quite capable of doing in a different context. Authority itself can be said to exert a certain tacit power over those subject to it, yet that power can quickly evaporate if the latter refuse to recognize it. What this tells us is that power is often more extensive than authority while formal authority may become an empty concept in the absence of the power to give it effect.

Because Michael is young and in the process of developing the capacities that come with adulthood, we may recognize him to be a powerful person—more powerful than the child he was a few years earlier but less powerful than he will be in the future. He appears to be cultivating well the several skills, or powers, needed to live the life he is growing into, including the abilities to manage his time, to research topics in more than one academic field, to write, to work hard at what he does, and to judge the propriety of contemplated actions. More basically he can walk, sleep, eat, play basketball, and use the computer. Yet as he grows into adulthood, he also recognizes that the proper exercise of these powers requires wisdom and discipline. He may, of course, decide on one occasion to skip a class to play basketball, but if he is mature enough, he will likely see that doing so repeatedly will hamper his education and make it more difficult to reach his longer-range life goals.

This is where authority enters the picture. We cannot exercise all of our powers whenever and wherever we please. There is a time and a place for everything, and we necessarily answer to authority in our use of these powers, even as we ourselves possess the authority to use them. Although there may be more such categories, we shall focus on six common ways of defining authority which have erroneously identified it with some form of power, namely, (1) psychological control, (2) persuasion, (3) physical power, (4) voluntary contract, (5) biological superiority and (6) superior knowledge. By contrast, we shall argue that *authority is resident in an office given us at creation. Indeed, when we encounter authority, we encounter nothing less than the image of God, which always points beyond itself.* The reality of this office is something firmly anchored in our common human experience but all too frequently denied by those attempting to grasp that experience theoretically. As we will discover in chapter 5, office is not a static position but a commission, an assignment, or a calling to which a proper response on our part is expected. It is other-oriented in that it is focused on service to God and to our fellow human beings, generally within a particular communal context. Nevertheless, although we often think of such offices as the presidency or chairmanship as loci of authority, we can also apply the notion of authoritative office to our very status as human beings, which the Christian tradition describes as the *imago Dei*, or image of God. Thus much of what the post-Kantian ethical tradition conceives of as respect for human rights in the face of external authority must rather be seen as respect for nothing less than an *authoritative office resident in the human person as person*. Where political authorities become tyrannical and impinge on what we would ordinarily think of as individual freedom, we might alternatively see this as a clash of authoritative offices, with one usurping responsibilities properly belonging to the other.

What of the relationship between authority and power? Authority is sometimes defined as the legitimate exercise of power. This is adequate as an initial description, as long as it is recognized that authority as such precedes the exercise of power. In human hands, power, we are persuaded, must logically follow authority. If authority is tantamount to responsible agency, then power is the capacity to give effect to that agency. To be sure once again, not every exercise of power is backed by authority, e.g., the ability of a thief to make off with someone else's property. The power possessed by animals, e.g., that enabling a bird to fly or a horse to gallop, is certainly God-given and appropriately exercised by them, although it cannot be tied to authority *per se*, since animals cannot be said to possess responsible agency. Nevertheless, although authority and power are distinct concepts, in the real world they tend to be closely connected. In the Bible we often read that, when God calls someone to a particular task, he equips or empowers them to do the task by his Spirit. When God called Moses to speak to Pharaoh on behalf of the Israelites, Moses protested: "Oh, my Lord, I have never been eloquent, neither in the past nor even now that you have spoken to your servant; but I am slow of speech and slow of tongue" (Exod 4:10 NRSV). Although God had called Moses to a particular prophetic office invested with authority, Moses feared that his abilities were lacking and that he was therefore not up to the task. Yet God promised to empower Moses and his brother Aaron for the task he had assigned them.

In addition to conflating authority with power, there is another widespread tendency which we shall take up in chapter 3, namely, to play off authority and personal autonomy as though these were in some fashion opposite principles or at least in tension with one another. As noted above, our undergraduate Michael is now out of the parental home. Within the broad parameters of university life, he is free to schedule his day as he sees fit. While at home, he may have clashed with his parents on this very issue. They perhaps wished him to complete his homework, while he preferred to go outside and play baseball with friends. Now he is free from the immediacy of parental supervision on this and other issues. Yet, as we noted above, he is in reality constrained on all sides by the multiple manifestations of authority that contribute to ordinary life.

The tradition of political liberalism makes much of the human desire for freedom. The recognition of this desire has conditioned the philosophies of Thomas Hobbes and John Locke, and, in somewhat different fashion, of Jean-Jacques Rousseau and Immanuel Kant. Even Karl Marx, who scorned the liberties championed by liberals as mere "bourgeois" freedoms, nevertheless held out hope for the arrival of a classless society, to be ushered in by a messianic proletariat, who will have liberated themselves from the oppression of capitalism. In such a society everyone will be much freer than before because the ancient division of labor, on which all class antagonisms are based, will have been transcended and abolished. Anarchists have taken the desire for freedom very far indeed, assuming that the authority of some over others can be altogether supplanted by an egalitarian mutuality.

Towards the end of the 1960s, secondary-school dress codes in North America were largely abandoned on the grounds that they impaired the freedom of the adolescent students to dress as they pleased. Especially in the United States, where the attainment of freedom has a strong place in the national civil religious narrative, this argument resonated with many, and those few defending the codes lost ground nearly everywhere. In such a context, if freedom and authority are conceived as polar opposites, then, whenever they are seen to come into conflict, freedom must necessarily triumph over the long term.

One of the more formidable challenges to authority of all kinds comes from Immanuel Kant and his heirs, including Stanley Milgram, Lawrence Kohlberg and John Rawls. Kantians believe that being subject to authority is a sign of ethical immaturity and that progress towards full adult autonomy requires that a form of moral reasoning known as the categorical imperative be applied to every human action. To accept the authority of a will not our own is to fail to live up to full adult responsibility. To be sure, not all Kantians will go as far as Robert Paul Wolff in embracing anarchism.[7] Yet Wolff may be correct in seeing this as the logical implication of Kant's theories. In any event, the Kantian school is a powerful one which has been extraordinarily influential and which we shall examine in some detail in chapter 3 below.

Over the past two or so centuries then, at least since the rise of nominalism in philosophy and liberalism in political theory, we have not been altogether comfortable with the notion of authority. Why indeed should we defer to a will outside of our own? Modern and postmodern human beings deem authority intrinsically demeaning and alienating, insofar as it apparently calls on us to suppress ourselves, our desires and our aspirations at the behest of something other than ourselves. In the worst of circumstances, authority might even call on us to do something we know to be wrong and injurious to others. This is the finding of Stanley Milgram's notorious experiments at Yale University in the early 1960s, with which we shall begin chapter 3.[8] If people believe that a legitimate authority is instructing them to act in a particular fashion, they will tend to obey this instruction, even if it calls them to inflict harm on another person. The pretext that they were only obeying orders was appealed to repeatedly by Nazi German functionaries who found themselves on trial for committing crimes against humanity. Given Milgram's findings, it is perhaps understandable that some might see the solution to such injustices to lie in a general minimization of authority's scope and the expansion of individual autonomy to as great an extent as possible.

Of course, such a solution—if it can be called such—presupposes that our own wills, liberated from a variety of immediate external authoritative impositions, will inevitably act virtuously when freed from

---

7. Wolff, *In Defense of Anarchism*.
8. Milgram, *Obedience to Authority*.

the latter's apparently corrosive influence. Much of the allure of such ideologies as liberalism, democratism, nationalism, and socialism lies in their claims that it is a fairly simple matter to remove impediments to human flourishing, by, e.g., maximizing individual freedom and expanding the scope of human rights, granting the franchise to increasing numbers of citizens, liberating a national community from foreign domination, or implementing collective ownership of property. In their initial stages, revolutions are often accompanied by popular euphoria at having been liberated from a tyrannical régime. But as they follow the logic of revolution, its leaders themselves all too often become tyrannical, sometimes outstripping the recently deposed rulers in their oppressiveness and in atrocities committed. Contrary to the claims for human autonomy, it turns out that authority is an inescapable reality for human beings. Even when the individual acts in her own interest without receiving explicit instruction from without, she does so under myriad influences which have formed her from birth. Those who liberate themselves from one authority must necessarily subject themselves to another. Even the personal authority so often described as individual freedom in the liberal tradition is a derived authority, as we shall see below.

If there is indeed such a thing as legitimate authority, where does this legitimacy come from? Perhaps the most famous recent account of authority's legitimacy is that of Max Weber in the early twentieth century. We shall explore this more thoroughly in chapter 4. At this point it will suffice to point out that, in a modern secular society, traditional accounts of authority's ultimate basis in a transcendent source or order must in some fashion be denied. The Apostle Paul could write two millennia ago that "there is no authority except from God and those that exist have been instituted by God" (Rom 13:1), a conviction which would echo down through the centuries in the western world. The political implications of the apostle's words are of course evident, but this dependence on transcendent authority was once deemed to apply to the whole of life, even those areas not immediately falling within the realm of, say, prince or pontiff. In those domains which we nowadays are accustomed to think of as subject to unique personal aspirations or callings, e.g., career path, place of residence, education, and marital partner, the lives of our ancestors were circumscribed by a fairly narrow set of conventions deemed to have the ultimate sanction of God himself. Under most circumstances, if one were born to peasant parents, one would continue as a peasant until death. Similarly to be born a noble meant to remain a noble. The possibilities for movement through the ranks were virtually nil.

Our ancestors, in short, were much more conscious than we are of being under authority in a wide variety of contexts, while their personal authority as individuals over their own lives was largely underdeveloped, if not entirely *un*developed. The scope for choosing a unique life path within the constraints of this tradition was small indeed, as marriages were arranged, occupations inherited, and the notion of leaving home meant at most moving to a spouse's ancestral village and possibly even into the paternal or maternal household itself. There was nothing unusual or peculiar in our forebears' culture which mandated this complex of authoritative traditions. Every society everywhere was similarly patterned. Not until fairly recently would this change in any large-scale fashion. This points to the phenomenon of historical development of which, since the nineteenth century in particular, we have become increasingly aware.

We shall discuss further the process of historical unfolding, and particularly the norm of *differentiation*, below. At this point we shall content ourselves with the observation that, as human beings, especially in the west, have increasingly unpacked and developed the potentialities implicit in God's creation, there has been a concomitant tendency to deny transcendent authority and to assume that we ourselves are capable of molding the world in accordance with our own subjective ambitions. It is no accident that the modern ideologies, with their proposals for reshaping humanity, have arisen when they have. The human capacity for adapting the environment to meet human needs, especially in the accelerated form we have experienced in recent centuries, has arguably tempted us to imagine that we are masters of the world and the authors of our own destiny. It has seduced us into forgetting, as Václav Havel famously put it, that we are not God. Somewhat ironically, however, this acceleration of human technical capacities has also placed new and unprecedented constraints around our lives and our ability to choose in ostensibly contingent circumstances, as Jacques Ellul and George Parkin Grant have pointed out.

Yet the empirical phenomenon of what might be called *individuation*, viz., the tendency for the individual to develop her own capacities distinct from the dictates of tradition and the communities of which she is part, must itself be acknowledged as legitimate, so long as it is not misconstrued as autonomy. If it is, then those within the grip of this misconstrual will tend to see the phenomenon as a continual expansion of freedom at the expense of authority rather than as *the balanced and proportionate coming into its own of a particular type of authority as distinct from others*. There will, concomitantly, come a tendency to assume that all authority is simply reducible to human will, either that of contracting individuals, as in Locke and Rousseau, or that of a sovereign with the means to back up his commands, as in Bodin and Hobbes. By contrast, we shall argue here that individuation is one more manifestation of the larger process of differentiation, which is the foundation for what we shall call the pluriformity of authority, to be treated at some length in chapter 6.

We are furthermore persuaded that only recognition of authority's transcendent origin can fully account for this pluriformity. This is because those who negate transcendent authority must of necessity seek a point of origin in what the Dutch philosopher Herman Dooyeweerd has called the immanent horizon of experience. Another way of expressing this phenomenon is to note that those denying the true God will tend to make for themselves another god out of something within his creation— an ancient tendency endemic to humanity and summed up in the term *idolatry*. If, as liberalism believes, all communities are reducible to the will of contracting individuals, then the differences we detect through our ordinary experience between state and church, marriage and family, school, and symphony orchestra, must be judged insubstantial and dependent on the *ultimate authority* of those individuals. If these communities in all their variety are nothing more than aggregate collections of individuals, then there is no basis for judging that one is essentially— or, perhaps more properly, *structurally*—different from another. This is nothing less than the negation of pluriformity.

Similarly, if we were to assume that all communal formations were simply arms of the state or nation, then such communities are ultimately subject *in all respects* to the potentially arbitrary will of state or nation. They can have no real claim to separate ontological status distinct from the ostensibly higher community of which they are part. At most they can claim only a certain conditional independence within the whole, the amount of which is at the latter's discretion. Again diversity must give way to uniformity.

Few people have difficulty telling the difference between turtles and elephants, oak trees and dandelions, sandstone and marble. The sort of physical and biological diversity we find all around us is readily accessible to ordinary experience. The persistence of zoology, botany, geology, physics, and chemistry as distinct scientific disciplines is testimony to this experience. However, despite the existence of distinctive fields of study within the social sciences, many theoreticians have difficulty accounting for the diversity we find within human society—a diversity which is nevertheless firmly anchored in our experience. As Oliver O'Donovan puts it, "unity is proper to the creator, complexity to the created world."[9] This complexity, especially as applied to the various social formations in which everyone is embedded, might well be called *pluriformity*. Each of these formations is a locus of authority, understood both externally and internally. From an external vantage point, each form must develop in a balanced and proportionate way, respecting the spheres of competence of the others. A healthy society consists of many such loci of authority; an unhealthy society is characterized by misguided efforts to expand one of these at the expense of all the others. Statist totalitarianism is one particularly egregious example of this, as manifested in Nazi Germany and communist Russia and China during the twentieth century. Another possibility is that the legitimate sphere of individual responsibility expands excessively, leading to a deprecation of community altogether. Ironically, the end result of the latter is likely to be not dissimilar to statist totalitarianism, as individual self-seeking produces conditions requiring increasing government intervention.

Internally, the communal forms themselves are united by a series of authoritative offices, capped by one person or an executive committee possessing the principal responsibility for coordinating the activities of the whole. If the community is large enough, there may be more than one body, each sharing authority over a particular element of the community's life. In some instances, of course, it is possible that a community is small enough to be governed by majority rule, which, as Simon correctly points out, is still a manifestation of authority. Yet even in such instances, as in a completely voluntary bird-watching society, which members join and leave freely, leaders will tend to emerge to take the initiative. Although authority and leadership are logically distinct, in the real world they tend to be closely associated, even in the absence of a formal office. This is what Weber understood in articulating the character of what he labeled charismatic authority.

What are these pluriform structures found in virtually every differentiated society? These are readily accessible to human experience, and there is nothing terribly exceptional about them. They range from

---

9. O. O'Donovan, *Desire of the Nations*, 177.

the most basic of human institutions, such as marriage, family, state, and church, to a variety of other communities and associations, such as schools, business enterprises, labor unions, charitable foundations, political parties, professional associations, hospitals, museums, dance troupes, universities, public libraries, chambers of commerce, symphony orchestras, revolving credit associations, amateur sporting clubs, neighborhood watch associations, animal welfare societies, publishing companies, yacht clubs, lobbying organizations, and a huge array of others. This list is, of course, far from complete, and it encompasses more than one type of communal formation. Some, such as philatelic societies and chess clubs, are not particularly essential to a society's continued survival and could easily be dispensed with. Others, including marriage, family, state, and (we would argue) the gathered church, are more central to society's functioning. Others still fall somewhere in between. An advanced, differentiated society might function without revolving credit associations, but not without financial institutions *per se*.

Each of these communities is administered internally by an arrangement of authoritative offices appropriate to that community. A local chess club might be governed directly by its members according to the principle of majority rule, or its members might elect a president and board to govern it. By contrast, a state is generally administered in accordance with principles embodied in a constitution, which may consist of a concise document or series of documents or, in the case of the United Kingdom, New Zealand, and Israel, of ordinary statutes and unwritten conventions possessing a foundational normative character. Church institutions are governed by a variety of polities, including episcopal, presbyterian, and congregational. Although some traditions, e.g., Lutheran and some Reformed, regard church polity as a largely indifferent matter, others, e.g., Roman Catholic, Eastern Orthodox, Presbyterian, and Baptist churches see it as necessarily implied by their respective confessions. Economic enterprises too are governed in different ways, from the highly structured transnational corporation to the small family-run business. Yet authority is present in all of these forms.

Finally, of course, it should be noted that the unique place of the individual and her personal authority over the conduct of her own life does not stand over against this pluriformity but must instead be seen as very much a part of it. In a highly differentiated society personal authority will have come into its own more than in a less differentiated one, along with the various distortions that accompany any legitimate development in human history. Such distortions, we would argue, are not reasons for repealing this personal authority and re-enclosing her within a less differentiated communal structure. The fact that Joanna may have chosen to marry a physically attractive man who nevertheless lacks personal integrity is not an argument for reinstituting parentally-arranged marriages. That consumers keep the pornography business going is no ground for abolishing the market. A monistic "tribalism" is no answer to the abuses of the various pluriform loci of authority. Rather each abuse must be addressed on its own terms and in ways appropriate to the type of authority at issue.

Authority, we shall argue, is one of God's good gifts making life possible in this world which he has created, redeemed, and sustained by his grace. We can no more imagine life without authority than we can conceive of it without sunshine, rain, or the fertility of the soil. More to the point, given that authority is intimately connected to the very image of God, authority is as integral to human life as humanity itself. *The deprecation of authority amounts to a deprecation of humanity; by contrast, the redemption of humanity entails, at least in principle, the redemption of authority in its pluriform manifestations.*

2

Authority and Power

Looking for Authority in All the Wrong Places

It is February 1917. The war effort is going badly for Russia. Germany occupies a huge swath of her territory in the west and looks set to score a final victory. Over a million Russian soldiers have been killed, with four times as many wounded and twice as many captured by the enemy. The winter is especially severe this year, and a lack of basic provisions for military personnel and civilians alike is taking a deep toll. People are hungry and morale is low. The troops lack the means to fight a major war, especially one lasting this long. Nearly a year and a half ago, the Tsar took over command of the war effort from his towering cousin Grand Duke Nikolai Nikolaevich, leaving the Tsaritsa and his ministers to govern the country in his absence. This was at the urging of the Tsaritsa herself.

Now, near the end of the month, strikes have paralysed the capital city of Petrograd. Strikers are occupying the streets and the police have not only been ineffective in quelling the disturbances; they are now in hiding. Soldiers of the Petrograd garrison have been summoned, but increasing numbers of regiments are mutinying and joining with the people they have been ordered to suppress. The capital is now in the hands of the Petrograd Soviet of Workers' and Soldiers' Deputies, an ad hoc *council established to govern in the midst of the chaos. Although the Tsar has dissolved the Duma, the parliamentary assembly established in 1906, some of its members have reconvened elsewhere and formed a Provisional Government.*

The Tsar is on his way back to Petrograd from the front. His train has been stopped, and the Tsar has been informed in no uncertain terms that he must give up the throne. Initially he agrees to abdicate in favor of his ailing young son, Aleksei, who has suffered from the effects of haemophilia virtually since birth. But he is told that, if Aleksei is made tsar, he will be separated from his parents and his father's brother, the Grand Duke Mikhail Aleksandrovich, will become regent until the boy reaches the age of majority. Unable to bear the thought of giving up his son, the Tsar renounces the throne for himself and the Tsarevich, in favor of the Grand Duke himself, who quickly declines the dubious honor. With the monarchy at an end, the Provisional Government under Prince Georgy Lvov is now supreme.

Or is it? In the capital alone the Provisional Government and the Petrograd Soviet quickly become rivals for political power, with the latter capitalizing on its more democratic support base and the latter handicapped by the popular perception that it is little more than a self-appointed continuation of the Duma and the old régime. Which of these, if either, possesses authority? The Provisional Government attempts to maintain Russia's war effort in the face of increasing domestic unrest. This policy ultimately cannot be sustained. By the end of the year the Provisional Government will be gone, and the constituent assembly charged with drafting a new constitution for Russia will be suppressed by January 1918. The Bolshevik faction of the Social Democratic Labor Party will be in power, under its leader, Vladimir Ilyich Ulyanov, better known by his assumed revolutionary name of Lenin. They will claim political authority mostly on the basis of their seizure of the reins of power, but also out of a claim to know that they are on the progressive side of an historical process leading to a liberating classless society.[1]

Authority and power are not the same thing. Nowadays many people pay lip service to this truism in some fashion, although political practice tends to lag behind this not quite universal recognition. If someone comes up behind you, holds what you have reason to believe is a gun in your back, and asks for your purse or wallet, you give it to him, not because you believe he has a right to it, but because you fear the consequences of refusing his request. If the robber should suddenly develop a disability in the use of his arm and drop the gun, you would, of course, keep your wallet and call for help, because there is no right involved in this attempted "transaction."

We know that in the real world of politics, governments come and go, and not always through legitimate means. Constitutional democracies prescribe legal mechanisms for appointing or electing government officials, specifying that, if these officials lack or lose their mandate to

---

1. For one among many accounts of this tumultuous era in Russia's history, see Salisbury, *Black Night, White Snow*.

govern, they must stand down and yield their posts to others now possessing this mandate. If these officials were elected to their positions, then the loss of a future election removes political authority from them and confers it on their successors. Yet not every constitution permits genuinely competitive elections, making it difficult to remove corrupt or ineffective officials possessing the reins of power. It is not unusual for political systems to break down, especially if the traditions of constitutional government are largely absent and if they perpetrate or otherwise permit injustices on a large enough scale.

In the case of Russia during the Great War, a number of stresses, both internal and external, converged to cripple the old imperial régime, which, while formally still in place, was rapidly losing popular support. This created an opening for any number of contesting parties to vie for political power and to make a claim to authority on this basis. Even after the Bolsheviks seized power in October 1917, their hold was initially tenuous at best, and many Russians refused to accept their claim to authority. This led to a civil war that lasted into the early 1920s. Boris Pasternak's celebrated novel, *Doctor Zhivago*, is set against this backdrop of war, revolution and civil war, vividly portraying the dilemmas of an ordinary family caught up in these events.[2]

Indeed contesting claims to authority based on power alone seem historically to be a recipe for civil conflict with its attendant dislocations and bloodshed. Where clearly recognized authority is lacking, ordinary life becomes difficult if not altogether impossible. In this respect, Thomas Hobbes's description of life in an hypothetical pre-political state of nature as "solitary, poor, nasty, brutish and short" takes on a certain plausibility.[3] Where Hobbes errs, however, is in assuming that the possession of unassailable power alone can settle these competing claims. At the very least we must admit that most people believe on some level that the exercise of power must come with the *right* to its exercise. This popular belief, of course, cannot by itself be the basis for such authority, but it is powerful testimony that the distinction between power and authority is anchored in something beyond mere personal preference.

Nevertheless, so many people still manage to confuse power and authority, even when they profess to understand that they are different things. This is due to a general tendency to assume that power manifests

2. Pasternak, *Doctor Zhivago*.
3. Hobbes, *Leviathan*, xiii.

itself primarily as coercive force. Not everyone is as blunt as Mao Zedong, who famously held that "Political power grows out of the barrel of a gun."[4] Yet even in the absence of overt reference to the *instruments* of coercion, there is an awareness that even the threat of their use constitutes a form of possibly psychological power, inevitably influencing a variety of human activities subject to it.

It may be that the heirs of Karl Marx and Friedrich Nietzsche are more conscious than most of the existence of power in its subtler forms, e.g., economic power of one class over another, of hallowed tradition over the current generation, or of unspoken social mores over the lives of others. Concepts such as capitalism, the establishment, the system, patriarchy, technique, and the like have been coined to describe the loci of such power. To these complex systems of power physical coercion is only ancillary, at most supporting power's more subtle manifestations, which are largely effective in keeping people in line and maintaining social order for the benefit of those at the top of the heap. Contemporary concern over gender and sexual harassment in the workplace comes from an understanding that, within an organizational environment, people relate to each other from different positions of power, which may compromise the voluntary nature of, say, romantic relationships that arise on the job.

What is missing from the neomarxist or deconstructionist vocabulary is an understanding that authority and power cannot be conflated. Claims to authority over others are treated as class, gender, or race-based mythological justifications for one's own superior place in an empirical arrangement of power. Thus for Marx the state under capitalism is little more than window dressing on the oppressive rule of the bourgeoisie, or the factory owners. Its authority is thus illusory, a product of a false consciousness induced by the rulers to protect their own power. Variants of this position can also be found among radical feminists, liberation theologians, and those for whom race is a central category.

Our argument here is that power and authority are indeed to be distinguished from each other, that authority in its primary sense is to be located in office, and that the authority of office is not to be identified with one of the capacities at its disposal, such as psychological power, persuasive ability, brute force, voluntary agreement or consent, biological differences, and superior knowledge. These capacities are multiple

---

4. Mao Zedong, "Problems of War and Strategy," 224.

and may not necessarily announce themselves as overt manifestations of power, which explains why so many overlook them as such.

If authority is something intrinsic to human life, then those willing to recognize this reality are bound to account for it theoretically in some fashion. We shall begin by arguing that *authority is resident in an office given by God to humanity at the creation, viz., the image of God.* This image is manifested in a variety of settings, both individual and communal, within a differentiated society. It is by no means coincidental that scripture connects this image to what the Reformed tradition calls the cultural mandate in Genesis 1:26–28:

> Then God said, "Let us make man in our image, after our likeness; and let them have dominion over the fish of the sea, and over the birds of the air, and over the cattle, and over all the earth, and over every creeping thing that creeps upon the earth." So God created man in his own image, in the image of God he created him; male and female he created them. And God blessed them, and God said to them, "Be fruitful and multiply, and fill the earth and subdue it; and have dominion over the fish of the sea and over the birds of the air and over every living thing that moves upon the earth."

Two things must be said of this image of God, an initially curious notion whose meaning may not be immediately obvious to the modern reader. First, it does *not* mean that human beings are themselves gods or have "bits" of God within them, like a batch of cookie dough with chocolate chips scattered throughout. There is a type of theologizing that focuses heavily on the so-called attributes of God, ascribing created qualities, such as justice, reason, will, etc., to the divine essence. Of course, God is indeed a God of justice, compassion, and mercy, as scripture affirms throughout. Yet if these qualities be understood as attributes of his *essence,* there is the ever-present danger of divinizing the attributes themselves, even when they appear in human beings, who are then thought to possess a spark of the divine. The obvious pantheistic (or panentheistic) implications of this are to be avoided by the Christian desiring to remain within the bounds of biblical orthodoxy.[5]

---

5. For an astute discussion of the image of God in the context of God's apparent attributes, see Clouser, *The Myth of Religious Neutrality,* 202–22. Here Clouser contrasts the view of Augustine, Anselm and Aquinas (AAA), which speculates concerning the essential properties of God, to that of the Cappadocian fathers and the Reformers (C/R), which focusses solely on God's free revelation of himself to his creatures and

Second, as J. Richard Middleton has pointed out, the biblical understanding of the image of God stands against the ancient near eastern worldviews, which ascribed the image of the gods to the king alone.[6] In his capacity as ruler, the king was the authorized representative of the gods, especially as understood in the ancient Mesopotamian cosmologies that formed the backdrop of the historical drama of Israel as God's covenant people. By contrast, the Old Testament, especially the first chapter of Genesis, radically democratizes the image of God to cover *all* human beings and not just their royal overlords. The image of God is a grant of responsibility to all people—male and female, rich and poor, king and peasant—as stewards of the earth. Middleton avers further that one cannot find a justification for human beings ruling each other in Genesis 1.[7] In this respect the biblical worldview constituted nothing less than a radical challenge to "the entire ruling and priestly structure of Mesopotamian society (and especially the absolute power of the king)."[8] Middleton further suggests that, because hierarchies of power are relativized by this first chapter of the first book of the Bible, "such hierarchies are not grounded in God's creational intent" for humanity.[9]

Although Middleton correctly points to the ontological equality of all God's image-bearers, such equality by itself does not rule out the differential status of the various authoritative offices in which ordinary human beings find themselves. To be sure, many of these offices are not arranged hierarchically *vis-à-vis* each other, but some clearly are, especially when located within the same communal or institutional context. God does indeed appoint specific persons to specific offices for specific purposes. Elsewhere scripture affirms his clear intention that others be subject to these offices (e.g., Rom 13:1–7, 1 Pet 2:13–17). The Pentateuch relates God's expressed displeasure at Miriam and Aaron's rebellion against Moses' authority on apparent egalitarian grounds: "Has the LORD indeed spoken only through Moses? Has he not spoken through us also?" (Num 12:2). Nevertheless, Middleton's basic observation is correct if properly qualified: all human beings, in whatever offices they find themselves, are created in God's image and bear authority as stewards over the rest of

---

eschews such speculation.

6. Middleton, *The Liberating Image*.
7. Ibid., 204–5.
8. Ibid., 204.
9. Ibid., 205.

creation. Man's basic authority as image of God is further dispersed into the several authoritative offices which we encounter on a day-to-day basis. This dispersal of authority we shall take up again in chapter 6.

It should immediately be noted that this dominion, or stewardship, is not to be reduced to the mere exercise of power, although it certainly requires power if it is to move beyond potentiality to action. It is in fact nothing less than a grant of *authority* to man over nonhuman creation, including other living things. Much as creation itself is portrayed as unfolding and developing in the first chapter of Genesis, so also is man's authority over this creation something which unfolds over time in the direction of greater complexity. In the event, of course, this increasing complexification, or *differentiation*, coincides with the working out of human sinfulness after the Fall (see, e.g., Gen 4:17–24). Nevertheless, the two historical trends should not be conflated. Had man not fallen into sin, differentiation would still have occurred. Cities would still have been built, children would have been raised, music would have been composed, novels written (though presumably not murder mysteries!), philosophies thought up, and so forth. But such activities would have occurred in a normative, legitimate way, free from the distorting effects of sin. Authority would have remained intact.

We are prepared to argue at this point that all people understand at an experiential level that authority is resident in specific offices associated with this differentiation. Anyone venturing into a classroom will immediately intuit who is the teacher and who are the students. Similarly, whoever attends an orchestra concert can easily tell the conductor from the concert master, quite irrespective of the sound of the music or the respective skills of the conductor and players. Even in ordinary language the concept of authority makes its presence felt in overt and less overt ways. Which child has not asked, "Can I go out and play?" only to have her mother correct her: "*May* I go out and play!" No one doubts the little girl's *ability* to play outside; what is at issue is whether she has her mother's permission, i.e., is *authorized*, to do so at that time. Authority, in short, is firmly anchored in our common experience.

At this point someone is likely to raise an objection: Might not human capacities, i.e., the various forms of power in our possession, be said in some sense to confer authority? This is especially evident with the specialized knowledge that makes a person an *authority* in a particular field of endeavor, e.g., medicine, law, or tool-and-die-making. Do not persuasive arguments carry a certain authority for those convinced by them? If one is skilled at wood-working, i.e., if one has the *ability*, or power, to work with wood, does this not make him an *authority* in that practical endeavor? These questions point to the complex nature of the relationship between power and authority. In many cases mere ability does appear already to imply authority.

However, we would argue that even in such cases in which authority and power are so closely tied together, authority nevertheless precedes power. Mary's ability to play classical guitar can be understood to make her an authority in her field, in which case her authority appears to be based on her possession of power. Yet her virtuosity as a guitarist is ultimately rooted in that authority granted her by God himself as manifested in the central office of divine image. Even from a proximate standpoint, her skill at the guitar has developed within the context of a web of interrelated authorities, including her parents, who may have encouraged her interest and financed her lessons; the music store, where they legally purchased the instrument for the agreed-upon price; the domestic monetary system that permitted the purchase; the legal framework which recognizes their ownership of the instrument; and of course the principles of music theory and the generally accepted methods of guitar-playing handed down from one generation to the next. Much of this still applies even if Mary is self-taught. She will still likely be playing recognizable pieces which in some fashion conform to the acknowledged—and authoritative—standards for guitar performance.

Power itself comes in many diverse forms, this diversity understood from more than one angle. The most basic form is the physical power that is found in the sun, wind, and water; petroleum, electricity, and nuclear energy; as well as the biological and mental capacities of animals and human beings. When there is a power failure, the electrical grid fueling a post-industrial society has ceased to function for a time. The power of a person to swim the English Channel or climb Mount Everest, or even simply to get up and walk across the room, exemplifies the truth of the ubiquity of power. Everything has a power-related aspect.

Power manifests itself in more subtle ways as well. A friend persuades us to accompany her to the art museum. One member of the board convinces the others to approve a particular marketing strategy for a company's products. An academic's work in a particular field bears the unmistakable imprint of a professor under whom he worked at graduate school. As we grow older, we recognize that we are more like our parents in a variety of ways than we are different from them, thereby exemplifying their continuing influence over us, even after they are gone. These manifestations of power do not call for the exercise of coercive means. *Persuasion* depends on the success of the persuader in moving a person voluntarily to consent to a proposed course of action. *Influence*, while sometimes seen as synonymous with persuasion, is more subtle, often working its way into a person's values and activities subconsciously. The success of advertising is based on both the more overt persuasion and the less obvious influence.

Power can, of course, be abused, and it is this abuse which often gives power, like authority itself, a bad name. In fact, it may be that authority's reputation is besmirched, more than anything else, by its association with that tainted phenomenon of power. Coercion itself can be misused, e.g., when one country invades another's territory unprovoked. But even persuasion and influence can become manipulation, which involves person A feeding person B selective or misleading information to secure the latter's assent to a deed to which she would not otherwise have agreed if she had had more accurate information. In 1898 US President William McKinley used the sinking of the *Maine* in Havana harbor as a pretext for attacking Spain. In 1939 Adolf Hitler concocted an international incident to bring the German people on side of an invasion of Poland. In 1964 President Lyndon Johnson used the Gulf of Tonkin incident to manipulate Congress into approving an escalation of US military action in Vietnam.

Power, especially when exercised over others, can also be used primarily to serve the interests of those holding it. It is perhaps this tendency which has most tainted its possession and exercise down through the centuries. Lord Acton famously averred that power tends to corrupt while absolute power corrupts absolutely. The ancient Greeks and Romans understood such self-interested power to constitute tyranny and oligarchy, degenerations from the legitimate forms of government, monarchy and aristocracy respectively. The more controversial elements of Plato's *Republic*, such as the communal ownership of property and the community of wives and children, were part of a grand effort to remove corruption from the body politic. If the city's guardians are deprived of private interests altogether, they will not pursue them at the expense of the larger community. Jean-Jacques Rousseau's republic, as set forth in his *Social Contract*, represents a similar scheme for subordinating particular wills to the general will. Yet the very concept of legitimate authority assumes that the possibility of leaders pursuing a common interest is not just an idealistic dream but falls within the realm of reality, even if it is nowhere perfectly realized. This justifies the differential possession of power by those in authority. If power were always and everywhere simply self-interested, with no possibility of rectifying this and bringing it into the service of a larger good, then some form of anarchic equal distribution of power would seem to be the logical implication.

However, the latter could only be an artificial imposition on society. In the normal course of a society's development, some people inevitably accrue more power than others, whether that power be defined epistemically, socially, lingually, economically, or politically. In this context, it might be more accurate to speak of the possession of *powers*, in the plural. Person A may be a member of parliament and thus have more political power than person B. But person B may be wealthier than person A and thus hold more economic power than the latter. Even with respect to knowledge, which is a recognized form of power, person C may know more than person D about quantum physics while person D may have the expertise in international relations which person C lacks. The irony of the anarchist vision, as we shall explore further below, is that any effort to distribute evenly these powers, even if restricted to economic and political powers only, would require a massive interventionist effort—by whom? the government?—leaving no corner of human life untouched. A huge concentration of totalitarian power would be needed to redistribute powers equally, which is of course as logically impossible as the attempt to walk and stand still at the same time. Such a totalitarian régime can hardly be what flesh and blood anarchists would wish to see, but it is almost certainly the practical consequence of their commitment.

The powers possessed by authority serve to support its legitimacy in the eyes of those subject to it. Thus when we encounter a police officer at an intersection, we reflexively comply with her directives. When the orchestra conductor raises his baton, the instrumentalists invariably take this as their cue to begin playing. When the foreman speaks, the members of the work crew listen and follow his instructions. The person possessing an authoritative office is changed by it in more than one possible way. Accordingly she could respond with a sense of personal superiority, allowing herself to be puffed up by her status, or with humility, as she undertakes conscientiously to fulfill its responsibilities. In the normal course of events, those under such authority do not engage in an elaborate reasoning process to determine whether their commands conform to Kant's categorical imperative or something similar.

They simply obey, because they intuitively recognize the legitimacy of the office issuing the command.

Authoritative office is also supported by an array of symbolic elements. Nation-states possess flags, coats-of-arms, and anthems intended to effect a sense of solidarity among their citizens. Royal authority has recourse to crowns, scepters, and precious metals and stones, all of which evoke a feeling of awe and respect among its subjects. Sword and mace are weapons of war but take on great symbolic importance when worn by a ruler or brought ceremonially into a parliamentary chamber. Letterhead on stationary carries with it the authority of an organization such as a church, business, charity, or university. Legal currency bears the image of a current or past head of state, along with other symbols of a country's identity, and must never be counterfeited. Clergy often wear distinctive garb, such as cassock, surplice, alb, and collar tabs. Soldiers and police officers routinely wear uniforms as markers of their office. To impersonate an officer by donning her uniform is a criminal offense in many jurisdictions, precisely because the offender is in effect claiming authority to which she has no right.

Such uniforms might tend to reinforce the popular misconception that only the leaders or guardians of a community bear authoritative offices. After all, ordinary parishioners do not generally wear identifying garb, although many people, especially older Protestants, do "dress up" to attend church. However, a number of private schools, such as England's Eton College, require uniforms among both faculty and students for at least some occasions. The uniforms are likely to differ between the two groups. Faculty may be expected to wear a modified academic gown, and students black trousers, white shirt, jacket, and tie. This underscores the different offices of teacher and student, but it impresses on both the seriousness of the respective offices to which they are called. The relationship between symbol and office would appear to be lost on the generations born after the Second World War, for whom education became a commodity to be purchased on the open market and dress a mere expression of individuality. Nevertheless, the original baby-boomers who eschewed dress codes and school uniforms in the 1960s well understood the symbolism of so doing—thereafter ironically making the ubiquitous blue jeans the new campus uniform! Authority had not been abolished after all, but reconfigured as mere power less obviously tied to awareness of the responsibilities of office.

Because this nearly ineffable power of authority defies easy explanation or rational justification, at least one observer has spoken of the belief in authority's legitimacy as superstitious.[10] Richard Sennett undertakes to break what he sees as authority's psychological hold on people so that they might disrupt the chain of command and obtain results more favorable to the interests of those subject to it. Kantians, in particular, believe themselves obliged to break through this mystical grip which authority so stubbornly exerts on people so that the latter might successfully "regain" their moral autonomy. Nevertheless, because of its subtle, inexplicable power, authority, particularly in its imperative form, does not generally have to resort to coercion or persuasion to legitimate its commands, although these are available to it as supportive means if needed. For the most part, its very status as authority is generally enough to secure obedience. Some may not like this reality, but without it the instruments of coercion would be far more visible than they are in most societies. In the real world we simply do not question every directive issuing from authority, any more than we could possibly question every tradition handed down from previous generations. Obedience is clearly the rule; disobedience, even if warranted in particular cases by the principles of civil disobedience against tyrannical commands, is just as obviously exceptional. It could scarcely be otherwise if a normal society is to survive for any length of time.

1. Authority As Psychological Power

More than one kind of reduction is at work in the ongoing attempts to account for authority which we shall survey here. We briefly alluded to the six categories in our proposed typology in chapter 1: (1) psychological control, (2) persuasion, (3) possession of the instruments of power, (4) voluntary contract, (5) biological superiority, and (6) superior knowledge. All of these appear deliberately to skirt around the notion of office, which, as we are arguing, is central to understanding authority. Each in its own way might be said to reduce authority to power—to some human capacity at the disposal of authority. Nevertheless each differs as to the type of power at issue, whether this be psychological, persuasive, instrumental, or some other manifestation.

---

10. Wolff, *In Defense of Anarchism*, 80.

Let us begin with the psychological reduction of authority, a position ably defended by Richard Sennett.[11] Sennett is not altogether clear whether authority is equivalent to power. On the one hand, he claims, authority is not precisely the same as power, "as when we say that a government official lacked the authority to engage in some venture."[12] This corresponds to the distinction between the *can* and the *may* of the little girl's question to her mother. So far so good. Authority, for Sennett, is not a thing but an interpretive process which undertakes to give meaning to the conditions of power, "to give the conditions of control and influence a meaning by defining an image of strength."[13] This image of strength is very much a subjective one resident in the minds both of those wielding authority and of those under it.

Sennett's analysis of authority is heavily dependent on a series of life examples he cites to bolster his case. We shall mention only three of them here, but these should suffice to show how the author points—somewhat lopsidedly—to the negative, alienating side of authority, along with the apparent need, if not to overcome it entirely, then at least to disrupt it periodically so as to make it more responsive to the demands of those subject to it. The first of Sennett's case studies concerns one Helen Bowen, a twenty-five-year-old caught up in what some would call a codependent relationship with her parents. Although she was no longer living in the parental home, Bowen had developed a pattern of dating men whom she knew her parents would dislike and then expending her energies challenging their expressions of disapproval. As a legal adult, she could, of course, simply have stayed away from her parents and dated whom she preferred. Yet something inside her drove her to live her life in ways deliberately defying her parents' wishes. Sennett calls this pattern one of disobedient dependence. Bowen was not truly independent of their authority, even as she continually challenged it. Their psychological hold on her was still considerable, although one might as easily interpret the opposite to be the case as well: Bowen exerted a certain psychological power over her parents, successfully antagonizing them on a regular basis over men in whom she might not otherwise show interest if she had only herself to answer to.[14]

11. Sennett, *Authority*.
12. Ibid., 18.
13. Ibid., 19.
14. Ibid., 28–41.

Yet is parental authority genuinely at issue here? Only in the sense in which parents never cease to be parents to their sons and daughters, even after the latter have grown up and left the home. Yet in a healthy extended family the active side of parental authority, i.e., the right to command obedience, properly diminishes as the children grow to maturity. As Yves R. Simon rightly indicates, where active parental authority does not aim at its own disappearance, it risks becoming abusive.[15] One assumes from Sennett's account that Bowen's upbringing may have been troubled—something which has extended inappropriately past adolescence and into young adulthood. Yet given that she is twenty-five, one has reason to doubt that authority as such is at issue. Or, if it is, the issue lies in Bowen's failure to assume the normal adult direction-setting authority over her own life. Indeed, if asked, her parents might actually prefer her to move away so as to be free from her antagonism. That both parties are locked in a difficult familial relationship, however much it might resemble the conflict over authority which undoubtedly occurred during the teen years, does not necessarily mean that *parental* authority is still at issue. At most it would appear to be an asymmetrical, dysfunctional psychological relationship which might—or might not—improve with counseling. However, if one identifies authority with mere psychological power, as Sennett appears to be doing here, one is unlikely to see this clearly.

The second of Sennett's examples is more evidently about what most people would recognize as authority. This one involves two famous conductors, Pierre Monteux (1875–1964) and Arturo Toscanini (1867–1957), who led a number of orchestras in Europe and North America during their long careers. Though both enjoyed the same official position relative to these orchestras, each had a quite different personal style. Toscanini inspired terror in his players, going so far as to scream, stamp his feet, and even throw his baton at them. He kept the orchestra in line largely through provoking fear of his anger. By contrast, Monteux had a quieter way of relating to his ensemble, conveying a more relaxed sense of self-mastery and a calm assurance of being in control, a style which Sennett obviously prefers to Toscanini's. Each conductor asserted his authority, albeit in different ways. Yet look at the phrases Sennett uses to describe this "authority": "relaxed, complete control of himself," "ease at being in control," "easy assurance," "inspiring terror," "aura," "strength," "superior judgment," and so forth. All of these have to do with the mental

---

15. Simon, *Philosophy of Democratic Government*, 9.

states of the people involved. What is missing is any reference to the concrete office of conductor without which an orchestra could not produce a pleasing sound.[16]

To be sure, a conductor who is unable for whatever reason to relate successfully to his players and to command their confidence will fill the office inadequately despite his formally occupying it. This will inevitably have an impact on, among other things, the quality of the music the group as a whole is able to produce under his direction. He may acquire a reputation for being difficult to work under, and his players may put forth only a cursory effort in his behalf. Yet at most the psychological ability to command the confidence of those under oneself must be seen as ancillary to authority, and not as standing at its point of origin. Again this is something Sennett seems to have missed. Having a commanding presence may indeed contribute to the smooth functioning of authority, yet by itself it can hardly confer that authority. The fact of the concert master having such a presence cannot *ipso facto* make of her a conductor. At some point, after the departure of the current conductor, the orchestra's board might decide to recognize her gifts and confer the baton upon her. She may end up performing more skillfully than her immediate predecessor, but her authority to do so will not have come until the board has made its decision.

Sennett's third example manifests an understanding of authority which is closer to the mark insofar as it recognizes that certain kinds of authority cannot rest on improper metaphors without incurring deleterious consequences for all concerned. George Pullman was the founder and president of the Pullman Palace Car Company, manufacturer of the famous railway sleeping and parlor cars used throughout the United States into the mid-twentieth century. Although the late nineteenth century is known to have been the classic era of high capitalism in that country, some of the early industrial giants sought to replicate the conditions of European feudalism, very nearly justifying their being styled as "barons" by some observers at the time. In 1880 Pullman went so far as to construct his own personal fiefdom: a planned city for his workers on the south side of Chicago, still to this day known as the Pullman neighborhood. Seeing himself as a father figure, he implicitly promised to care for them. But when depression struck in 1893, he was forced to lower wages even as he maintained rents in his Pullman community at previous

---

16. Sennett, *Authority*, 16–19.

levels, thereby squeezing the workers and contributing to their decision to strike the following year. Although Pullman may genuinely have believed himself to have his workers' best interests at heart, his promise to care for them fell by the wayside as the economy took a nosedive. Rather than blaming impersonal economic forces, the workers blamed Pullman himself, since he was the one who had tacitly assumed responsibility for their wellbeing.[17]

The falsity of the paternal metaphor is indicated, *inter alia*, by the fact that a real father desires to strengthen his children as they grow to maturity and independence. He rejoices as they assume each new capacity, from walking to talking, to dressing themselves, to getting their first job, to establishing their own families. In a paternalistic company workers are kept in a state of submission and dependence; they have become, in effect, permanent children, unable to grow and move beyond this relationship. This is perhaps the strongest part of Sennett's analysis, because, despite the defects of his psychologizing approach, he correctly understands that metaphors appropriate to one communal setting may not be well suited to another. This, we would argue, amounts to a tacit recognition of pluriformity.

All the same, Sennett paints his larger portrait of authority in dark hues, viewing it primarily as self-interested strength resting on psychological power over others having a deep need for, and emotional dependence on, them. There seems to be nothing intrinsic to a particular office making it authoritative. Whoever finds himself in that office is forced to resort to shows of strength in order to get people to do his bidding. Because authority seems to be intrinsically alienating to such people, the only means by which they can achieve freedom—a freedom conceived as autonomy—is to break its hold in some fashion. This calls for subjecting it to a periodic disruption in the chain of command. Given such a negative portrayal, the question remains whether authority might be necessary as a positive good for the preservation of communities requiring some form of united action. This possibility does not seem to figure into Sennett's analysis.

At this point we turn to political scientist and systems analyst David Easton, whose view of authority is similar to Sennett's, albeit without the necessarily negative associations the latter attaches to it. Given that Easton defines politics as "the authoritative allocation of values," he must

---

17. See chapter 2, "Paternalism: An Authority of False Love," in Sennett, *Authority*, esp. 62–77.

undertake to define the meaning of the authority behind the allocative process. He does so by recourse to what he calls images of authority on the part of those subject to it.[18] Authority itself he describes as a kind of relationship based on influence. It is "not a characteristic that attaches to a member of the political system regardless of its consequences, but . . . a type of power relationship between two or more members or groups."[19] Authority thus depends, not so much on the person or office, but on the relationship between persons. A principal characteristic of this relationship is the presence of intent or awareness on the part of the two parties. In the absence of such awareness, we can speak only of manipulation. If this awareness is indeed present, then we can speak of either force, persuasion or authority. Authority occurs when person B alters his behavior at the behest of person A without being forced to do so and without evaluating her injunction according to his own standards of what is and is not appropriate to the situation.[20]

Where does this authority come from? Clearly, acceding to an ostensibly authoritative office is insufficient, since it says nothing about the relationship between the officeholder and those over whom the office is set. This is where the perceived images, symbols or mental pictures of those subject to authority come into play. Something has to occur within the minds of the respondents to invest those claiming authority with the legitimacy conferred by such images and symbols. This points, once again, to psychological factors. In their absence authority is nonexistent. If person B obeys the commands of person A because he fears the consequences of not doing so, then their relationship is not one of authority, but of mere force. If person B follows person A's directives because he is convinced of the rightness of those directives themselves, then the relationship is one of persuasion.

Easton clearly sees persuasion as preferable to authority, which he tends to view as a somewhat archaic relic of pre-modern societies. If authority cannot be dispensed with entirely, it is more in accordance with modern democratic attitudes to replace it whenever and wherever possible with persuasion, presumably because this takes seriously the rationality of the respondents. One detects in Easton something of the influence of Kant's preference for arriving at independent judgments free

---

18. David Easton, "The Perception of Authority and Political Change," in Friedrich, ed., *Nomos 1: Authority*, 170–96.

19. Ibid., 177–78.

20. Ibid., 179.

from the supposedly unthinking submission to the judgments of others. If this is so and if we take seriously Easton's preference for persuasion over authority, then we may have reason to conclude that his ultimate desire would be for the sphere of politics itself, given the "authoritative" component in his definition, to diminish with the passage of time.

2. Authority As Persuasive Power

If Easton is careful to distinguish between authority and persuasion, as we believe he is correct to do, certainly not everyone is willing to do this. Writing in the wake of the student rebellions of the 1960s and early '70s, Carl J. Friedrich argues that authority must be firmly connected with rationality.[21] Any concept of authority demanding blind obedience to someone simply because she is held to *be* an authority is not evidently rooted in such rationality. For this reason Friedrich believes that authority cannot be said to reside in specific persons but in their communications only. Anyone claiming authority for her command but unable to produce clear reasons in its defense does not have genuine authority. Here Friedrich is undertaking to respond to the partisans of the French Revolution who deprecated authority as a source of evil and sought to replace it with reason. This is wrong, argues Friedrich, partly because the revolutionaries themselves claimed to speak with authority in favor of their proposed social and political agenda. Much of this negative view of authority is due to a perennial tendency to confuse authority with power. Authority has sometimes been defined as rightful power or the rightful exercise of power. It has been claimed for persons and for things, such as the law.

From Friedrich's perspective, this is inadequate. Authority must instead be anchored in reason and the process of reasoning, particularly in defense of a proposed course of action. Only insofar as good reasons are offered for something, or are at least capable of being offered, can a command be considered authoritative. Authority is thus defined as "the capacity to offer reasons for what is being done and said."[22] It must be identified, not so much with persons or things thought to possess the power to get something done, but with the authoritative *communications* themselves. An authoritative communication is capable of

---

21. Friedrich, *Tradition & Authority*.
22. Ibid., 49.

reasoned defense. One which is not so capable lacks authority irrespective of its source.

As for the origin of authority, Friedrich argues that this is to be found in the subjective values of those under it. A fundamental shift in values leads to a change in authority, as in revolutionary situations, when old authority figures are replaced by new ones. This is what happened in the 1960s when Charles de Gaulle and Konrad Adenauer lost much of their authority in France and Germany respectively. It happened even more dramatically in Russia in early 1917 when the Tsar effectively lost his authority, eventually to be replaced by Lenin's Bolsheviks. These coincided with a change of values in the people themselves. Are these values mental constructs similar to Easton's images and symbols? If so, then Friedrich might be held to be entertaining the psychological reduction and would thus fall into our first category above. Yet unlike Sennett and Easton, Friedrich places his emphasis on the communications themselves issuing from those claiming the possession of authority. Where those communications are defensible, authority can be said to be present. Where they are not, authority evaporates.

In foreign affairs authority is more limited than in the domestic realm, because no one person or institution can claim "full or comprehensive authority."[23] This is due to the fact that it is too wide a field for anyone to grasp in its entirety, but also because in a nuclear age no government is able to provide the security traditionally expected of a government. Thus its claim to authority in the field of defense is severely limited, especially after 1945. That such a judgment would be made in the midst of the Vietnam debacle is perhaps understandable. The administrations of Presidents Lyndon Johnson and Richard Nixon in the US sought to pursue a policy of containment of communism in Southeast Asia—a policy which eventually met with failure in 1975. By 1968 Johnson's defense policies were already losing credibility with increasing numbers of Americans. If Friedrich's analysis is correct, this loss of credibility entailed nothing less than a loss of authority. Although Johnson formally held the office of the presidency and was thus in an apparently authoritative position to set his country's defense policies, he found himself unable to offer the public a rational justification for these policies, a necessary prerequisite for the existence of authority. Friedrich's analysis would seem to account for those extreme situations in which someone continues formally to

---

23. Ibid., 74.

occupy an office claiming authority but whose injunctions are no longer generally believed to be authoritative. A failure of communication has occurred, and this makes the exercise of authority less plausible in such a context, or possibly in any context.

At this point Friedrich addresses challenges to authority. These have usually been advanced in the name of freedom, based on the supposition that authority and freedom are, if not opposites, at least in tension with each other. But Friedrich believes that freedom can never be against authority *per se*, only against false authority, i.e., that which does not possess the capacity for reasoned communication, in favor of true authority, i.e., that which does possess this.

Of course, any discussion of the relationship between authority and legitimacy calls to mind Max Weber's famous discussion of the sources for authority's legitimacy, including the traditional, legal, and charismatic. Weber's categories, however, are not as neat as they seem, for, as Friedrich points out, even a law-governed constitutional political order (i.e., legal authority), if it has endured long enough, carries all the force of hallowed tradition, as we shall see in chapter 4. As for legitimacy itself, Friedrich argues that it enjoys an interdependent relationship with authority, even as each is a distinct concept. Authority helps to confer legitimacy on the exercise of power, although it is possible for someone to retain legitimate power after he has lost his authority, something which occurs in revolutionary situations.

Friedrich's principal error, as we see it, lies, not only in his inability to distinguish between what might be called imperative and epistemic authority, but to ignore the extent to which both are dependent on office. As a consequence he appears unable to distinguish between authority proper and persuasion. Persuasion necessarily relies upon the offering of reasons by person A to person B with the expectation that person B will agree to person A's proposal. But the very notion of persuasion presupposes the possibility that person B will not so agree and retains the freedom to do so in virtually every circumstance. Yet imperative authority, both as traditionally understood and as manifested in ordinary experience, issues directives which are mandatory, meaning that they must be obeyed and cannot be ignored with impunity. It is, of course, possible to imagine a political order based largely on persuasion, perhaps along the lines of the ancient direct democracy of the Athenian polis, where citizens had to be convinced of the virtues of a particular policy proposal. Nevertheless, once a vote is taken and a majority has decided on a course of action, the resulting decision necessarily has an authoritative character—unless, that is, one is willing to embrace Robert Paul Wolff's anarchistic vision, in which every individual must be brought voluntarily onside of a common agenda. Wolff argues that authority can and should be dispensed with, to be replaced by persuasion. Friedrich, by contrast, makes a somewhat unusual case for identifying authority with persuasion itself.

Is such an identification plausible? We believe it is not, or at least not completely. To be sure, there is much to be said for those filling various authoritative offices providing reasons for their commands under most circumstances. Such reasons can only bolster authority, and they do indeed *carry* authority in some sense, much as a layman might be said to be an epistemic authority on, say, politics or economics based on his personal command of those fields of knowledge. If someone bearing a recognized authoritative office issues a directive the soundness of which huge numbers of people have come to doubt, she would be foolish to rest on her office alone without providing some explanation for the program whose implementation she is mandating. This is the grain of truth behind the observation that President Johnson had lost his authority over American foreign and defense policies by the end of his term.

Nevertheless, as Oliver O'Donovan observes, authority's "moral claim is to a degree independent of the moral claim of its particular demands taken on their own."[24] This he sees as one of its paradoxical qualities, something that Friedrich overlooks. Furthermore, if the opposition leader in parliament makes a more persuasive case than the prime minister on a particular issue, he may well succeed in getting his party elected to government come the next election. In the meantime, however, his better grasp of that issue is not by itself sufficient to make him prime minister or to invest his communications with authority. Only established legal mechanisms, e.g., election and appointment, associated with the office of prime minister can achieve that. Friedrich's opinion to the contrary notwithstanding, authority does indeed reside in specific offices and not only in the communications issuing thereof. The office must come first and only then come the communications issuing thereof.

---

24. O. O'Donovan, *Resurrection and Moral Order*, 131.

3. Authority As Instruments of Power

Although each of these approaches to authority involves some form of power, whether psychological or persuasive power, one form would reduce authority to the exercise of a fairly simple and not very subtle form of power consisting of incentives and disincentives, that is, the mere capacity of person A to make person B do her bidding by either issuing threats or promising benefits. Although there is a superficial resemblance between this category and the previous, viz., the conflation with persuasion, the focus of each is different. Those focusing on persuasion emphasize the capacity of the agent enjoying pre-eminence to connect with those under him based on common rationality. Defensible arguments play a central role here. On the other hand, those focusing on incentives and disincentives emphasize the instruments themselves employed by those in authority. It matters not whether a leader's directives are rationally justifiable or even in the public interest. What does matter is her capacity to withhold and extend benefits to those within her power. Self-interest plays a significant role even if it comes in the guise of persuasion.

Within political science this instrumental approach to authority is characteristic of the school known as political realism, whose central assumption is that human beings are self-interested agents expending their energies attempting, on the one hand, to flee a variety of disutilities and, on the other, to accumulate as many capacities as possible in their own hands. One side of this political realism reveals a rather blunt edge: Do this or else, is the implicit or explicit message. Here the focus is on military and police power, i.e., the coercive instruments at the disposal of the state, or what the Apostle Paul calls the power of the sword (Rom 13). The mere fact of its possession of these means gives it the right to its subjects' obedience. With respect to parents, the fact of their being larger and stronger than their children is all that is needed to give them the right to discipline them. In Plato's *Republic*, the character Thrasymachus famously exemplifies an approach to political order which rests on mere strength. If Socrates was able, with some effort, to defeat Thrasymachus's position early on in the dialogue, the latter has nevertheless persisted throughout history in some form.

In the early modern era, Machiavelli and Hobbes argued in rather more sophisticated fashion than Thrasymachus for the identification of right with might. Karl Marx and his heirs, despite the evident undercurrent in their writings favoring freedom from oppression, see the history of mankind as one of a power struggle for control over the means of production. While history will ultimately vindicate the oppressed proletariat, it proceeds, not by argument from premises based on, say, a natural law or divine mandate, but by a concrete empirical intensification of class struggle with greater power defeating lesser power. More recently those claiming the postmodern label, including such deconstructionists as Jacques Derrida and Michel Foucault, have extended the Marxist emphasis on class to a variety of other group identities, including gender, race and sexual orientation. But the power struggle remains a sustaining theme.

If the use of disincentives, also known as "the stick," is determinative in securing obedience to authority, there is a flip side which is just as important, if not more so. This is, of course, "the carrot," which involves the holding out of concrete incentives to obedience. The boundary between incentives and disincentives is, of course, fluid. If a political leader threatens citizens with the withdrawal of certain rights and privileges as a price for disobedience, in effect she is promising to extend these rights and privileges if they do obey. To promise to protect law and order—a positive good—at election time is to threaten voters with chaos if they fail to vote "properly." Whichever the strategy, the leader is put in the position of treating her relationship to subordinates as one of exchanging desired goods, albeit between unequal partners. Each party has something to offer the other, and the extent to which their desires are mutually compatible will come to define and solidify the position of the person or body possessing authority.

Plato's most famous dialogue, Πολιτεία, or *The Republic*, is about justice and not, of course, about authority as such.[25] Yet as Socrates and his companions seek knowledge of the true identity of justice, authority necessarily makes an appearance, as it does also in *The Statesman*. If justice has an intrinsic meaning and worth to the person undertaking to practice it, then it must be rooted in an authoritative order transcending the subjective preferences of human beings. That order, to which the word φύσις (*physis*), or nature, is attached, inevitably makes a claim on the individual. In Plato's account, Socrates devotes his intellectual energies to seeking this order and calling on his followers to live by it, even if this conflicts with the conventions of the city. At the beginning of *The Republic*, the characters of Cephalus and Polemarchus represent these conventions, whose inadequacy for living the good life Socrates easily

---

25. For an English translation see Plato, *The Republic*.

demonstrates. Well into the first book, however, Thrasymachus makes his appearance, arguing for a radically historicist understanding of justice. Justice, he avers, is nothing but the advantage of the stronger. Those who are in positions of authority in the city have attained them through superior strength. Although they may make a pretense of ruling in the public interest, they are in reality governing in their own interest at the expense of the larger political community. This, of course, renders meaningless the distinction between the three lawful forms of government and their unlawful counterparts, as explicated in Plato's *Gorgias* and elsewhere. Might makes right, as the old cliché puts it.

Some two millennia later the Florentine statesman and philosopher, Niccolò Machiavelli, notoriously argues that conventional standards of right and wrong, justice and injustice, might have to be flouted by the prince in the interest of securing and maintaining political stability within his realm.[26] Machiavelli's is not an argument for cruelty and ruthlessness, as is sometimes thought by those who have turned his name into a pejorative adjective. Rather it is better for the means of violence to remain in the background. If they have to be used too frequently, the prince's authority is almost certainly in danger. Yet such means should remain visible enough to inspire a healthy dose of fear in the subjects. All of this is in the interest of upholding an otherwise fragile political stability, which is to the benefit of all, and not merely to the prince himself.

Writing in the following century, Thomas Hobbes (1588–1679) articulates a vision of society which owes something, not only to Thrasymachus and Machiavelli, but to Epicurus and his followers.[27] Nature is no longer a normative order, as it was for the Greeks; it is merely the movement of matter and energy, to which we can attach no prescriptive judgments and which can be analyzed only in terms of material causes and effects. There are no virtues possessing an intrinsically normative character. A virtue is only a human quality esteemed by others, nothing more. The key to understanding human beings is that they are moved by a variety of passions, all of which are reducible to a single motivating force: the fear of a violent death and the desire for self-preservation. Hobbes' account of the pre-political state of nature as a war of all against all is familiar enough not to require further elaboration here. Suffice it to say, however, that the extreme insecurity produced by such a condition eventually prompts individuals to

---

26. Macchiavelli, *The Prince*, 1–37.
27. See especially Hobbes, *Leviathan*, 41–283.

enter into political society. They do so by means of a contract whose terms are enforced by a sovereign power monopolizing the means of coercion. Without this sovereign power, the contract is null and void because it is unenforceable. With this sovereign power, the contract continues in force, but the sovereign himself is not subject to its terms. He remains above the law and is the ultimate arbiter of right and wrong, just and unjust. He cannot be legitimately questioned, because his monopoly of the instruments of force makes him effectively unassailable.

Hobbes' emphasis on contract is not sufficient to place him in our fourth and next category, which reduces authority to a voluntary contract. This is because, despite his influence on the subsequent development of social contract theorists such as Locke and Rousseau, for Hobbes the mere making of a promise can never be adequate to invest someone with authority. You and I may both pledge to obey the decrees of person A. But if person A is unable to remove the mutual fear that darkens our lives and replace it with the more manageable fear of himself, then our obligation to him ceases. The old common law maxim has it that promises made under duress are null and void. Hobbes turns this on its head: promises made *apart* from such duress are null and void. They simply cannot be believed, especially if fulfilling one's promise threatens one's life and livelihood. The fact that all people, when pushed to the brink, will fight to preserve themselves means that the only certain way to ensure social stability is to invest the sovereign with sufficient instruments of force to strike fear in his subjects' hearts and so prevent them turning on each other. Fear is never banished from the Hobbesian commonwealth; it is merely localized in the person of the sovereign and thus made more manageable.

What the proponents of this view have in common is the conviction that human beings are fairly simple creatures, responding in predictable ways to the exertion of force or the extension of incentives. Often these incentives are of a brute physical character, as the mere possession of coercive power is assumed to confer the right to govern. However, one more question should be addressed before we move on: Even if rulers do possess instruments to provide incentives and disincentives, and even if it be assumed that their authority is reducible to this power, is not the power at issue really psychological in nature? After all, power is being exercised *by extending threats or promises*, an action which focuses on changing people's mental states in an obedient direction. Nevertheless, it is the instruments backing up those threats and promises that would justify placing this conception in a different category from our first, as described above. Idle threats and false promises are naked examples of psychological manipulation. If, on the other hand, those subject to such threats and promises see them carried out—occasionally with respect to the former and consistently with respect to the latter—then they will obey because of this.

One more feature needs to be noted with respect to this approach. The focus on instruments of power does not create *community* as such. The extension of benefits and administration of punishments is quite compatible with an aggregate of persons retaining a fairly narrow and atomized view of their own particular interests. Here people obey the law and vote for particular candidates in order to gain favors or to avoid unpleasant consequences for themselves alone and not for any larger public interest. Authority is obeyed, not because it is right to do so, but because the subjects believe that obedience will procure certain advantages for themselves in their private capacities.

Most basically, the central flaw in the instrumental approach is that it is unable to justify obedience to one party rather than to another when both evidently possess the instruments of power. What, for example, does the Canada Revenue Agency possess that an ordinary thief who also demands my money does not? This the instrumental approach is unable to answer.

4. Authority As Voluntary Contract

Although Hobbes laid the foundation for the subsequent development of social contract theory, his successors took it in a somewhat different direction. If Hobbes focused on the instruments of power undergirding political order, later contractarian thinkers stressed the act itself whereby the wills of the parties were united to establish freely society and government. The means of enforcing the terms of the contract are clearly ancillary to this act, which is sufficient to place the contractarians in a new category.

It is appropriate to begin with John Locke, whose ideas are familiar to especially Americans because Thomas Jefferson incorporated them in his *Declaration of Independence*. Locke is something of a synthetic figure, clearly dependent on Hobbes for his foundational categories, yet unable to bring himself to abandon the older notions of right undergirding so much of the pre-modern western tradition of political theorizing.

Accordingly, for Locke the pre-political state of nature, rather than necessarily being a state of general warfare in which force and fraud are the chief virtues, is somewhat more pacific than for Hobbes. Indeed the principles of right retain their validity, despite the absence of a mechanism of enforcement. In particular, human beings retain the right to life, liberty, and property, the last of which plays a central role in Locke. Yet because the protection of property is in the hands of individuals, all of whom possess the "executive power of the law of nature" and must thus depend on their own varying degrees of strength, people are motivated to leave behind the state of nature, to contract with each other to enter into society, and eventually to establish civil government.[28]

Though we believe the contractarian view of authority to possess a distinctive character of its own, it must be admitted that, superficially at least, it bears some similarity to two previous categories, the conflations with persuasion and with the instruments of power. How so? However one conceives the social contract, it is generally *about* perceived goods valued by the parties to the contract. Thus in Locke, as long as civil government succeeds in protecting private property, it retains its legitimacy. This would seem to be similar to Hobbes' conflation of authority with the instruments of power. To be sure, the government's legitimacy rests in the consent of the governed, but Locke clearly assumes that this consent will be forthcoming as long as the government protects its subjects' privately-owned property. If it fails to do so, the subjects are justified in appealing to heaven, as Locke euphemistically calls an act of rebellion against the political rulers. Yet what if the subjects consent to government despoiling them of their own property? This they will not do, and this is where the contractarian approach appears to resemble the conflation with persuasion, with its appeal to reason. It would not be reasonable for the parties to a contract to agree to something which would harm their lives and possessions. Thus an element of persuasion must necessarily enter the picture, as rulers—at least at the initial stage of the contract's formation—appeal to their potential subjects' rationality as a ground for assuming empirical power over them.

However, the notion of a ruler persuading her subjects to follow her lead does not begin to do justice to the contractarian position, which views authority as flowing upwards from the parties themselves rather than downwards from the rulers' initiative. If human beings are truly

---

28. Locke, *Second Treatise*.

rational, and if they exercise their reason properly, they will voluntarily imbue their governing institutions with the authority they themselves already possess by nature. This is more than the claim that those subject to authority must approve its directives through persuasion; it goes so far as to claim that the person or institution asserting authority can claim at most a commission from the people, from whom all authority must originate. Following Paul-Louis Courier, philosopher Yves René Simon labels this the "coach-driver" theory of authority.[29] Because the coach-driver is hired by his passengers to take them where they wish to go, he possesses no authority in the genuine sense. Though he may appear to be leading, his authority is illusory. The same can be said of all governing authority within a larger body of persons. Such authority is always derived from the whole.

Yet one cannot take the coach-driver metaphor too far and still remain within the contractarian position. After all, the coach-driver's passengers are free to exit the vehicle if they change their minds as to where they wish to go. By contrast, Locke's appeal to heaven notwithstanding, the parties to the social contract, once they have entered it, are bound by the decisions made by the governors and are not at liberty to disobey simply because they dislike or disagree with the decision. This would seem to indicate that the authority possessed by political rulers is genuine, if ultimately derived, authority.

The contractarian position takes different forms in Jean-Jacques Rousseau and Immanuel Kant, and more recently in Hannah Arendt and John Rawls. Rousseau, though using liberal terminology, takes it in a markedly illiberal direction by investing the general will of the people with a status superior to the individuals comprised by it. Here the contract is not a limited one, as it is in Hobbes, where there are practical limits, and in Locke, where there are moral and legal limits. Rousseau's contract is a total one, in which the parties give up the whole of themselves to the sovereign, retaining not even the right to defend their own lives or their right to property.[30] The sovereign, of course, is not an all-powerful ruler or autocrat. It is not a king or even a parliament. It is the totality of citizens assembled for the purpose of legislating. It is only in making the law that the sovereign comes into its own. The general will

---

29. Simon, *Democratic Government*, 147; quoting Courier, *Lettres au rédacteur du Censeur*, 62–63.

30. Rousseau, *Social Contract*, I.6.

of the sovereign animates the law and confers legitimacy on what would otherwise be a mere decree emanating from a particular will.

The general will has a rather precarious existence even under the best of circumstances, which are difficult enough to articulate in theory, and perhaps impossible to effect in reality. It cannot come to be in a large state where the people are too numerous to gather together for purposes of legislating or too heterogeneous with respect to their interests. It thus requires a small city-state of like-minded citizens who are unlikely to be overawed by the particular will of a single would-be ruler. In contrast to Hobbes, the mere possession of might is not sufficient to create right.[31] In fact, where a particular will has overpowered the general will through superior force, there is no legitimacy to this form of political rule, and the subjects are at liberty to throw off their shackles when and if they are able to do so. Rousseau has a somewhat restricted conception of the threat of tyranny, which occurs only when a particular will destroys the general will. However, the general will itself cannot become tyrannical, because it cannot will to hurt its members. This means that the mechanisms Rousseau employs to preserve the general will cannot themselves become tyrannical. Even his notorious civil religion, which in effect calls for banishing all orthodox believers in revealed religions, can never be defined as oppressive, even if people on the receiving end might feel it to be so.

Kant follows Rousseau in his emphasis on will, though Kant more carefully articulates the character of this will and how it legitimates a proposed action. When an individual contemplates an action, he must refrain from simply deferring to authority, which amounts to an abdication of personal responsibility, and think through its implications by means of the categorical imperative. According to the categorical imperative, a proposed action is right insofar as it can be universalized, that is, insofar as the agent could wish to see it practiced by every other moral agent.[32] This categorical imperative functions in a way similar to Rousseau's general will, though it functions at a higher level of abstraction and obviates the need for a literal assembly of the whole to pronounce something just. Its success is guaranteed by the universal possession of reason, which leads all human beings to come to the same or similar conclusions with respect to the content of right and justice. Though Kant intends his categorical imperative as a guide to all ethical decision-making, it certainly has relevance to political judgments

---

31. Ibid., I.3.
32. Kant, *Fundamental Principles of the Metaphysic of Morals*, § 2.

in particular. Kant is by no means an antinomian, but he does view law as rooted in the autonomous wills of individuals acting in concert through their common possession of reason.

Hannah Arendt bears at least a superficial resemblance to Rousseau insofar as she favors a small-scale body politic in which citizens can meet face-to-face for the purposes of acting and speaking in the company of their fellow citizens. Though action is potentially limitless in its impact on the subsequent unfolding of human history, the citizens are bound together by mutual promises, the first of which is the very act of foundation calling the political community into being.[33] This act provides the authority necessary to legitimate subsequent acts by the citizens, whatever their content. For Arendt the small public space is necessary for the possession of genuine political freedom where there is neither ruling nor being ruled. The authority for law, based for the ancients on natural law or a claimed revelation from above, must be rooted in this initial foundational act if genuine participatory freedom is to be preserved.

John Rawls adapts Kant's ideas and carries them to an even higher level of abstraction, if that were possible. Once again, for Rawls, as for Kant, there need not be an actual popular assembly to ratify the principles of justice. It is only necessary to demonstrate that all human beings, stripped of their historically contingent particularities, would assent to a specific rule if they were properly exercising their reason. Placed behind his famous veil of ignorance in his original position of equality—counterpart to the early contractarians' state of nature—rational individuals would choose rules of justice to which all would be bound.[34]

If individuals—or the collected people—are not the originators of the laws under which they are expected to live, then there is doubt as to the validity of these laws. The mere claim to legal status is not enough to secure their authority, because authority is believed to issue from below. The conflation of authority with voluntary contract is especially attractive in a polity influenced by liberalism or by what Russell Kirk labels "democratism," i.e., the belief in the sovereignty of the democratic people.[35] A central difficulty with this school is that it cannot account for what might be called the coordinative function of authority in a community of diverse members with varying interests. Contractarians tend to assume

---

33. Arendt, *On Revolution*, 179–215.

34. See Rawls, *Theory of Justice*, and our discussion of Rawls in chapter 3 below.

35. Kirk, *The Politics of Prudence*, 272–86. Elsewhere I have labeled this latter phenomenon "democracy as creed." See my *Political Visions and Illusions*, 124–51.

that the natural state of man is one of primitive anarchic equality, wherein no one is intrinsically subject to another.[36] Only their mutual agreement can create such bonds of obligation between them, including the bonds of authority and obedience.

There is, of course, an element of truth in this. Authority does not arise out of some natural or biological superiority of one person or a class of persons over all others, as the racist ideologies of the past have averred.[37] No one would arbitrarily select two people off the street and claim, based on a combination in each of perceived personal qualities such as intelligence, ethnicity and skin color, that one must therefore be permanently set over the other as a sergeant would be over a private in the military. In real life each person would be in a complex web of authoritative relationships with each other and with many others besides. Rousseau asserts that, in the absence of such natural authority, "conventions form the basis of all legitimate authority among men."[38] This is true as long as one understands that such conventions are not purely arbitrary and self-seeking but answer to a genuine need built into the fabric of community itself. The existence of conventions and the authority associated with them are, in short, not optional even if the specific forms they take are variable according to time and place.

5. Authority As Natural Or Biological Superiority

This approach is manifested in two different schools, one of which has been thoroughly discredited in the past half century or so. We shall begin with the latter. Recall Rousseau's dictum that "no man has a natural authority over his fellow," which would seem evident to us now.[39] This can only be understood against a backdrop in which it was widely, if not universally, assumed that society is an ordered hierarchy with everyone occupying a fairly set position within it, often on the basis of ascribed and unchangeable qualities. Those who are at the bottom rung of the social ladder instinctively defer to their "betters," however this "better-ness" be defined. Aristotle had argued for the existence of "slaves by nature," i.e., those possessing sufficient reason to understand but not to issue

---

36. See Rousseau, *Social Contract*, I.4.
37. See, e.g., the next section immediately below.
38. Rousseau, *Social Contract*, I.4; trans. Cole, 389.
39. Ibid.

commands.[40] He similarly maintains that "the male is by nature superior, and the female inferior; and the one rules, and the other is ruled" and that "this principle, of necessity, extends to all mankind."[41] Though Plato, at least in his *Republic*, admitted the possibility of movement through the ranks, he too viewed society as a hierarchy, with "iron" and "bronze" classes deferring to the "silver" and "gold" classes,[42] the last of which is occupied by his famous philosopher-kings.

One needs to be cautious in tarring every notion that distinguishes "us" from "them" with the chauvinist or racist brush. Ethnocentrism is often thought to be a peculiarly western vice, but in truth every culture is and must be ethnocentric in some sense, much as communion between individuals must begin with consciousness of the self and its identity. In the biblical record the ancient Hebrews distinguished themselves from the surrounding gentile nations and believed themselves to be chosen by God from among those nations. Although the ancient Greek city-states were politically fragmented and quarrelsome, there was a consciousness of at least linguistic commonality over against non-Greek-speaking "barbarians." It is also scarcely unusual for a particular people to believe that its own ways are best, a conviction perhaps born more of familiarity than of a malicious xenophobia. However, there is an ever-present possibility that the universal fondness for the familiar will turn into something much more distorted, if a belief in the natural superiority of one's own people and its customs leads to the conviction that this people must, therefore, rule over other, inferior peoples.

Well into modern times the ruling houses of Europe were populated by those boasting "royal blood," which was presumed to fit them to govern mere commoners. Those less royal, such as the Dukes of Norfolk, might have "noble blood" flowing through their veins, which justified their local rule over the non-noble subjects living within their domains. It is difficult for us to recall a time when political leaders could get worked up over a forthcoming morganatic marriage between a prince and a commoner. Into the mid-twentieth century the European colonial empires were predicated on a general belief in what Rudyard Kipling famously called *The White Man's Burden* (1899), viz., that Europeans as a superior race were charged with the responsibility for civilizing the peoples of Asia and Africa who had

---

40. Aristotle, *Politics* I.1254b.20.
41. Ibid., I.1254b.15; trans. Jowett, 1132.
42. Plato, *The Republic* III.415.

come under their rule. Here the paternal metaphor was often employed, albeit without the recognition of its obvious limits given that minor children eventually grow up and leave the parental household.

The nationalist movements of the nineteenth and twentieth centuries were often motivated by a similar sense of cultural, or even racial, superiority over other neighboring nations. This belief often came at the expense of ethnic minorities living within the claimed territory of a particular nation. The cinematic character Gus Portokalos, from *My Big Fat Greek Wedding*,[43] is a caricature of the ethnic nationalist, claiming that the etymological root of the word *kimono* is Greek and that "[t]here are two kinds of people - Greeks, and everyone else who wish they was Greek." More dangerously, of course, conflicting territorial claims of ethnic nationalists led directly to the Balkan Wars of 1912 and 1913 and, indirectly, to the outbreak of the Great War in 1914. Such conflicts resumed on a smaller scale after the collapse of communism at the end of the century.

The most extreme example of twentieth-century chauvinism was that of Adolf Hitler's national socialists, or Nazis, as they are better known. The Nazis believed that history was a record of struggle among the various races of the world for supremacy. In Darwinian fashion, they were convinced that the "Aryan race," i.e., the Germanic people, was destined, through its innate superiority, to triumph over presumed inferior races, such as Slavs and Jews. This belief in Germanic superiority fueled the Nazi effort to conquer Europe and, eventually, to exterminate the Jews.

More recent examples of racist policies can be found in the "Jim Crow" laws of the American South and the apartheid policies of the Afrikaner-dominated National Party in South Africa between 1948 and 1994. Both once more were based on the presumed inferiority of the subject races, although the rhetoric of apartheid was often dressed in the language of plural development and the self-determination of distinct cultural communities, something wrongly assumed capable of appealing to nonwhite South Africans, as well as to liberal westerners. The Southern states' policies of racial segregation were a holdover from the era of slavery before 1865, initially ratified by the United States Supreme Court's decision in *Plessy vs. Ferguson* (1896), but overruled in *Brown vs. the Board of Education of Topeka, Kansas* (1954). Efforts by Nelson Mandela's African National Congress in South Africa and by Dr. Martin Luther King's Southern Christian Leadership Conference in the

---

43. Joel Zwick, *My Big Fat Greek Wedding*, Golden Circle Films, 2002.

US eventually cast such racist policies into permanent disrepute. As late as 1968 it was possible for Alabama Governor George Wallace to campaign for the presidency on a segregationist program, but by the end of the twentieth century overt segregationist rhetoric had declined to nearly nil, at least in polite company. The notion, in particular, that the rights of citizenship should be limited to the members of a single dominant race was effectively dead.

The general pre-modern view of the position of women in society provides the second major example of this view of authority, particularly in its later historical stages. In a primitive tribal or agrarian society a gendered division of labor is nearly universal, due to the different physical capacities of men and women—all-important in a community living close to the soil and at the mercy of the vicissitudes of nature. If the eldest male of the community is chieftain, assuming a number of roles, including those of political leader and priest, it may not be only his maleness that has a bearing on his status. His strength in battle, his perceived success in placating the gods, the number of his wives and children, and his relationship to the old chieftain may all play a role.

Such undifferentiated male-centered authority continued to play a role as societies developed further over the centuries. In medieval and early modern Europe, monarchies developed such that females were generally excluded from the throne, especially in those jurisdictions, such as Hannover and Luxembourg, bound by Salic Law. This was due to the expectation that a prince must lead his troops into battle. The story of King Henry VIII's obsession with producing a male heir for the throne of England is familiar enough that we tend to forget that he was motivated, not merely by what contemporary feminists would call "sexism" or by his avaricious sexual appetite (though that may have been a factor), but principally by a desire to avoid a recurrence of the dynastic wars of the previous century. Where the legal preference for a male heir continues, e.g., in the British and associated Commonwealth monarchies until recently, it does so as a vestige of a much older practice that made sense in its historical context.

By the late nineteenth and early twentieth centuries, however, the situation had clearly changed, primarily due to the further differentiation or complexification of society. Offices once reserved for men were assailed by those who rightly believed women qualified to hold them. The extension to women of the right to vote was a key achievement in especially the English-speaking democracies in the immediate aftermath of the Great War. Increasingly it was no longer obvious that women as a group should be permanently subordinate to men apart from a specific authoritative office an individual man might occupy. Here the contribution of feminism in its various forms can hardly be overestimated. Now it seems evident to at least westerners living in advanced, post-industrial societies that women and men should be guaranteed legal equality and have comparable opportunities in seeking to fulfill their life's callings and aspirations.

There is a second school less obviously racist or sexist but which nevertheless believes in an ineffable quality elevating some persons over others. Bertrand de Jouvenel is a good example of this approach. He begins by affirming that authority is born of the need for human cooperation. Such cooperation is effected by authority, by someone in a position of "natural ascendency." It cannot arise spontaneously and simultaneously in everyone. Rather, any collective initiative must originate with a single person, who in turn exercises influence over an expanding circle of his fellow human beings. Some observers mistakenly assume that the impetus to action comes through the threat of violence. Yet even in the case of an actual conquest, this interpretation cannot explain how the original company of conquerors was established in the first place. Jouvenel believes that human association comes about "by the summons of a man."[44]

The element of consent is significant here. In fact, Jouvenel defines authority as "the faculty of gaining another man's assent." It is "the efficient cause of voluntary associations,"[45] "the ability of a man to get his own proposals accepted."[46] Authority is embodied in a "natural ascendancy" possessed by some over others. This appears to be something like innate leadership abilities enabling their possessor to get others to do their bidding. The similarity to Weber's charismatic authority would seem evident. Authority is surrounded with a "halo" which bestows prestige on its holder.

However the exercise of this authority is not to be equated with the use of power. Authority is distinguished from mere power by the fact that the former "is exercised only over those who voluntarily accept it,"[47] which brings up the element of persuasion. Because of Jouvenel's emphasis on persuasion as the efficient cause of obedience to authority, one might at first glance tend to place him in the same category as Friedrich,

44. Jouvenel, *Sovereignty*, 29.
45. Ibid.
46. Ibid., 31.
47. Ibid., 32.

who believes that authority can be ascribed, not to persons as such, but only to their communications. Yet this is not exactly the same as Jouvenel's argument. Whether or not the persuasive efforts of the leader stand up to rational scrutiny is beside the point. The salient criterion is whether or not these communications are believed by those to whom they are directed. Jouvenel would freely admit that authority belongs to specific persons, even if the voluntary principle is the origin of this authority. The key element here is the *natural ascendancy* which the born leader possesses over others. Some people have got it; most have not. This natural ascendancy is enough to procure the consent of the governed, almost irrespective of the content of the communications flowing thereof.

The mainstream of the contractarian approach posits a natural equality of status among the parties to the contract. All inequalities of authority are interpreted as entirely conventional, that is, as rooted in normative precepts reducible to the mutual consent of the parties themselves. There is nothing intrinsic to human society requiring such inequality. However, by employing the word *natural* Jouvenel is already admitting the existence of pre-conventional inequality among human beings, something Rousseau explicitly denies. Person A and person B may argue for identical proposals in the assembly and may even defend them in exactly the same way. Yet person A lacks the natural ascendancy of person B and therefore fails where person B succeeds. The latter possesses an ineffable personal quality enabling him to persuade effectively, quite apart from the content of his communications. It is this quality that we call authority.

Once again, as in the previous conflations, there is something missing from Jouvenel's analysis, viz., authoritative *office*. Assuming the reality of natural ascendancy, one might nevertheless dispute its identification with authority as such. At most it is one of the ancillary means at authority's disposal, along with rational persuasive abilities, psychological power, coercive power, etc. Once more, the fact that the Secretary of State might be a strong personality with natural leadership skills does not in itself make her the President. Where a president's leadership is weak, his office may be attenuated accordingly, with others being required to fill in as needed. In such cases the office at issue may become but a formality, as the locus of effective responsibility comes to reside elsewhere. Yet even in such cases natural ascendancy alone is insufficient effectively to sideline the President apart from specific offices that might be able to assume such powers in extremity. A Secretary of State with acknowledged leadership abilities could conceivably make a credible claim to exercise effective authority, while an electrician from Sandusky, Ohio, could not, simply because he lacks, not only the relevant skills, but the relevant office.

6. Authority As Superior Knowledge Or Expertise

This may be the most widespread of the recent reductive accounts of authority, and it appeals strongly to a technologically sophisticated society where positions are distributed according to skill. The old patterns of nepotism and patronage, whereby offices are allocated according to family relationship or friendship, seem obviously atavistic and likely to curtail the growth of a dynamic economy and society. In Canada there are always complaints during a cabinet shuffle when a sitting prime minister moves a minister from one portfolio to a completely unrelated one, seemingly irrespective of his or her field of expertise. Reforms of the public service in North America in the late nineteenth and early twentieth centuries established the merit principle as the basis of hiring staff for the bureaucratic departments at the center of government. Universities hire faculty based on their attainment of a terminal degree in their field, as well as on previous experience and a good publication record. Isn't it evident that if one is an *authority in her field*, she should be heard and perhaps followed?

Plato's *Republic* may well be the most ancient example of the identification of authority with knowledge. Famously unsympathetic towards Athenian democracy, Plato's Socrates favors a political order in which everyone does that for which he is best fitted and philosophers rule as kings based on their knowledge of the good, the true, and the beautiful. Because most people are incapable of acquiring such knowledge, government must be placed in the hands, not of the many, but of the virtuous few. This argument is further bolstered in *The Statesman*, where rulership is given to those skilled in the art of statesmanship. The rule of law is clearly second best as compared to the rule of those possessing the requisite knowledge for true statesmanship.

There is a sense in which this knowledge already carries authority quite apart from a specific office occupied by its possessor. Because philosophy is much more than the capacity to think abstractly but holds the promise of lifting its practitioner above the sensible world to the very source of being, the philosopher's authority is very nearly of a priestly sort, communicating truth to those unable to attain it for themselves through the socratic method. Hence Socrates' concern to join the kingly office with philosophic wisdom, to invest those with epistemic authority with the authority of high political office, i.e., to make philosophers into kings.

This, of course, presents difficulties for democracy, as Aristotle recognized. According to Aristotle, "a citizen is one who shares in governing and being governed," though he admits that the definition of citizenship differs according to the form of government.[48] If, however, one finds within the polity a person of exemplary virtue who is obviously superior to his fellow citizens, it would be profoundly unjust to treat this "god among men" as their equal. In such cases there are only two alternatives: either all should submit themselves eagerly to his rule, or he himself should be subject to ostracism, i.e., banished from the polity for the sake of preserving its form of government.[49] Neither of these is precisely just, so the dilemma remains.

In fact, even without the occasional appearance of philosopher-kings on the stage of human history, recent centuries have only sharpened the tensions between authoritative office and those claiming the authority of perhaps a higher knowledge. This has opened a chasm between two very broad categories of approaches. First we find those who stand on established offices and legal precedents in the face of those who might subvert their authority. Second are those who denigrate such authority, claiming it to be in conflict with justice and truth understood in the abstract. Although the first school is often labeled conservative, the most thoughtful of progressives generally comprehend their own dependence on a stable political order characterized by the existence of a reliable legal framework within which the various offices find their place. Virtually everyone eschewing the revolutionary label would fall into this first category.

On the other hand, would-be revolutionaries arguably belong in the second school, assuming that, if a status quo political order is found to conflict with justice—or perhaps more properly: if *they* find it to do so—it may have to be abolished in its entirety and replaced with something more evidently just. This assumes, of course, that the revolutionaries themselves have a superior knowledge of what justice requires than do the duly constituted officials of the much maligned existing régime. In effect, epistemic authority is held to trump the authority of political office when the two

---

48. Aristotle, *Politics* III.1284a.
49. Ibid., III.1284a-b.

come into conflict. Refusing to submit their claims to a higher adjudicating authority that might be able to judge as to their rightness, the revolutionaries profess absolute confidence in their own epistemic authority, expecting that others will simply acquiesce in their claims.

Karl Marx famously believed that the historical process followed a particular pattern detectable by the enlightened observer sufficiently aware to look for it. Believing the economic class struggle to provide the key to understanding this process, he was convinced of his own knowledge of its workings. Marx believed in the inevitability of the victory of the oppressed proletariat over their bourgeois oppressors. Lenin, on the other hand, was forced to give history a bit of a push, seemingly admitting the failure of Marx's prognostications. The tool of this effort was an élite vanguard of the proletariat who would perform something of a prophetic, or even priestly function in representing the messianic proletariat. Believing in the higher authority of their own knowledge, Lenin's Bolsheviks had no qualms about seizing power in Russia from the elected, and thus presumably authoritative, constituent assembly in late 1917.

A number of observers are sufficiently disturbed by the claims of superior knowledge on the political realm to engage the issue in their own writings. Some of these, though certainly not all, go by the conservative label. Many adhere to a vague populism, while others claim to be recovering the classical tradition of civic republicanism. Christopher Lasch is one of the more eloquent opponents of the ongoing efforts of self-appointed élites to act as "would-be liberators" of the masses and to engage in "large-scale social engineering"[50] aimed at expanding possibilities and pushing back natural and conventional limits. Instead he places his confidence in ordinary people, who understand that mutual respect, and not a weakening of standards in the interest of being "compassionate," can be the only foundation for a civil society and a democratic state.[51]

Sir Bernard Crick fears a variety of non- or even antipolitical forces that would impair the functioning of politics. He is at pains in particular to defend ordinary politics, in all its untidiness, from the imposition of various visions that would curtail or eliminate the deliberative process that goes into the making of public policy. The principal threats he sees coming from technology, or rather the naïve belief that the significant problems facing society are merely technical and thus soluble by technical

---

50. Lasch, *The Revolt of the Elites* , 27.
51. Ibid., 92–114.

knowledge, and from ideology, which attempts to remake society based on abstract goals implemented by the state.[52] Both of these threats are based on the claim to a higher knowledge by élites. Hannah Arendt similarly fears technology and ideology, taking care to maintain the distinctiveness of political speech and action over against, on the one hand, those who would reduce them to labor and fabricating work and, on the other, those who would try to subject them to the categories properly belonging to the life of the mind.[53] Indeed it may be that the conspicuous absence of justice as a general concept in the thought of both Crick and Arendt is based on their reticence to admit the imposition of transformative gnostic visions into the give-and-take of political deliberation.

However, the mere presence of deliberation does not necessarily exclude the pretense of superior knowledge to those with a concern for the health of politics. Amy Gutmann and Dennis Thompson write in favor of dialogue among citizens in a process called deliberative democracy.[54] They make an eloquent plea for people to talk out their disagreements, seemingly echoing the concerns of Crick and Arendt to protect an open public realm. However, following John Rawls and ultimately Kant himself, Gutmann and Thompson suppose that all rational persons will come to the same conclusions if they follow the procedures of deliberative democracy. This gives them the confidence to assert the outcomes of such deliberation in advance, e.g., that opponents on the abortion issue will come to a moderate pro-choice position. It is, of course, one thing to urge citizens to dialogue; it is quite another to tell them beforehand what the results of such dialogue should be, a curious notion that would appear to render the dialogue itself superfluous.

There is, of course, a moment of truth in the tendency to locate authority in the possession of knowledge. Knowledge does confer on a person a certain *epistemic* authority, to use Richard De George's expression. Epistemic authority is a nonexecutive authority that does not issue in action, but rests solely in a person's superior knowledge.[55] A huge amount of what we claim to know comes from what we hear from others. We trust their claim to knowledge and on that basis make a similar claim to the same knowledge. The fact that people believe what other people tell

---

52. Crick, *In Defence of Politics*, especially chapters 5 and 2.

53. See especially Arendt, *The Human Condition*, and her incomplete trilogy, *The Life of the Mind*.

54. See, e.g., Gutmann and Thompson, *Democracy and Disagreement*.

55. De George, *The Nature and Limits of Authority*, 27.

them makes the latter *de facto* epistemic authorities. In this respect we are surrounded by epistemic authorities on all sides. If John has taken up the study of anthropology on his own, he may be justly said to be an authority in that field. If, however, he were to show up at the local university and attempt to teach courses in anthropology, all his expertise would not make him a *professor* of anthropology, because he lacks the relevant office enabling him to teach this field in an academic setting. If his knowledge of a certain subfield is greater than that of one of the tenured faculty, this still does not give him the authority to teach in that university. The possession of epistemic authority cannot by itself confer the executive authority of office.

Conclusion

In exploring the conflations above, the reader should not take me to imply that the elements with which authority is frequently identified do not play a role in authority. All of them do, though not always to the same extent within each communal context. For example, although authority is not to be confused with persuasion, the latter is certainly among the means available to authority, particularly when there is general doubt concerning one of its particular directives. A good case study of this is the campaign by governments to publicize seat belt laws, which are otherwise practically unenforceable. Government efforts to disseminate knowledge of the dangers of smoking are a similar form of persuasion, although in this case such persuasion does not bolster obedience to a law as such, since use of tobacco is legal. Similarly, the focus on contract is not entirely misguided, particularly with respect to organizations that genuinely do have a voluntary basis, e.g., housing cooperatives, choral societies, amateur football clubs, etc. Even the state's authority to a very large extent presupposes at least the tacit *consent* of the citizens/subjects, even if it is not reducible to contract as such. Moreover, natural or biological differences certainly play more of a role in marriage and family than in the more obviously organized communities. As for the role of expertise and superior knowledge, this is certainly important with respect to the filling of offices requiring specialized skills and education. Most obviously the person filling the office of teacher should have the requisite credentials. A physician must have graduated from medical school with an MD. Many positions have prerequisites calling for previous training and experience. In the absence of these a person will not be invited to fill the position. If he or she is already in such an office and proves to lack the qualifications and capacities to exercise it effectively, this will inevitably have an impact on the office itself and the respect for it from those formally subject to it. It may even be grounds for dismissal. On the other hand, the mere fact of a student speaking up in class and offering a piece of information new to the teacher does not diminish or terminate the authority of the office of teacher.

If we were to summarize the basic flaw in all six of the above-mentioned conflations, we would probably have to conclude once again that authority is being identified with mere power, even if the types of power necessarily differ. Political realists in the line of Hobbes have often said that might makes right. Though we discussed Hobbes under the third category, there is a sense in which the ability to manipulate someone psychologically or to persuade someone is each a manifestation of power in the larger sense. Authority can thus be said to be something more than power. Power is ancillary to the exercise of authority, but it is not the same thing.

3

Authority and Autonomy

Does Authority Inhibit Freedom?

THE CITY OF NEW Haven, Connecticut, is home to Yale University, one of the traditional "Ivy League" schools in the United States. In 1961 a junior professor in psychology, Stanley Milgram, places an advertisement in a local newspaper soliciting participants in what is purported to be a study of memory. John Doe has answered the ad and is ushered by a white-coated experimenter into a room where another person is seated. Both are told the nature of the experiment in which they have elected to take part. One person is to be a teacher, the other a learner. They draw straws and Doe is to be the teacher, and the other man the learner. Both are taken to an adjacent room where the learner is seated at a table. A strap attached to an electrode is placed around his arm, with the teacher looking on. The experimenter explains that the teacher will be reading through a list of word pairs, which the learner will then have to read back to the teacher in the correct order. If he misses one of the pair, the teacher, who will be seated in the other room, will administer an electric shock, beginning at 15 volts, increasing the voltage with each successive error up to a high of 450. The experimenter assures the teacher that the shocks are not dangerous to the learner.

The experiment proceeds with the teacher reading the first pair of words. This continues until the learner makes the first mistake. As expected, Doe administers the initial shock to the learner, who is behind a closed door in the adjacent room. At some point after the learner has made a number of errors, the teacher hears the first audible, if somewhat muffled, indication of discomfort from the learner. The teacher looks hesitantly at the experimenter, expecting some guidance. The experimenter tells him to continue, which he does obediently. After more errors what started out as grunts from the learner become increasingly urgent cries of pain, coupled with a protest that he has a heart condition and wishes to end the experiment. Doe becomes increasingly agitated, expecting that the experimenter will intervene and put a halt to the project. But the experimenter remains calm, assuring him that he himself assumes all responsibility for what happens, instructing him to continue.

The teacher reads the next set of word pairs, the first of which the learner misses. The teacher administers 365 volts to the learner, who screams in pain. The learner now indicates that he does not want to go on.

"Please continue," says the experimenter, at which Doe protests.

"The experiment requires that you continue."

Taking a deep breath and rolling his eyes, Doe reads another set of word pairs, anxious to hear the result from behind the door. This time there is no sound at all, which alarms the teacher, who once again expresses a desire to quit and to check up on the health of the learner.

"It is absolutely essential that you continue," insists the experimenter, who is unperturbed by the protests. Doe objects once more.

"You have no other choice; you must go on."

The teacher proceeds to read the remaining word pairs up to the maximum voltage of 450 volts, despite his obvious fears that the learner may be unconscious and unable to respond. At the end Doe mops his brow with his handkerchief, his fears tempered by a feeling of relief that the ordeal is finally over.[1]

Virtually every first-year psychology student learns about the notorious Milgram experiments, which were undertaken, not to study memory as purported, but to gauge the extent to which people will obey authority, even under conditions that appear to compromise their moral commitments. Of course, the entire situation was a set-up. The "learner" was in reality an actor hired to play the part. The drawing of straws was fixed, with "teacher" written on both slips of paper. The "teacher" was given a mild shock before the start of the experiment to give him a sense of what the learner would be experiencing, but, apart from that, the elaborate console in front of him was a façade. The switches he threw did not shock the "learner" at all. The sounds emitted from the other room came from a tape recorder, timed to run after each "shock" was delivered.

---

1. This is a free summary of a typical case found in Milgram, *Obedience to Authority*.

How far would the "teacher" go in carrying out orders, even when hearing the agonizing cries of the victim/learner at the end of the "electrode." Would the subject break off the experiment, thereby defying authority, because he believed he was being commanded to do something wrong? Or would the subject, upon being assured by the white-coated experimenter that he assumed full responsibility, continue to administer "shocks" even up to the "dangerous" level of 450 volts?

Milgram had gone into the experiment believing that virtually all decent people would at some point refuse to proceed any further, because their moral convictions would not allow them to do so. However, what he found was both surprising and dismaying:

> Many subjects will obey the experimenter no matter how vehement the pleading of the person being shocked, no matter how painful the shocks seem to be, and no matter how much the victim pleads to be let out.... It is the extreme willingness of adults to go to almost any lengths on the command of an authority that constitutes the chief finding of the study and the fact most urgently demanding explanation.[2]

Milgram concluded that, for people to be brought to the point of performing such an action, they must first abandon their autonomy and enter into what he calls an *agentic* state, in which they see themselves as no longer responsible for their own actions and as nothing more than an agent for carrying out someone else's instructions. Thus authority, which is necessary for human survival insofar as it enables the achievement of cooperative endeavors, also has a dark side insofar as it facilitates the rise of tyrannies and totalitarian régimes, which rely for their very existence on the cooperation of vast numbers of citizens.

Like many people who had lived through the horrors of the Second World War, Milgram was appalled by the fact that so many ordinary Germans played their part in the Nazi death machine in obedience to orders issued by higher ups. Arendt's coverage of Adolf Eichmann's trial in Jerusalem seemed to confirm that, far from being cruel or sadistic, Eichmann was a mere bureaucrat functioning within an extensive chain of command.[3] How is it possible that otherwise ordinary, decent people can be brought to the point of doing harm to their fellow human beings? They do so, according to Milgram, by subordinating their own wills to

---

2. Ibid., 5.
3. See Arendt, *Eichmann in Jerusalem: A Report on the Banality of Evil*.

those of others, thereby becoming mere agents of the latter. Their ability to reason morally is thus impaired by the felt need to defer to authority. In the case of these experiments, the presence of authority was conveyed by the white lab coat of the experimenter, by the official-looking venue and by the prestige of the university under whose auspices they were conducted. All of these elements combined to induce the unwitting subjects to give up their freedom and to commit acts they would otherwise not do.

The first major error addressed in the previous chapter is the tendency to confuse authority with one of the capacities at its disposal. In this chapter we shall address a second major error, which consists of the tendency to oppose authority and freedom. Those working from within this perspective tend to view freedom or liberty in a positive light while viewing authority negatively. The experience of Nazi Germany and Milgram's experiments have only reinforced this point of view. The common assumption, since at least the French Revolution, is that, even in its most benevolent form, authority is intrinsically alienating, preventing the person from living in accordance with his own will. As noted in chapter 1, Yves René Simon speaks in this regard of authority's bad reputation.

Simon is at pains to demonstrate that authority and autonomy, the latter of which must be understood in the Thomistic and not the Kantian sense, are complementary and ought not to be conceived as polar opposites. The two are opposed only with respect to authority's substitutional function, that is, when parental authority substitutes for the absent maturity of the child under its care. Here the freedom of the latter must continually expand at the expense of the authority of parents. However, when authority's function is essential, e.g., in choosing among equally good means to a given end or in willing the form and content of the common good, then authority and freedom are rightly to be regarded as supplementary.[4] Yet even Simon, who has otherwise done so much to recover a robust appreciation of authority's place in human society, persists in viewing authority and freedom *as different things* needing to be related to each other in some fashion.

Those in the grip of a liberal ideology, whether this be understood in the rhetorical North American sense or in the larger western sense, are wont to assume the reality of a redemptive historical trajectory whereby personal liberty must continually expand at the expense of authority conceived in a generic, undifferentiated form. Authority, deemed

---

4. Simon, *Democratic Government*, 139–41.

something of a relic of an oppressive past, is to be continually superseded by social forms facilitating voluntary cooperation among persons in a state of equality *vis-à-vis* each other. Hence David Easton, as noted in the previous chapter, believes that authority must increasingly be replaced by persuasion. Sennett advocates the periodic disruption of the chain of command stretching from authority downwards and connecting it to those under its jurisdiction. Arendt wishes to establish an open political space where citizens can freely come together and where there is neither ruling nor being ruled.

Not everyone we have looked at thus far actually aspires to abolish authority. Some wish merely to diminish its scope, while others identify it with one of the capacities at its disposal, as noted in chapter 2. The latter strategy enables them to affirm authority in some sense while repudiating the claims usually made on its behalf, particularly the expectation of obedience from those under it. This is Carl Friedrich's approach. The contractarians undertake to soften the reality that authority impinges on an individual's will by basing its legitimacy on a collective manifestation of such wills. By contrast, our argument here is that, far from being polar opposites, freedom and authority are related to each other in the following way: *What we often think of as personal freedom is itself a type of authority, finding its own legitimate place within the pluriform manifestations of authority comprised by an ordinary human society*. Thus when we experience a conflict between authority and freedom, we are in reality seeing a *conflict between the claims of two different authorities*. In this respect the contending claims between personal authority and, say, political authority are not essentially different from those between church and state, or state and business enterprise. Those following the modern tendency to privilege the individual and her liberties are generally unable to see this clearly.

The Allure of Freedom

There can be no doubt that freedom is something people find deeply attractive. When we were growing up under the authority of our parents, it was often grating to have to follow their instructions when we preferred to be doing something different. In the middle of an impromptu baseball game, how often did we receive the parental call to come in and do our homework or practice the piano or eat supper. We knew from experience that there were consequences for not doing as we were told. These were consequences we preferred to avoid, so we abandoned our play and came into the house. During these years of childhood and adolescence, we looked forward to the time we would be fully grown and thus, we assumed, able to do as we please.

Yet once we were adults and on our own, we quickly discovered that we had come into a wide range of responsibilities that limited our ability simply to follow our own proclivities. These responsibilities cut across the full array of life's activities, including work and family. In the workplace we found ourselves under immediate supervision for eight hours a day, five days a week. Even if we thought our work should proceed in a certain way, our own judgment might be overruled by the supervisor or by company policy, which called for something different. Similarly, in planning holidays, we were constrained by the needs and wishes of a spouse and children as to destination and timing. All of these can be said to constrain our freedom—if, that is, freedom be defined as the mere right to act as we wish.

If freedom is a desired condition, then of course its achievement must be secured against a potential or genuine rival, which may be viewed either passively, as the lack of ability to do something, or actively, as an agent bent on suppressing this freedom. The various ideological visions that compete within the contemporary political landscape generally agree that freedom is a good thing, but they define its contours somewhat differently. The early liberals, including Thomas Hobbes, John Locke, and Adam Smith, viewed liberty largely as the absence of external impediments. These impediments could come from a variety of sources, all of which might become so *in the name of freedom itself*, a condition labeled the *state of nature*. In this hypothetical state, human beings in principle have perfect freedom to do as they wish, but their liberty of action is in reality threatened by the presence of others possessed of the same freedom. Hobbes, of course, argued for the enhancement of state power as the best means of freeing people from their fear of each other.

By contrast, Locke and Smith believed that the greatest threat to freedom comes from government, a stance maintained by such recent libertarians as Friedrich von Hayek and Ludwig von Mises. Writing in the middle of the eighteenth century, Montesquieu believed that the best way to preserve freedom is to divide sovereignty among three branches of government: the legislative, the executive, and the judiciary, a position that had a large influence on the founders of the American federal system a few decades later.[5] Not every American state necessarily accepted the sufficiency of this division of powers and, as a price for their ratification of the new constitution, successfully argued for a bill of rights explicitly guaranteeing freedoms of religion, of speech, of the press, and so forth.

Sir Isaiah Berlin made a famous distinction between negative and positive freedom—between *freedom from* and *freedom to*. The former he associated with the early liberal figures mentioned above, while the latter he identified with individual self-mastery as extolled by Rousseau and Kant.[6] These two concepts might also be tied to Leo Strauss's two initial waves of modernity, the first being primarily English in origin and the second having French and German roots.[7] This difference indicates already that the mere trumpeting of freedom as an ideal to be sought after may end up as little more than empty rhetoric unless we can agree upon a common definition, which is not easily forthcoming. Hegel believed that history was moving towards the progressive realization of freedom, but for him freedom was not to be identified with the classical liberal focus on expanding the sphere of individual prerogatives against an overweening state or an excessively powerful neighbor. Rather Hegel's freedom could be realized only within the larger framework of history, moving, under the direction of the state, towards a higher political unity over the chaotic forces of civil society.

Marx similarly assumed that the world historical movement towards the classless society would eventually free everyone from bondage to the oppressive division of labor and the class system it spawned. Freedom of speech, religion, the press, and so forth he disparaged as mere "bourgeois freedoms" masking the reality of class-based oppression in a capitalist society. In his somewhat irate and hairsplitting annotations to the 1875 Programme of the German Workers' Party, Marx lambasted its authors for their advocacy of religious freedom of conscience, instead preferring to "liberate the conscience from the witchery of religion."[8] Marx perhaps assumed that this would be readily accomplished, once the classless so-

---

5. Montesquieu, *Ésprit des lois* 11.

6. Sir Berlin, "Two Concepts of Liberty," 118–72. The essay itself was originally delivered in 1958 as his inaugural address at Oxford as the Chichele Professor of Social and Political Theory.

7. Strauss, "What Is Political Philosophy?," in *What Is Political Philosophy*, 9–55.

8. Marx, "Marginal Notes to the Programme of the German Workers' Party," in Marx and Engels, *Selected Works*, 333–34. These notes are popularly known as the Critique of the Gotha Programme.

ciety had eliminated the need for an opiate of the people, i.e., a painkiller to soften capitalism's oppression. Yet if people persisted in believing the tenets of their inherited faith traditions, this "freedom" might have to be accomplished through coercive methods, which goes some way in explaining the periods of religious persecution during the seven-decade Soviet era.

Following the Greeks of the classical era, Hannah Arendt defined freedom largely in terms of political participation. The right simply to be left alone is not freedom, which rather consists of acting and speaking in the company of one's fellow citizens within the context of the public realm. Thus Arendt might be seen to advocate Berlin's concept of positive freedom, were it not for her expressed hostility to Rousseau's notion of sovereignty and its tendency to quash the expression of individuality within political community.

Freedom As Autonomy: Rousseau and Kant

Despite the contemporary tendency to identify freedom with mere license, i.e., with the right to do as we please, the most thoughtful of political theorists, including those in the liberal tradition, understand that freedom must have some form of normative content and must be compatible with others' exercise of their own freedom. This necessitates the positing of limits—certainly external limits and perhaps internal as well. The case for external limits is often expressed in a pithy way: my right to swing my fist ends where your nose begins. Here my interior motive for swinging my fist is beside the point and cannot be called into question. But if it comes into contact with your nose, thus causing you injury, I have abused my freedom by exercising it beyond its proper limits. There is no question that my fist-swinging activity is by itself legitimate; no one can rightly criticize the content of my freedom. This accords with Berlin's notion of negative freedom.

Yet the reality is that freedom, like everything else, is frequently subject to abuse. This is no cause for abolishing it altogether, but it is reason to call into question its popular definition as the right to do as we please. In the ongoing development of liberalism, we have seen a pronounced shift in the conception of freedom from Hobbes up to the present. In Hobbes freedom means the ability to fulfill one's desires, which produces continual conflict. This conflict must be ended from without—by an all-powerful sovereign with the means to do so. The content of this widely-held freedom is not yet at issue. By the latter part of the eighteenth century, we find a renewed attempt to infuse freedom with some sort of content, but within the context of a distinctively modern worldview. St. Paul wrote of freedom in Christ (Gal 5), while the scholastic philosophers tied freedom to the virtue of practical wisdom or prudence. Both conceived of normative, internal constraints on the exercise of liberty.

When we get to Rousseau and Kant, however, we find these two philosophers attempting to go beyond the Hobbesian conception of freedom while continuing to work within the modern assumptions of the Hobbesian project. Rousseau does this by recourse to the general will, which he sees as the source of legitimacy in a polity. Against Hobbes he argues that the right of the strongest is insufficient to create political right. Yet law must nevertheless originate in the will and not in a higher law or reason outside that will, as the scholastics had held. That this will is not merely arbitrary is evident from Rousseau's distinction between the general will and the will of all. Because the latter is merely the aggregate of particular wills within a polity, it is incapable of creating right as such. By contrast, the general will "must be general in its object as well as its essence."[9] If one's own favored position loses in the vote of the sovereign assembly, it only proves that one has misjudged the general will. Should someone persist in pursuing one's preference after the general will has been determined, he will then be forced to be free,[10] suggesting that freedom definitely has substantive content and is not merely the *individual* exercise of the will.

For Rousseau then the social contract is nothing less than a means of enabling cooperation among people while preserving and even enhancing their freedom. In Rousseau's famous expression, "Man is born free; and everywhere he is in chains." The only way to legitimate these "chains," or limits to personal autonomy, is to ensure that the individual, as member of a sovereign people, retains the power to make the laws under which he must live. If the general will, which creates the sovereign, should be eclipsed by a particular will, then the individual loses his autonomy and is within his rights to try to liberate himself from these chains, which are no longer legitimate but are now oppressive.

---

9. Rousseau, *Social Contract*, II.4; trans. Cole, 397.
10. Ibid., I.7.

Kant follows the Rousseauan account of authority and its origin but puts his own unique twist on it. As a typical liberal, Kant undertakes to maximize individual freedom at the expense of authority, at least within the realm of ethics. The danger with such maximization is, of course, that human society will descend into a Hobbesian state of nature, that is, a state of general warfare, as individual self-seeking overwhelms all social constraints. But this danger is present only if freedom is defined as *mere* self-seeking—as the self doing no more than to follow its own proclivities irrespective of their moral status. This is not what Kant has in mind with his concept of *autonomy*, which entails a strong sense of duty. Kant's solution to this problem is found in the categorical imperative, which declares as morally right any act that one could will to become a universal law.[11] Far from producing a "do your own thing" form of morality, as some members of the baby boomer generation once put it, Kant's categorical imperative places an exacting duty on the responsible agent to think through every proposed action to ensure that it is rationally defensible from a universal standpoint. This includes the demands of those in authority, which are not to be taken *merely* on authority. Like everything else, these too must be weighed in the balance by the autonomous individual in accordance with the precepts of the categorical imperative. If not, then these demands might be rightly refused.

The quest for moral autonomy presupposes a certain maturity on the part of the reasoning subject. This connection between autonomy and maturity is brought to the fore by Jean Piaget and Lawrence Kohlberg, whose theories on the moral development of children exemplify this Kantian influence. According to Piaget, the development of moral reasoning in the child can be understood to occur in two basic stages. In the initial stage the young child believes naïvely that the rules of so simple a game as marbles are of adult or even divine origin and cannot be changed. Nevertheless she understands these rules in an egocentric way and is not yet capable of making them her own. They are strongly associated in her mind with adult constraints imposed externally, yet she does not actually practice them. Any innovation she herself makes she understands as merely discovering a heretofore unknown rule present from the beginning.[12]

---

11. Kant, *Fundamental Principles of the Metaphysics of Morals*.
12. Piaget, *The Moral Judgement of the Child*, 9–103.

By contrast, the older child has come to view rules quite differently. Rather than the vertical sociability of the earlier stage, the child at the more advanced stage is increasingly comfortable with a horizontal sociability, in which his and his peers' felt need to cooperate generates mutually acceptable rules. These rules do not come from adult authority but arise spontaneously in the midst of various social activities. Now procedures become important. Rules can easily be changed as long as proper procedures are followed and there is a consensus in favor. The older child has outgrown his previous belief in the mystical origins of these rules but is now more likely than the younger child to internalize them and to function within them. This entails nothing other than the attainment of autonomy and the relinquishing of heteronomy.

Piaget is by no means loath to draw parallels to adult societies, comparing the small children among his subjects to "many conservative adults who delude themselves into thinking that they are assisting the triumph of eternal reason over present fashion, when they are really the slaves of past custom at the expense of permanent laws of rational cooperation."[13] Similarly he attributes the "belief in the divine origin of institutions" to childish egocentrism and speaks, somewhat condescendingly, of "conformist communities, whose laws and customs are always attributed to some transcendental will."[14] Thus in a mature society of mature people, political democracy replaces theocracy and gerontocracy. Reason replaces reliance on tradition.

Kohlberg's approach is similar to Piaget's and traces the development of moral reasoning through six stages in the progression towards adulthood.[15] Kohlberg characterizes the first two stages as pre-conventional. In the first stage the child's actions are governed by fear of punishment. In the second, her actions are governed by the incentives attached to exchange in a marketplace: "You scratch my back and I'll scratch yours." The third and fourth stages are at the conventional level. In the third stage the child seeks the approval of others, and motives are taken into account for the first time. At stage four the child—or possibly by now adolescent—becomes oriented to the need for law and order. "Right behavior consists of doing one's duty, showing respect for authority, and maintaining the

---

13. Ibid., 67.
14. Ibid, 89.
15. Kohlberg, *The Philosophy of Moral Development*, 17–22.

given social order for its own sake."[16] At the post-conventional, autonomous, or principled level come the fifth and sixth stages. In stage five the person becomes oriented to the social contract deemed to be holding together the larger society. The emphasis is still on law, but with an added stress on flexibility due to "rational considerations of social utility." Democracy and consent of the governed are concerns for those reasoning at this fifth level. As Kohlberg puts it, "[t]his is the 'official' morality of the American government and Constitution."[17]

Finally, at the sixth stage the moral agent reasons in accordance with abstract self-chosen principles and acts accordingly, apparently without reference to authority, but simply out of a general regard for human dignity. Anyone following Kant's categorical imperative or Jesus' Golden Rule has placed herself at this most advanced moral stage. Tellingly, however, anyone following the Decalogue definitely finds himself at an earlier stage of moral development: possibly the fourth or even the first. Moreover, these stages can be readily matched to the major historical epochs of the west, beginning with an almost childlike medieval humanity believing in and fearing God, progressing through Hobbesian self-seeking, on to the Lockean social contract, and culminating in the Kantian project. The clear implication is that virtually all adults prior to the eighteenth century, with the notable exceptions of the Buddha, Socrates and Jesus, were moral infants, reflexively obeying authority and, for the most part, living unexamined lives.

Clearly Piaget and Kohlberg follow Kant in seeking a moral autonomy in which the individual person may live in accordance with her own self-imposed principles. Accepting something on authority is not appropriate for the mature adult capable of thinking rationally.

What are the political implications of this approach? As noted above, the human developmental stages closely parallel the larger historical trend of secularization in the west—albeit cut short well before the advent of Leo Strauss' "third wave" of modernity, viz., the era dominated by Friedrich Nietzsche and his heirs.[18] The political side of this development

---

16. Ibid., 18.

17. Ibid., 19.

18. Strauss, *What Is Political Philosophy*, 54–55. Existentialism, historicism, and postmodernism certainly represent an affirmation of the individual actor within history, but because each act performed is a singular act for which there are no readily applicable pre-existing rules, the actor must rely on his own intuitive judgment and not on something as elaborate as the categorical imperative.

indicates a movement away from overlapping patterns of patrimonial rule to early modern absolute monarchy to late modern democracy. Max Weber discerns in this an across-the-board transition from traditional forms of authority, such as kingship and hereditary aristocracy, to legal authority, with its focus on legal rules governing appointment or election to specific offices. We shall take this up more fully in the next chapter.

Yet even here authority as such remains firmly in place. Only its political basis has changed. Whether a ruler has inherited a throne or been elected president in no way affects the authority of the office itself. True, an elected official may have more discretion than an hereditary monarch where the popular consensus favors democracy. In contemporary constitutional monarchies, such as Canada and the United Kingdom, the Queen or her representative never takes the initiative and almost always follows the advice of her ministers. Yet at one time kings had considerable political power, as much as or more than an American president, whom Samuel Huntington likens to a Tudor monarch.[19] Although the differences between Henry VIII and Franklin D. Roosevelt were considerable, no one can doubt that both possessed political authority within the framework of their respective constitutions. Similarly, whether one is taxed by an elected parliament or by an absolute ruler may not make any difference with respect to the amount of money left in one's pocket. Both have the authority to collect revenue, irrespective of how they attained that authority. But might this authority be dispensed with altogether?

Kantian Anarchism: Robert Paul Wolff

From at least the nineteenth century, anarchism has been an alluring vision for some, as it holds out the prospect of living in a socially cooperative fashion, yet without the coordination of a higher—and presumably oppressive—political authority. If Rousseau attempted to legitimate the chains of obligation, anarchists would cast off these chains altogether, relying instead on spontaneous horizontal cooperation and the building of community from the bottom up. Proponents such as Mikhail Bakunin (1814–1876) and Prince Peter Kropotkin (1842–1921) split early with the socialists, with whom they otherwise shared a vision of social and economic equality, precisely over the issue of authority in a post-revolutionary world. Socialists recognized the need for authority to coordinate

---

19. Huntington, *Political Order in Changing Societies*, 93–139.

collective human activities,[20] while anarchists were certain that humanity, placed in a more favorable social environment, would naturally nurture the necessary ties enabling them to work and live together without authority's intervention. Once again, as do other ideologies, anarchism strongly appeals to the desire for freedom.

Although the Kantian element is by no means a major contributor to the anarchist movement, Robert Paul Wolff believes that Kantian moral autonomy necessitates philosophical anarchism. Believing that the obligation of moral autonomy stands in considerable tension with the existence of authority, he raises the possibility that "all beliefs in authority may be wrong."[21] Why? Because they conflict with the moral requirement that all human beings take responsibility for their own choices. If one acts solely because an authority commands it, and if one does not take the time to evaluate personally the rectitude of such an act, then one effectively abdicates one's own moral responsibility, which is ongoing and cannot be extinguished by authority's claims. Whenever someone commands obedience based on authority, he is calling on the person under him to suspend this responsibility, if only temporarily. Even democratic states attain legitimacy only by requiring that citizens forfeit their autonomy, which Wolff believes is unacceptable.

What are the alternatives? Only two. We must either "embrace philosophical anarchism and treat all governments as nonlegitimate bodies whose commands must be judged and evaluated in each instance before they are obeyed," or we must "give up as quixotic the pursuit of autonomy in the political realm and submit ourselves (by an implicit promise) to whatever form of government appears most just and beneficent at the moment."[22] Wolff opts for the former over the latter. Only anarchism is suitable to a polity composed of morally mature persons. Anything other than this entails treating adults as children incapable of reasoning for themselves as to what is right and wrong.

The language Wolff uses to defend his choice is revealing: "The moral condition *demands* that we acknowledge responsibility and achieve autonomy wherever and whenever possible...."[23] "The primary *obligation*

---

20. See, e.g., Engels, "On Authority," 730–33.
21. Wolff, *In Defense of Anarchism*, 10.
22. Ibid., 71.
23. Ibid., 17; emphasis mine.

of man is autonomy, the refusal to be ruled."[24] "It is *out of the question* to give up the commitment to moral autonomy. . . . I am then guilty of what Kant might have called the *sin* of willful heteronomy."[25] The use of the word *sin* is telling. It points to a basic tension in Wolff's endeavor. In speaking of the *obligation* of moral autonomy or the *sin* of failing to live up to this obligation, he is tacitly reintroducing the language of authority, though he of course cannot bring himself to admit it. Much as a child continually asks "why" of his parents, Wolff would have us engage in something similar with respect to commands issued by someone claiming to possess authority. Yet, much as the parent must eventually say, "because I'm your mother and I say so," an end point must ultimately be reached in the continual questioning of authority which the Kantian project would appear to call for. One can envision the following conversation, with Kant and Wolff initiating with what in effect is a command:

"You must be morally autonomous."

"Why?" we might ask.

"Because it's a mark of mature adulthood."

"Why?"

"Because it just is."

"Why?"

In exasperation: "Because I say so!"

Even the distinction between childishness and adult responsibility presupposes a universal normative order on which such a distinction is dependent and in whose context it makes sense. This order must inevitably possess an authoritative character commanding assent from those subject to it. Otherwise it becomes a matter of mere preference: if I want to remain childish in my middle age and have the financial means to do so, what is that to anyone else? Or if I wish to call a child an adult or vice versa, why not?

The irony, of course, is that the imperative to remain morally autonomous is issued with all the authority of the philosopher who has come to this conclusion through long years of study and reflection. Here is where something of the circularity of the argument comes into play. Kant's categorical imperative would presumably necessitate that we evaluate even Kant's advice if we hope to remain autonomous. Yet since we must

24. Ibid., 18; emphasis mine.
25. Ibid., 72; emphasis mine.

fall back on the categorical imperative to learn that we must remain autonomous *vis-à-vis* all imperatives, there would seem to be nothing firm undergirding the categorical imperative itself. The categorical imperative would seem to lack the authority needed to make it anything more than a will o' the wisp—or the pious wish of Kant himself.

Towards the end of Wolff's essay, he argues for adopting "a system of voluntary compliance with governmental directives" in which "superstitious beliefs in legitimacy of authority have evaporated." But would this be enough to secure the coordinated action necessary for any polity to survive? Wolff believes it would, even in the military, and claims that he would feel safe in a country "whose soldiers were free to choose when and for what they would fight."[26] There are obvious difficulties, even assuming the reality of the autonomy he defends. For example, what if some or many people chose not to use the categorical imperative to evaluate their own or others' actions? Would they be free to do this or would they have to be compelled by others to do so? What, further, if employing the categorical imperative does not lead everyone to the same conclusion on a matter requiring united action? Would this not reintroduce authority into the picture? John Rawls appears to think so.

Kantian Liberalism: John Rawls

By no means do all the followers of Kant agree with Wolff that their mentor's political ideas imply anarchism. More influential is the work of the late Harvard political philosopher, John Rawls (1921–2002), whose writings have had a profound influence on at least two generations of professed liberals in the United States and elsewhere in the English-speaking world. Unlike Wolff, Rawls never envisions that the state should be anything other than the state and tacitly assumes that the apparatus of government will remain in place. Indeed, "the legal order exercises a final authority over a certain well-defined territory."[27] The issue for Rawls is how these rules embodying this order are chosen and by whom. Whereas Wolff believes that we *as individuals* are obligated to assess the rightness of each ostensibly authoritative prescription, Rawls believes that the validity of the laws issues from their origin in freely- and *communally*-chosen principles.

26. Ibid., 80.
27. John Rawls, *Theory of Justice*, 207.

Rawls calls his approach "justice as fairness." For him society is "a cooperative venture of mutual advantage" characterized by both identity and conflict of interests. Its members "recognize certain rules of conduct as binding" and generally follow these rules,[28] recognizing that it is in the common interest for them to do so. But all societies distribute advantages and disadvantages among their members, and this distribution is never altogether satisfactory to everyone. Rival conceptions of justice call for differing principles of distribution, all of which will inevitably please some and disappoint others. Thus the central issue for Rawls is how to choose the rules whereby the "benefits and burdens of social cooperation" are justly distributed. Although general agreement on such rules is a prerequisite for human community, choosing them is not a simple matter, due to the tendency of persons to seek to revise them in their own favor.

Drawing on the social contract theories of Locke, Rousseau and Kant, Rawls proposes to alter the aim of the contract, which is no longer to enter society or to establish a form of government as such, but to formulate the undergirding principles of justice. Rousseau's oft-convening sovereign assembly of the citizenry is not literally needed to guarantee the justice of the laws. Instead Rawls asks us to engage in a high level of theoretical abstraction in which we imagine ourselves in an original position of equality behind a veil of ignorance. This roughly corresponds to the early liberals' state of nature, although it is purely an hypothetical situation whose aim is ancillary to effecting justice. Within this original position "no one knows his place in society, his class position or social status, nor does any one know his fortune in the distribution of natural assets and abilities, his intelligence, strength, and the like." Furthermore, no one knows his "own conception of the good" or his own psychological makeup.[29]

The purpose of placing everyone behind this veil of ignorance is to remove anything that might bias the selection process. Rawls assumes that the parties are "rational and mutually disinterested," with rationality defined as "taking the most effective means to given ends."[30] All members seek their own good, doing what they can to advance that good and avoiding anything that might diminish it. If, while choosing the rules of justice, one already knows that he stands to inherit considerable wealth, he might conceivably opt for a rule that would keep wealth in existing hands, ir-

---

28. Ibid., 4.
29. Ibid., 11.
30. Ibid., 12.

respective of its impact on the larger community. The veil of ignorance is intended to eliminate this possibility. Thus if one does not know where she will stand with respect to the possession of wealth, and if she knows there is a chance of being poor once the veil is lifted, she will choose rules that will at least minimally benefit the poor, perhaps through progressive taxation coupled with redistributive social programs.

Rawls is confident that in this original position of equality rational persons would not opt for a utilitarian approach that would impose excessive hardships on some for the greater benefit of the majority. Such an arrangement would be unjust. They would instead choose two basic principles as foundational for the fashioning of positive laws:

> First: each person is to have an equal right to the most extensive scheme of equal basic liberties compatible with a similar scheme of liberties for others. Second: social and economic inequalities are to be arranged so that they are both (a) reasonably expected to be to everyone's advantage, and (b) attached to positions and offices open to all.[31]

The first principle necessarily takes priority over the second, as Rawls believes that no rational person would exchange basic liberties for compensating economic gains.

While Rawls believes in personal autonomy, he is no anarchist. This is evident in his statement that justice as fairness cannot imply absolute respect for each person's conscientious judgments or unlimited permission for everyone to form their own moral convictions. If there is a conflict between two or more sincerely held moral beliefs, we cannot afford simply to allow the holder of each to live in accordance with them; we must instead attempt to discern which is correct. This we can do only by appealing once again to the original position of equality and the principles of justice chosen therein, which everyone must be held responsible for maintaining. It is fully in accordance with respect for personal autonomy to compel the person with a misguided conscience to live up to the principles agreed to in the original position.[32] Although Rawls believes that justice as fairness comes closer than any other scheme to remolding society along voluntary lines, the meaning of *voluntary* is not to be reduced to mere desire. One is reminded again of Rousseau's

---

31. Ibid., 53.
32. Ibid., 254–55.

dictum that a person differing with the general will must be forced to be free—something with which Rawls evidently agrees.

Rawls' difference with Wolff is obvious. While Wolff is willing to trust individuals to think through moral decisions for themselves along Kantian lines, Rawls trusts the process more than he does those claiming to exercise it. If the process is followed scrupulously, i.e., as Rawls believes it should be, then there should be few disagreements on the principles of justice. If, on the other hand, citizens come to different conclusions on these principles, it is because some have not properly followed the process. Who determines whether this is the case? One might assume that Rawls himself would be happy to assume this role. In any event, he could scarcely envision a polity lacking some sort of authority, which for him is likely to take on more of a judicial than legislative flavor, despite Kant's emphasis on the legislative character of the autonomous will.

Some observers have noted that Rawls' account of the human person is excessively abstract, divorcing her from all of the particularities that go into making her who she is and thus influencing her decisions. Glenn W. Olsen charges Rawls with robbing us of "most of our humanity in the name of an impossibly abstract, mathematical, and procedural view of what life in society, what community, is about."[33] Our very capacity to choose in contingent circumstances does not exist in a vacuum; in all sorts of ways it is conditioned by our upbringing, our education, our peers, our religious beliefs and a variety of other beliefs about the world that we have acquired in the course of our lives. George Parkin Grant in particular argues that Rawls fails to take into account the global reality of transnational corporations and "the public corporation [i.e., government] which coordinates their welfare," and the impact these "dominating powers" have on the calculating individual.[34] Furthermore, Grant argues that, despite his effort to distance his own theory from the utilitarianism of Jeremy Bentham and the Mills, Rawls' account of self-interest is itself utilitarian at base, insofar as it identifies the "primary goods" sought by calculating individuals with "the maximising of the cosy pleasures."[35]

Human rationality does not quite speak with one voice in every respect. To be sure, the laws of logic hold for everyone. One cannot deny such laws with impunity. Yet reason is less a faculty, as in the traditional

---

33. Olsen, "John Rawls and the Flight from Authority," 423.
34. Grant, *English Speaking Justice*, 41.
35. Ibid., 45–47.

view, as it is the *logical aspect* of a total human experience, which is at base much more than rational. Logic may take us from point A to point B, but it cannot tell us why we should start at point A, or even why we are in motion to begin with. Nor can it tell us whether point B is a worthy goal to set before ourselves or which criteria should be used to determine this. Most basically, it is unable to tell us the meaning of points A and B within the context of reality as a whole.

Moreover, accepting Rawls' principles of justice presupposes that all participants in the process whereby they are chosen share a certain view of equality, which may or may not be the case. To observe that by nature people are *un*equal, possessing different aptitudes and capabilities and thus deserving different treatment, is not intrinsically unreasonable, even if it runs against the grain for most people today. Prior to the modern era many polities privileged certain classes of people, and even today in those same countries at least the *titles* of nobility survive, even if their political power does not. There are good and defensible reasons why such a country as the United States might constitutionally proscribe such titles, but within the context of the medieval and early modern European constitutions it is difficult to argue that their recognition was genuinely *irrational*. A commitment to equality is precisely that: a pre-theoretical commitment very much dependent on a particular philosophical anthropology that cannot itself be the product of a purely formal reason.

The Quest for Autonomy

The most basic difficulty with Wolff's—and Kant's and Milgram's—approaches is that they assume the possibility of moral autonomy—an assumption based in a particular worldview that may not after all adequately account for our lived experience and, ultimately, human nature itself. This can be seen in Milgram's analysis of his own experiments. Milgram admits that hierarchical organization confers a definite advantage on a group with respect to survival. An organized tribe will easily overcome a disorganized tribe when they come into conflict. Furthermore, a tribe characterized by a division of labor, with persons specializing in different occupations, is more likely to endure than one lacking such division. Hierarchy also provides internal stability to the group, lessening the possibility of civil discord. Milgram concludes that, through many eons of evolutionary adaptation to our environment, we human beings come into this world with the potential, if not precisely the instinct, for obedience,[36] which allows us to live and function within communities.

This means, in effect, that we are hard-wired for relationships based on authority and subordination. Here Milgram shifts from an evolutionary model to a model based on cybernetics, "the science of regulation or control."[37] In its independent state, the organism regulates its own impulses to secure its continued existence. However, when it becomes part of a larger systemic whole, it must enter a state in which its self-regulation becomes subordinate to an external regulator capable of coordinating relationships among the several members. To be sure, the internal conscience functions in part to prevent individuals turning on each other. Yet something more is needed from without. This is provided by authority acting within a hierarchical organization. For the person within this setting and subject to authority, the impact of conscience must itself be inhibited as directions from the top necessarily take precedence. Were this not the case, coordinated group activity would become difficult if not impossible. If communal action were based only on what could be agreed on by everyone, achieving anything more than the least common denominator would be out of the question. Not only would this be inefficient; it would endanger the survival of the group itself, especially in the competition with other similar groups.

Milgram describes the psychological shift as a move from *autonomy*, i.e., "when a person sees himself as acting on his own," to an *agentic state*, i.e., "the condition a person is in when he sees himself as an agent for carrying out another person's wishes." The latter "occurs when a self-regulating entity is internally modified so as to allow its functioning within a system of hierarchical control."[38] Within the agentic state people give up the self-imposed restraint of conscience and come to evaluate their own actions, not by whether they are good or bad, but by whether they conform to the expectations of authority and function well within the systemic whole. The agentic state is a mental condition enhancing the probability of obedience in the subject.

The problem arises, of course, when the two inhibiting mechanisms come into conflict, which is what Milgram's experiments were intended to explore. Their results showed, once more, that most people will go

36. Milgram, *Obedience to Authority*, 123–25.
37. Ibid., 125.
38. Ibid., 133–34.

rather far in obeying authority even when its commands violate their own conscience. Nevertheless, in the laboratory Milgram finds that the agentic state remains incomplete, for it does not induce *unthinking* compliance with such commands. If conscience and command conflict in the mind of the subject, the subject experiences considerable tension, which is manifested in expressions of discomfort or unease. Even when the subject fulfills authority's directive to the end, she is visibly agitated and unhappy with what she believes she must do. In this respect, Milgram finds "residues of selfhood" in the subject.[39] By contrast, in the totalitarian system the agentic state is more thoroughgoing, with selfhood nearly completely submerged into the pervasive mindset of the collectivity. Here obedience becomes not only willing but even enthusiastic as one's moral judgment is entirely suspended.

Nevertheless, there are good reasons to question whether Milgram's dichotomy between autonomy and the agentic state is warranted. Milgram himself admits that, as the child matures, she is subject to various socializing agents,[40] from family to school to the workplace to government, all of which aim at the "internalization of the social order."[41] In this way, the person's conscience is formed by the very structures of authority with which it may eventually come to stand in tension. In other words, the individual's inhibitory mechanism is formed from the outset by various external inhibitors, all of which can be grouped under the broad heading of authority. Even when people believe they are acting on their own, i.e., autonomously, each decision they make is conditioned, either directly or indirectly, by numerous authorities, the most significant of which have made their impact long before.

This is illustrated by two subjects whose actions and responses Milgram himself cites, while nevertheless failing to draw out their full implications. The first subject is "Jan Rensaleer,"[42] an industrial engineer who was born in the Netherlands and immigrated to the United States after the war. Rensaleer stops the experiment after 255 volts, refusing to

---

39. Ibid., 155.

40. I here use the term agent in the more generally accepted sense of someone who is an active, responsible person—precisely the opposite of Milgram's meaning. Somewhat idiosyncratically, Milgram uses the term agency as synonymous with the agentic state, as in someone being transformed to "an unalloyed state of agency" (ibid., 155).

41. Ibid., 138.

42. This is undoubtedly intended to represent the Dutch surname *Rensselaer*, which Milgram appears to have misspelled following anglicized pronunciation.

go on. He expresses regret that he has gone as far as he has in response to authority, assuming full responsibility for his own actions and refusing to blame the experimenter. Yet, having lived through the Nazi occupation of his native country, he is not surprised by the level of obedience in the other subjects of the experiment. According to Milgram, Rensaleer is "a member of the Dutch Reformed Church."[43]

The second subject is the "Professor of Old Testament," who discontinues the experiment after 150 volts, surprisingly asserting that "I'm taking orders from him," i.e., the protesting "learner." Milgram notes that the Professor does not precisely claim to be disobeying as much as shifting his allegiance—from the experimenter, whom he appears to view as merely a "dull technician" of limited intelligence and imagination, to the learner/victim. Moreover, when asked the best means of fortifying resistance to unjust authority, the Professor replies, "If one had as one's ultimate authority God, then it trivializes human authority." Milgram's response to this statement is remarkable, both for what it indicates about the nature of authority and for his apparent failure to make any more of it: "Again, the answer for this man lies not in the repudiation of authority but in the substitution of good—that is, divine—authority for bad."[44] This could have summed up his analysis of the experiments as a whole, had Milgram treated this observation as more than just the passing comment of the subject of an experiment.

Both "Rensaleer" and the "Professor of Old Testament" were evidently Christians, having been formed in accordance with a Christian worldview to distinguish between right and wrong. Their claim to selfhood would thus lie, not in pretending to act autonomously, but in acting in accordance with principles taught by another authority or a series of authorities, whose presence is felt more vividly than that of the experimenter.

Thus Milgram's claimed mental shift from autonomy to the agentic state may not, after all, be an accurate way of accounting for what occurs in the person, either in the laboratory or in ordinary life. Our consciences are formed in such a way as to recognize and obey legitimate authority. Our very selfhood is fashioned in large measure by others, including our parents, schools, churches, peers, the media, and many other socializing agents. To be sure, we are not simply the products of our environment,

---

43. Ibid., 50–52.
44. Ibid., 47–49.

along the lines argued by radical behaviorists, such as B. F. Skinner. We grow into and retain our responsibility at every stage of the process of growth. Thus when we come to see ourselves as part of a larger communal whole, we do not so much suppress our selfhood as adjust it to the realities of living among our fellow human beings. The recognition that we are not alone in the world and therefore must curtail our desires for the sake of getting along is integral to the development of the mature self. Or, as our parents might have told us, it's all part of growing up.

Moreover, every authoritative claim made upon us is itself subject to higher authority. We are embedded in a pluriformity of overlapping communal contexts, each of which makes an authoritative claim on us. Sometimes we have voluntarily assented to live under a particular authority, as in, e.g., the bylaws and executive of a local bird-watching society, which we are free (or, as I prefer, authorized) to enter and quit at will. But the most significant authorities, such as our parents, our political communities and, in many cases, our church communities, make claims on us without our necessarily having assented to be subject to them. These authorities are themselves far from being autonomous. Our parents raised us in accordance with principles given to them by their own parents, as reinforced, perhaps, by school, church, etc. Our political leaders are bound by the precepts of the law and the constitution, and by longstanding conventions passed down as part of a larger political culture, all of which can be said to have authority over these leaders. In other words, all human authorities are themselves subject to authority.

Though some might be inclined to label this a hierarchy or chain of command, of which each of us is merely one link, this is misleading and fails to do justice to the full complexity of interrelationships among the multiple authoritative agents in society. Those traditionalists favoring hierarchical views of society tend to assume that the hierarchy is singular and uniform in character, when in reality one person exercising authority over another in one context, e.g., the workplace, may be under the authority of the second person in another context, e.g., the church institution. We shall explore this pluriformity of authorities at length in chapter 6 below.

Freedom As Authority

In our story in the first chapter of Michael, the undergraduate university student, we noted, among other things, that at one point he phoned his parents to inform them that he would be delaying his visit to them because of volunteer duties at a local food bank. We suggested then that Michael's parents, in assuring him of their support for his decision, were respecting their son's fresh attainment of authority over the direction of his own life. Recognizing, as Yves Simon indicates, that parental authority properly aims at its own disappearance, his parents do not try to interfere with his plans or make him feel guilty for them. Given their greater experience, they are undoubtedly open to his requests for advice. Yet in its active sense their authority over him diminishes as he assumes greater responsibility for himself.

There is, of course, something profoundly right in this. Parents who continue to attempt to control their adult children's lives are the stuff of soap operas, advice columns, and psychoanalysis, but they do not make for the formation of mature persons and, concomitantly, a healthy society. As each of us grows up, he gradually takes on more responsibility, not only for himself, but for the communities of which he is a member. This is a constant in every society, normatively speaking.

However, there is a related development that is quite new and largely restricted, at least until recently, to the western world. This has to do with the gradual expansion over the course of centuries of the sphere of personal responsibility, or, as I would put it, *exclusive personal authority*. Young people today are unlike their forebears in that they have before them a huge range of choices to make in a variety of areas. They are likely to live longer than their ancestors and thus have more time to make and live out their decisions. They may choose their education, their mate, their career, their home, and even their religion. They have a huge number of electronic gadgets to facilitate their communications across vast distances and to provide entertainment 24/7. They shop in supermarkets boasting an unprecedented variety of foods from every part of the globe, some of which were practically unknown to their parents. The automobile and the superhighways that were built for them have increased their mobility to a degree hardly imaginable to their grandparents. Previous generations may have had some leeway in deciding how to live their lives, yet they did so within fairly narrow limits inherited from their forebears. The place of the individual *qua individual* had yet to come into its own.

Peter Berger sees this new world as subject to what he calls the heretical imperative.[45] Originating in the Greek word αἵρεσις (*hairesis*), meaning *choice*, heresy once meant putting oneself in the position of picking and choosing among the elements of one's own tradition, which is thereby deprived of its authority over one.[46] This is not so much a matter of critiquing one tradition by another commonly-held tradition, but rather a somewhat idiosyncratic and eclectic construction of an opinion deviating from the accepted worldview. In pre-modern times heresy was the exception in a world of religious certainty. Now, however, the modern world is characterized by a "pluralization of plausibility structures" "in which picking and choosing become imperative."[47] We are all heretics and furthermore have been compelled by modernity to become such. Doubt has replaced faith as the default position, with the individual increasingly expected to rely on her own resources. Whether this development of individuality represents a fall from grace or liberation from the dead weight of the past depends on who is making the assessment. In our view, the development of a sphere of individual authority is a positive good appropriate to the stage of history at which it came about. Nevertheless, like every new occurrence in a sinful world, it has not been an unmixed blessing.

Three parallel developments have contributed to this greater status of the individual: (1) the process of societal differentiation; (2) the spread of liberalism; and (3) the steady expansion of technological capacities beginning in the seventeenth century.

Differentiation—We shall take up this phenomenon more fully in chapter 6. Suffice it here to observe that, as the various human cultural activities began to unfold within their own distinctive spheres, such as schools, business enterprises, labor unions, artists' cooperatives, and the like, it is not surprising that a sphere of life accorded to the individual person should develop as well. This was manifested initially in the extension of a series of negative rights against government, as embodied in the English *Bill of Rights* of 1689 and especially the American *Bill of Rights* of 1791. These provided, among other things, for freedoms of speech, of religion, and of association; for the right to a fair trial, the presumption of innocence, and *habeas corpus*. Government need not have undertaken actively to provide these freedoms; it simply stepped back and refrained

---

45. Berger, *The Heretical Imperative*.
46. Ibid., 25.
47. Ibid., 24, 25.

from interfering in citizens' rights to speak and worship freely, to associate with their fellow citizens for their own chosen purposes, etc. Of course, these could be said to have a certain political aim, as free speech was originally accorded only to members of the English Parliament to facilitate open and critical debate over policy proposals. Yet the right to speak freely would eventually be expanded to include the entire citizenry and to become a more general freedom of expression, as in section 2 of Canada's *Charter of Rights and Freedoms*.

Along with this expansion of the personal sphere has come the contraction and eventual disappearance of, e.g., the professional matchmaker, whose services were made obsolete by the increasing social acceptance of prospective partners finding each other and falling in love on their own. Similarly, while family businesses still exist, it is far more common now for the young person to choose a field of employment for herself, usually on the basis of her own perceived gifts and predilections rather than on parental expectations. It is no simple matter to discern whether this development is an unadulterated good or whether there might be a dark side, for much of what falls under the rubric of differentiation may in reality be a manifestation of anti-normative fragmentation. This brings us to the next factor, the spread of liberalism.

Liberalism—It is difficult to disentangle the legitimate expansion of the sphere of the individual from the parallel development of the political philosophy of liberalism, as associated with the teachings of Hobbes, Locke, Rousseau, and Kant. We explored this phenomenon in chapter 2 as we looked at the reduction of authority to voluntary contract. As we have noted elsewhere, liberalism in all of its forms undertakes to reduce the full complexity of social formations to a collection of voluntary associations which do not differ from each other in any meaningful way.[48] Thus family, marriage, state, and church alike can be defined as associations formed by rationally self-interested individuals for specific agreed-upon ends. Of course, because such associations are precisely voluntary, they can be quit or altogether disbanded at the whim of the members. Because the benefits of such associations can presumably be had elsewhere and on easier terms, there is a tendency for prospective sexual partners, for example, to forego marriage and to live together informally. Such unions are less likely to produce children, which may in part account for the

---

48. See my own *Political Visions and Illusions*, esp. 42–71.

recent decline of the birthrate in many western countries to below replacement level.

Nor is it accidental that, while the United States has the highest rate of church attendance in the western world, those churches dominating its religious landscape are ones boasting a congregational polity and emphasizing individual conversion as a precondition for membership, usually at the expense of a more robust sense of the communal character of the faith, as manifested in the binding character of creeds, confessions, and liturgies. There the institutional church carries no real authority in itself, other than that granted to it by its members, who are at liberty to go elsewhere if it fails to meet their needs. Accordingly, the local church is viewed as an association of regenerate believers and is to be governed democratically.[49] While it would be unwise to ascribe the growth in such churches entirely to the impact of liberalism,[50] it seems more than coincidental that their polities should reflect the associational patterns extolled in much of the rest of society.[51]

The paradox of an *individualist* account of society is that, while in one sense too much is made of the individual person, in reality the sphere of exclusive personal authority is not at all secure from encroachment by other spheres, especially that of the state. At first glance this does not obviously seem true. In his defense of human rights, Michael Ignatieff goes so far as to argue that rights must always belong to individuals and not to groups. The very language of rights "cannot be translated into a

---

49. See, e.g., Southern Baptist Convention, *Baptist Faith and Message*, esp. §VI: "The Church."

50. In fact, such bodies as the Southern Baptist Convention have proven to be bulwarks against the confessional liberalism that has impacted so many other large Protestant denominations.

51. On this issue see, e.g., O. O'Donovan's comments in response to Yoder's Anabaptist approach:

> A voluntary society is one that I could leave without incurring grave or irremediable loss, which might seem a strange thing for a Christian to think about the church. Finally, does the concept of the church as a voluntary society not commend itself chiefly because it fits late-modern expectations of how civil society will be organised? Is Yoder, in the name of non-conformity, not championing a great conformism, lining the church up with the sports clubs, friendly societies, colleges, symphony subscription-guilds, political parties and so on, just to prove that the church offers late-modern order no serious threat? (*Desire of the Nations*, 223–24)

Of course, O'Donovan's use of the term church assumes its definition as a particular differentiated community rather than in the more encompassing sense of *corpus Christi*.

nonindividualistic, communitarian framework. It presumes moral individualism and is nonsensical outside that assumption."[52] Rights have meaning "only if they can be enforced against institutions like the family, the state, and the church."[53] They furthermore defend the autonomy of the individual "against the *oppression* of religion, state, family, and group."[54] There can be no doubt, of course, that members of a group can be subject to abuse at its hands. Nevertheless, there is much more to Ignatieff's approach than meets the eye, as his use of the word *oppression* already indicates. Rights are intrinsically adversarial, in that they are always held *over against* some other external authoritative agent. Individuals must constantly be vigilant against the pretensions of the groups of which they are part, jealously guarding their personal sphere of competence. Yet the word *enforced* necessarily implies an agent possessing the capacity to protect and advance this sphere over against the threatened encroachment of these various authoritative communities. There can be little doubt that the only agent with this ability is the state itself.

McGill University's Douglas Farrow notes the appeal to libertarians everywhere of John Stuart Mill's harm principle: "the only purpose for which power can be rightfully exercised over any member of a civilized community, against his will, is to prevent harm to others."[55] Of course, no society has ever existed for which this harm principle forms the primary, much less the sole, basis of freedom. In a mature differentiated society there are myriad nonstate communities each of which has its own identity and its own standards for membership. These standards necessarily impose constraints on those subject to them. To belong to an Orthodox Jewish community requires one to follow Torah and, more specifically, centuries of rabbinic interpretation of its precepts. If one violates these, one is likely to face sanctions from the community and perhaps even expulsion.

Is there something intrinsically oppressive in the reality that communities impose standards on individual members? Though few, apart from postmodern philosophers, would go so far as to assert this overtly, the logic of the harm principle must eventually give a positive answer to this question. And, if so, the state must then intervene to protect these individuals from having to submit to norms unrelated to this principle. As

---

52. Ignatieff, *Human Rights as Politics and Idolatry*, 67.
53. Ibid., 66–67.
54. Ibid., 83; emphasis mine.
55. Mill, *On Liberty*, 9. See Farrow, "The Audacity of the State."

Farrow correctly understands, this formulation must cut out "the oppressive middle term between the individual and the state," i.e., the nonstate communities that command the loyalties of ordinary persons, thereby reducing the scope of our obligations to encompass ourselves and the state alone. Farrow continues: "This begs the question, however, as to what does or does not harm another, and who will decide that." Again the state must take on this role of liberating the individual from the authority of those institutions that have come collectively to be called civil society. Although Mill's writings strongly appeal to libertarians, Farrow concludes that "Mill's ideas aren't really very libertarian after all,"[56] given that their implementation requires an ever-expanding state exercising an increasing number of capacities beyond its proper sphere of competence. Therefore, although liberalism has expanded the sphere of individual competence, it has done so in a way that has made its continued existence precarious indeed.

Technology—It would be difficult to underestimate the role technological developments have played in expanding the range of personal choices in recent decades. It has done so largely by freeing up time and energy previously devoted to such basic but time-consuming tasks as providing food, clothing, and shelter. To be sure, the division of labor, the market, and international trade have also made their contributions, but there can be no denying that, e.g., the invention of the sewing machine revolutionized the apparel industry by making clothing more affordable to ordinary consumers, who could now buy not only attractive, well-made garments but more of them. Electric refrigeration made it possible to store perishable foodstuffs for longer periods of time, reducing the necessary number of visits to the grocer. The advent of the automobile and the ubiquitous expressways built to accommodate it have expanded the range of possible places to live for westerners, as commuting for work and pleasure alike is now feasible over much greater distances than in the past. All of this means that the individual is confronted with many more choices than were available to her forebears, which, like everything else, has its up and down sides.

On the one hand, fewer people than ever before are involved in backbreaking, and possibly life-shortening, manual labor and many more are in professions that allow for some creativity and innovation. Marx and Engels famously envisioned the future communist society as one in which "nobody has one exclusive sphere of activity but each can become accomplished in any branch he wishes, [in which] society regulates the general production

---

56. Farrow, "Audacity of the State."

and thus makes it possible for me to do one thing today and another tomorrow, to hunt in the morning, fish in the afternoon, rear cattle in the evening, criticise after dinner, just as I have a mind, without ever becoming hunter, fisherman, shepherd or critic."[57] In a profound sense, technological development has brought especially western countries as close to this ideal as it is possible to get. The early twenty-first-century economy finds many people making mid-life career changes, as they deem appropriate to their own circumstances. To be sure, such a decision is sometimes forced upon people who find their jobs have become obsolete due precisely to the process of technical innovation that created the jobs in the first place. Yet over the long term, and despite the continued existence of poverty and disadvantage, more people than ever before are liberated from the unrelenting régime of biological necessity, cushioned in large measure by private insurance plans and the welfare state, and able to pursue at least moderately fulfilling career paths.

On the other hand, the rapid expansion of technology has encouraged a certain hubris and a dangerous illusion of human invincibility. That such developments are related to the spread of liberalism is undeniable, even if the causal connection is not immediately obvious to everyone. In principle, we strongly believe that the development of technology is a positive good, drawing as it does on the dynamic potential that God has woven into the very fabric of his creation. In contrast to the views of, say, Jacques Ellul, we believe that the cultural formation that produces technology is due, not to the fall into sin, but to the original good creation of God.[58] In the Reformed tradition of Christianity this is known as the Cultural Mandate and is rooted in Genesis 1:28. However, this dominion over the earth has too often become an excuse for exploitation and mere self-assertion, which has wrought destructive consequences on the larger social fabric as well as on the physical environment. As the language of liberalism has exalted individual rights at the expense of communities of all sorts, technological development has expanded the number of alternatives across virtually the entire range of life activities. Keeping one's options open becomes the supreme virtue, and having fewer choices than one would like is now identified with the worst of oppression.

---

57. Marx and Engels, *The German Ideology*, excerpts, in Marx and Engels, *Basic Writings*, 246–60, esp. 254.

58. See, e.g., Ellul, "Technique and the Opening Chapters of Genesis," in Mitcham and Grote, *Theology and Technology*, 123–37, where the author develops most clearly his understanding of technological development as a postlapsarian phenomenon.

Given this dark side, some observers have gone so far as to question the very legitimacy of rights. Robert Kraynak has pointed out the "subversive power of rights," noting that their focus on the individual has inevitably eroded authorities of all kinds. Rights amount to "ungrateful claims against authority, either for protections and immunities against the interference of authority or for entitlements from authority." They entail a "belief that man is born free and can determine his own destiny without being dependent upon others or beholden to higher powers."[59] Rights breed in the person a sense of entitlement and suppress the expressions of gratitude that ought to flow from the blessings God has provided. They encourage a false sense of independence and even an "impatience with God's providence."[60] Technology plays into this by inhibiting a sense of gratitude for the bounties of nature and tempting man to conquer it instead.

In 1999 the World Health Organization (WHO) and the International Agency for Prevention of Blindness (IAPB) launched VISION 2020: The Right to Sight, a global initiative to eliminate avoidable blindness by 2020.[61] In 2006 an organization called Right to Sight was established in Ireland,[62] and the slogan has also been picked up by the CNIB, formerly the Canadian National Institute for the Blind, as part of its own campaign to prevent blindness.[63] Although the campaign is unquestionably worthy of support, it should be noted that the use of the term *right* is not necessarily an obvious one in this context. The campaign might just as easily have adopted the following slogan: "The *Gift* of Sight," thereby emphasizing the truth that all we have is gift. The use of *gift* rather than *right* would seem to be more in accordance with Kraynak's preference, as it connotes gratitude rather than entitlement.

Although Kraynak makes a persuasive case for his position, we believe he would be better served by admitting the legitimacy of a sphere of exclusive personal authority *taking its rightful place alongside other manifestations of authority*. He is correct to note that, as popularly understood, rights are indeed subversive of authority, but the latter also covers the

---

59. Kraynak, *Christian Faith and Modern Democracy: God and Politics in the Fallen World*, 172.

60. Ibid., 173.

61. The International Agency for the Prevention of Blindness, "Vision 2020: The Right to Sight." Online: http://www.iapb.org/vision-2020.

62. Right to Sight (website).

63. CNIB. Online: http://www.cnib.ca/.

exclusive personal authority for which we argue here. In other words, the claims for individual rights, if disconnected from the web of communal relationships and the obligations flowing thereof, can only call forth the overweening state, whose interference in the institutions of civil society effectively erodes the authority even of the person in his own domain. The prejudice against authority entails a paradox: *whereas it appears superficially to advance the autonomous individual, in practice it is contemptuous of his authority, properly understood in its limited normative sense.*

Could it be that genuine respect for the human person is inconceivable apart from a general respect for authority in all of its pluriform manifestations? This is indeed our argument here. If the *imago Dei* entails a grant of authority, and if this is what makes for the uniqueness of human beings in God's world, then to fail to recognize and honor this authority is nothing less than a failure to esteem the human person in all his complexity. The history of the twentieth century was littered with totalitarian revolutionary régimes claiming to liberate people from the perceived oppression of predecessor régimes and to secure their autonomy. Yet in the name of an abstraction called *the people* they have shown themselves willing to dispense with those ordinary flesh-and-blood persons they have come to deem obstacles to the realization of their goals, whether the latter be the classless society, the triumph of the master race, national glory or some other overriding agenda item.

In the face of the abuses of totalitarianism, some have sought, following Kant once again, to affirm that human beings must be treated as ends rather than as means, which is one of the precepts of the categorical imperative. Yet this too is inadequate. Our very being as human creatures is a conditional, dependent being; we are dependent on the grace of God for our very existence. Dutch philosopher Herman Dooyeweerd prefers to limit the word B*eing* (*zijn*) to God alone, describing creation as *meaning* (*zin*), "the dependent mode of reality or existence."[64] As one of the principal Reformation catechisms puts it, "the chief end of man is to glorify God and enjoy him forever."[65] Or as an earlier such catechism expresses the matter, we are not our own but belong, in everything we are, to God in Christ.[66] Although not everyone acknowledges this radical dependence on God, we are nevertheless created by him to seek the divine somewhere. If we do not

---

64. Dooyeweerd, *A New Critique of Theoretical Thought*, 1:73n1.
65. Westminster Shorter Catechism (1647), Q. & A. 1.
66. Heidelberg Catechism (1563), Q. & A. 1.

do so in the Creator himself, then we are bent willy-nilly on doing so in the creation.[67] This explains the near religious language attached to, e.g., the "sanctity" of human rights or of the person, which is supposed to evoke a certain awe or deference in those hearing it. As Mary Ann Glendon has argued, rights talk is treated as a trump card, i.e., as something to put a stop to deliberation rather than to move it forward.[68] It is the functional equivalent to "thus saith the Lord." Grant points to the general liberal tendency to appeal to the word *person* to cover for a lack of an adequate account of what makes human beings worthy of respect.[69]

Ignatieff is perhaps more honest than most in admitting that, "[i]f idolatry consists in elevating any purely human principle into an unquestioned absolute, surely human rights looks like an idolatry."[70] Rejecting what he calls the "humanist idolatry" of the person, he believes that, to be consistent, the humanist would have to affirm that "there is nothing sacred about human beings" and that the only foundation for the protection of rights is historical utility: "Human rights is the language through which individuals have created a defense of their autonomy against the oppression of religion, state, family, and group."[71] Ignatieff opts for an historically-conditioned and conditional "faith in our species" as the only effective means to protect its members,[72] yet by embracing a worldview that insists on playing off individuals against the communities that form their core identity, he is effectively advancing an approach that must ultimately reach a dead end.[73] Against Ignatieff and his fellow liberals, we continue to affirm that *a genuine esteem for the human person requires a respect for authority in all of its pluriform manifestations, including, but not limited to, exclusive personal authority.*

---

67. See, e.g., Clouser, *The Myth of Religious Neutrality*, in which the author argues that all theories are rooted in belief in a nondependent divinity of some sort.

68. Glendon, *Rights Talk: The Impoverishment of Political Discourse*.

69. Grant, *English-Speaking Justice*, 33.

70. Ignatieff, *Human Rights as Politics and Idolatry*, 83. It should be noted in passing that Grant was Ignatieff's uncle on his mother's side. See Ignatieff, *True Patriot Love: Four Generations in Search of Canada*.

71. Ignatieff, *Politics and Idolatry*, 83. Note once more his use of the word oppression.

72. Ibid., 87.

73. In Ignatieff's earlier book, *The Needs of Strangers*, his professed liberalism is more nuanced in that he recognizes more explicitly the individual's need for the collectivity (13).

4

Authority and Legitimacy

Tradition, Law, and Charisma

Shirley Mackenzie has been a member of Canada's Parliament for the past seventeen years. Representing a safe urban riding (constituency) for the federal Liberal Party, she has easily won re-election against her Conservative and New Democratic opponents. After a brief period of Conservative government, the Liberals have now returned to power, and the new Prime Minister has slated Mackenzie to serve as Minister of Transport in his government. Because this is her first time in Cabinet, she must take a privy councillor's oath, after which she will become a member of the Queen's Privy Council for Canada. On the designated day, she recites the oath in the presence of the Governor General, the Queen's representative:

> *I, Shirley Mackenzie, do solemnly and sincerely swear that I shall be a true and faithful servant to Her Majesty Queen Elizabeth the Second, as a member of Her Majesty's Privy Council for Canada. I will in all things to be treated, debated and resolved in Privy Council, faithfully, honestly and truly declare my mind and my opinion. I shall keep secret all matters committed and revealed to me in this capacity, or that shall be secretly treated of in Council. Generally, in all things I shall do as a faithful and true servant ought to do for Her Majesty. So help me God.*

After this she is now designated the Honourable Shirley Mackenzie, P.C., a title she will retain for life. Once she leaves Cabinet, her official duties will be minimal, restricted to the rare state occasion, such as the accession of a new monarch. In the meantime, and until the Prime Minister decides otherwise, she will be up to her neck in government business, presiding over the Department of Transport and actively contributing to Cabinet deliberations, in addition to servicing her own constituents back home.

According to Canada's *Constitution Act, 1867*, "There shall be a Council to aid and advise in the Government of Canada, to be styled the Queen's Privy Council for Canada" (§ 11). Somewhat oddly, this document makes no mention of the Prime Minister or Cabinet, leaving the unfamiliar reader to assume that the Governor General and the Privy Council are the principal agents responsible for making the important executive decisions of the day. Even the language of the oath gives the impression that Mackenzie will be a personal advisor to the Queen herself, entirely overlooking her dependence on the leader of her party and of the new government. If at some point the Prime Minister decides to shuffle his cabinet, that is, to add to or subtract from the ministry, or to transfer the ministers between departments, she could easily find herself without a job. Yet she will remain a Privy Councillor, her active advisory capacity effectively dormant for the time being. No longer a part of the Government of the day, her continuing status will be largely honorific.

Of course, the Prime Minister himself has no formal authority to appoint her or to remove her from office. He merely advises the Governor General, who will then issue the appointment in the name of the Queen. However—and this is significant—as the Queen's representative she almost never seeks out Her Majesty's opinion, and only rarely does she ever refuse such advice from her first minister. Were she to do so, she would touch off a constitutional crisis with profound ramifications for the political system as a whole.

Citizens of a republic like the United States may express puzzlement over this curious duality at the heart of Canada's constitution, which reads one way but functions in quite another. The Queen, as an inherited head of state, is legally the fount of sovereignty in her several realms, including Canada. Indeed "Sovereign" is one of her titles. Nevertheless, her effective powers are carefully circumscribed by unwritten convention and by the country's status as a democracy. The Prime Minister and his Cabinet actually govern the country. Thus, though Mackenzie is *formally* dependent on the Queen for her position, she is *actually* dependent on the Prime Minister, whose lack of mention in the *Constitution Act* in no way hampers the exercise of his considerable powers, which, during a majority government,[1] exceed those of the US President.

---

1. In a majority government, the party in power has an absolute majority of seats

Because the American constitution was deliberately planned by representatives of the thirteen original states in the 1780s, Americans are accustomed to thinking of a constitution as a legal document drafted to prescribe the arrangement of basic political institutions. From this perspective, it would make no sense to establish a largely figurehead monarch or a seemingly atrophic body with so few duties. Yet constitutions, in the empirical sense, are not created as such; they evolve slowly over the course of many years—and sometimes centuries. Americans did not so much set up a new constitution as adapt an existing constitution embodied in the original colonial bodies politic. The Constitution of the United States of America, that is, the document bearing this title, borrowed heavily from both English and colonial usage, establishing, with ample precedent, a bicameral legislature, a chief executive (modeled on both the King and the colonial governors), and an independent judiciary, along with the principles of the Common Law with their guarantees of the rights of citizens.

By contrast, both Britain's and Canada's constitutions developed incrementally and, until recently in Canada's case, were never intended to be enshrined in a single document claiming to *be* the constitution. The authority for America's written constitution is clear enough: "We the people of the United States . . . do ordain and establish this Constitution for the United States of America." The authority for Britain's unwritten constitution is not nearly as obvious. To be sure, it is rooted in longstanding tradition, but nowadays it is generally doubted that tradition provides an adequate authority for anything of significance. If we have come to accept democracy as an unquestioned good, and if democracy means the rule of the people, how indeed can we tolerate a heritable monarchy or an appointive upper parliamentary chamber, such as Britain's House of Lords or Canada's Senate?

Max Weber: Traditional Authority

Nearly a century ago the German sociologist Max Weber (1864–1920) observed what he took to be a grand historical movement away from

---

in the House of Commons. In a minority government, a rare occurrence in Great Britain, currently governed by a coalition government of Conservatives and Liberal Democrats, but not uncommon in Canada, the ruling party has only a plurality of seats in the Commons, relying on one or more additional parties holding the balance of powers. Canada enjoyed—or perhaps suffered through—three minority governments between 2004 and 2011.

traditional manifestations of authority towards legal (sometimes legal-rational) authority. Traditional authority (*traditionale Herrschaft*) is based on "the sanctity of age-old rules and powers."[2] The possessor of such authority attains it by traditional means, which generally entails inheritance, as in the case of the British or Prussian monarchies. The king is part of a royal family, membership in which entitles one at least to potential access to authority, depending on his position in the line of succession to the throne. The king possesses, not so much an office, as a *status* which he retains for the rest of his life. There is no mandatory retirement age, and there are no pension benefits for an emeritus king, because the king remains such until death. The rules governing succession may not be written down but are nevertheless generally known and accepted. For example, a number of continental European monarchies were governed by Salic Law, which held that a female could not ascend to a throne. This put an end to the personal unions between Great Britain and Hanover in 1837, and between the Netherlands and Luxembourg in 1890, when Victoria and Wilhelmina became queens of England and the Netherlands respectively. This was because Hanover and Luxembourg were governed by Salic Law.

In an hereditary monarchy loyalty is sworn to the king himself and not to the nation, and even less to an abstraction such as the constitution or the laws, as we saw in Minister Mackenzie's oath above. Service to the government or to the citizenry is expressed in terms of service to the personal embodiment of the nation. The king is bound, not so much by formal rules and principles, as by unwritten conventions hallowed by ancient tradition and generally accepted by political actors and ordinary people alike. The boundaries between public and private are elastic, if they can be said to exist at all. What would be considered corruption in a more advanced, republican constitution is simply a normal mode of operation here, perhaps comparable to today's restaurant tips. When a person occupies an exalted post, it is expected that, while undertaking to serve the public, he will in the course of his duties line his own pockets as well. Even if self-aggrandizement is not exactly a virtue, it is no vice either, as long as the ruler continues to pursue the common good and avoids becoming overtly tyrannical.

Relationships with subjects take on the character of those between patron and client, and each such relationship is likely to develop its own unique pattern. There is no effort at implementing equality under the

---

2. Weber, *Economy and Society*, 226.

law or uniformity of treatment. Notables of the realm are, as a matter of course, treated differently from peasants and artisans. Of course, the ruler, in his general beneficence, may see fit to grant a favor to a particular person or group of persons, at their request. For example, Grand Duchess Olga, sister of the last Tsar of Russia, was once approached by the keeper of the forests on her estate, complaining that his children lacked enough milk and requesting an extra cow for his family. Days later he awoke to find twelve cows outside his house, enough to provide milk for the entire village.[3] This story was related by the Grand Duchess's daughter-in-law, who used it to illustrate her kindness to her subordinates. Yet it also demonstrates one of the perennial features of traditional rule, viz., the dependence on personal beneficence and the absence of the more systematic legal provisions, such as minimum wage laws and social assistance, that one would find in a modern welfare state.

What makes this traditional authority legitimate? Tellingly, Weber uses the word *Herrschaft* rather than *Autorität* to describe the forms of rule he undertakes to analyze. Not surprisingly, there is no exact equivalent for *Herrschaft* in English, though one commonly-used German-English dictionary defines it as "dominion, mastery, control, power, government, sovereign authority, command."[4] Power is and always has been unevenly distributed across society and is differentiated such that it is manifested in a variety of ways in different settings. Some observers, under Marxian influence, are wont to speak of *the powerful* and *the powerless*, as though everyone could be placed in one of these two categories. The assumption is that power is a single, continuous entity subject to a zero-sum distribution or competition. If someone increases her possession of power, it must be at another's expense. Yet this masks the genuine complexity in the distribution of what should more properly be called *powers* (in the plural) throughout an ordinary society. Someone who has mastered the skill of auto mechanics has a certain power over the academic psychologist who knows nothing about motor cars. But the academic who is knowledgeable in psychology has the advantage over the mechanic whose intellectual gifts may be limited.

Although power is not to be altogether identified with authority, the empirical possession of power is in most cases generally perceived to be legitimate and, save under exceptional circumstances, will likely go

---

3. "To Be and Not to Seem," 15.
4. *New Cassell's German Dictionary*, 228.

unquestioned. The man who wears a crown, holds a scepter, and claims royal authority is very likely really to be king and is recognized as such. The burden of proof lies, not with those accepting his claim, but with those doubting it. Society's working assumption is that Sally's violin virtuosity, Lloyd's sculpting skills, Roland's knowledge of chemistry, and Miranda's grasp of accountancy are legitimately in their possession. We admire people for their abilities, which we properly call *gifts*, even if we often fail to acknowledge the Giver.

It is precisely this divine Giver to whom appeal is often made by traditional authority in Weber's sense. Why is Henry VIII king? Because God wills it. Case closed. No further explanation needed. If a usurper becomes king instead, his victory only proves that God was on his side and willed that he rule. Similarly in the traditionalist *Weltanschauung* the act of legislating makes no sense; the laws exist from time immemorial, the gift of God or the gods. Mere human beings have no authority to change them or to adopt new ones, because that would entail an illegitimate repudiation of the divine gift. In this respect, laws are *found* rather than *made*.[5]

At the dawn of the twentieth century Europe was governed largely by hereditary monarchies, some constitutional and some less so. In 1910 Portugal's King Manuel II was toppled and a republic established instead. In 1917 Nicholas II abdicated, leaving Russia's political future to a briefly serving provisional government, itself quickly supplanted by Lenin's Bolsheviks. In 1918, in the immediate wake of its loss in the Great War, Germany abolished its monarchy, its emperor Wilhelm II fleeing to exile in the Netherlands. By any standard the British monarchy has been the most successful, with Queen Elizabeth II reigning over sixteen of the world's forty-four monarchies.

Yet there is an unmistakable pattern to the development of most of the members of the Commonwealth of Nations, as exemplified in the case of India. India became independent in 1947, originally as a "dominion," in the language of the era, with a status identical to those of Canada, Australia and New Zealand. George VI continued as King-Emperor, and shortly thereafter just King, of India, appointing a Governor General, initially Lord Mountbatten, to represent him. However, in 1950 India declared itself a republic, a precedent followed by most of the member

---

5. See, e.g., Sabine and Thorson, *A History of Political Theory*, 196. But see also Brague, *The Law of God*, 49–50, in which the author argues that, outside of ancient Israel, the king made the laws and that the Torah had no counterpart in other parts of the ancient world.

states of the Commonwealth, with the exception of those formed largely through European settlement. The Governor General was replaced by a state President to be elected by the members of the federal Parliament and the State Legislative Assemblies. If monarchy is not precisely extinct, the trend in this direction is unmistakably clear.

Weber: Legal Authority

Obviously something of significance has occurred in the world over the past century. As the Great War was in the process of upending the old order, Weber, already in his last years, wrote of a new world coming into being—one in which deference to tradition would give way to legal authority. He would not live to see this world, but in retrospect his observations seem prescient, as today European monarchies survive only in Scandinavia, the Low Countries and Spain. Where it has managed to hold its own, monarchy has become something of a vestigial institution, retaining a semblance of formal authority but without the effective power that once went with it. In the Netherlands, moreover, Queen Wilhelmina set a precedent for her successors by abdicating—in effect retiring—in 1948, living another fourteen years thereafter. The Dutch monarchy has evolved into a hereditary state presidency, largely shorn of the ceremonial and mystique once surrounding royal figures in the late medieval and early modern eras.

Legal authority (*legale Herrschaft*) is characterized by the supremacy of offices and of abstract rules by which they are ordered. The status of the person occupying an office is immaterial to the latter's authority. Not only is an hereditary noble no more fit than a commoner to govern; the commoner may actually be *better* qualified because ability and qualifications have likely been taken into account in the hiring, election, or appointment process. Patronage and nepotism are holdovers from traditional rule: you will be favored for a position if you are a personal friend of the ruler or are related to him. In legal authority, by contrast, offices are filled through known general rules applicable to all. In a democracy rulers are elected by the people, who, at least in theory, choose those they believe to be best suited to their respective positions. Yet most other government posts within what has come to be called the bureaucracy are subject to appointment in accordance with the merit principle, which provides for equality of opportunity for all citizens as well as competitive examinations and interviews to determine ability to do the job.

Once a person has attained to office, she is subject to the rules governing that office. If this is a public office, the rules are constituted by administrative law regulating the various departments and agencies of government. If it is a corporate office in the private sector, the rules will be the internal bylaws which establish and maintain such offices. Each office has its "specified sphere of competence" in which the discretion of the office-holder is carefully circumscribed by impersonal rules applicable to all.[6] If the office entails authority *over* someone or a body of persons, certain coercive powers will also be assigned to it, but once again these are strictly delimited and the types of coercive means will necessarily differ from one context to the next.

Here written constitutions take on supreme importance. The existence of ancient usages is deemed insufficient to guarantee the rule of law and to prevent arbitrary rule. Those drafting such a constitution assume that this single document is capable of prescribing all of the institutions of government and their mutual interrelations. The American founders famously designed various checks and balances among the three principal branches of government: the legislative, the executive, and the judicial. This was intended as a means of dividing sovereignty and preventing any one office or group of offices acquiring unaccountable power. Prior to 1940 the two-term presidency had been an unwritten convention followed by every president from George Washington, who set the precedent, to Franklin Roosevelt, who broke it by standing for a third term. Rather than reverting to previous precedent after the crises of the Great Depression and Second World War had ended, many believed that the Constitution itself had to be changed to prohibit a third term, which resulted in the adoption of the Twenty-Second Amendment in 1951. Changing the constitution, in the larger empirical sense, called for amending the Constitution, i.e., the document bearing that title. Leaving the matter up to what might be considered individual caprice was deemed insufficient.

While the Privy Councillor's Oath is filled with the language of personal loyalty and service to the Queen, the Oath of Office for the President of the United States is quite different, reflecting the shift from traditional to legal authority:

---

6. Ibid., 218.

> I do solemnly swear that I will faithfully execute the office of President of the United States, and will to the best of my ability, preserve, protect and defend the Constitution of the United States.

Here the focus is not on a person possessing a certain status, but on loyalty to a set of laws—indeed "the supreme law of the land"[7]—to which the office is intimately bound. Those taking the oath of American citizenship similarly swear to "support and defend the Constitution and laws of the United States of America against all enemies, foreign and domestic" and to "bear true faith and allegiance to the same."

An implication of the rule of law is that rights replace privileges. While privileges are enjoyed unequally by persons of different ranks, rights are said to be possessed equally by all citizens. Foremost of these is the right to vote, a basic precondition for democracy. But other rights, such as free speech, freedom of the press, freedom of religion, and so forth, are also held to belong to everyone on an equal basis. Furthermore, in a variation on the social contract position, some would argue that the citizens' recognition of each other as equal rights-bearers is the only realistic, if somewhat thin, foundation for political community. Admitting that the western notion of human rights has its roots in natural law theories,[8] Michael Ignatieff nevertheless affirms human rights on two bases: first, *moral reciprocity*, a secularized version of the Golden Rule that would have us judging human actions by whether or not we would want to be the recipients;[9] and second, as noted in the previous chapter, historical utility, i.e., that such rights have demonstrated their usefulness in protecting individuals against group oppression.[10]

Although many of us would tend to think of democracy as the form of government most congruent with legal authority, Weber instead cites as the purest form *bureaucracy*, a term often used in a less than positive sense in much of the English-speaking world. The bureaucracy is properly organized hierarchically, with lower offices clearly subordinate to the higher. It thus constitutes an aristocracy of merit, with the lines of accountability set forth by and subject to strict applications of law. Low-level officials are "personally free," subject to their superiors only with

---

7. *Constitution of the United States*, article VI.
8. Ignatieff, *The Rights Revolution*, 43.
9. Ignatieff, *Human Rights as Politics and Idolatry*, 88–89.
10. Ibid., 83.

respect to the conduct of their offices and possessing what we have called exclusive personal authority over their own lives outside of these. Candidates are to be appointed, not elected, because that is the only way to ensure that positions are filled by the technically competent. Officials should be remunerated based on a fixed salary scale, with promotion based on seniority or achievement or both.[11]

By contrast, there can be no hierarchy among democratically elected officials, because the legitimacy of each would then rest on a separate popular mandate giving him a certain independence from his supposed superiors. If he fails in the conduct of his official duties, he has the electorate to fear, not a higher-up. For this reason bureaucracy is the most rational form of organization and perhaps even most in conformity with the rule of law. Bureaucratic rule entails "domination through knowledge" (*Herrschaft kraft Wissen*),[12] which ensures its rationality, the form of knowledge once again being technical competence.

In chapter 2 we noted, among the several erroneous ways of conceiving the relationship between authority and power, the tendency to confuse knowledge with authority, along with the assumption that authority is based on knowledge. While not quite making this identification himself, Weber does believe that a society valuing the goods that come with especially scientific knowledge will tie its authoritative offices to those able to provide these goods. Legitimacy is conferred, not by natural law or divine fiat, but by a populace willing to recognize the authoritative position of a given official. Where an official is unable to deliver, her legitimacy will evaporate as the society ceases to recognize her position. A lack of legitimacy in this sense will erode the claims of both traditional and legal authorities. Legitimacy, in Weber's understanding, is not conferred by God or by a higher law; it is conferred by those willing to acknowledge and respect a claim to authority.

Status to Office: The Differentiation of Society

How do we account for this historical movement away from traditional to legal authority? Can this movement be considered an unmitigated progressive development? Is the contrast between the two as stark as Weber portrays it? Since the Enlightenment of the eighteenth century,

11. Weber, *Economy and Society*, 220–21.
12. Ibid., 225.

our western societies have come to be dominated by a prejudice against tradition, as much as against authority itself. Tradition as such can be said to carry a certain authority in every pre-modern society. An agrarian community living close to the land and dependent on the vicissitudes of changing climate and weather cannot afford to depart from the ways of the elders who have gone before them. The latter have passed down the ancient methods of tilling the soil, of sowing, watering, fertilizing, and harvesting, and these must be followed if the community hopes to survive. There is little margin for innovation and error when so many lives are at stake. Past experience is guide to present and future.

In such a context the authority of the person over his or her life is insufficiently differentiated from the authority of the larger community of which he or she is a member. Marriages are arranged, occupations are inherited, there is a highly gendered division of labor—the entire course of an individual's life is set by the community's tradition. The twentieth-century phenomenon of adolescent rebellion, exemplified dramatically in the classic film *Rebel Without a Cause*,[13] is inconceivable in such a context. Childhood ends early and adult responsibilities are assumed immediately thereafter. There is no time for the luxury of sowing one's wild oats or for finding one's identity, activities that would endanger the entire community. Hindsight tends to make such communities looked cramped and intolerant. Yet if they were such, it was not without good reason.

The trend that Weber observes corresponds to what philosopher Herman Dooyeweerd labels the *differentiation of society*.[14] As an historical process differentiation begins with the primitive tribal or undifferentiated society, a small, possibly nomadic community in which leaders exercise several functions at once without distinguishing among them. In Genesis 14:18–20 we read of the mysterious Melchizedek, who was simultaneously king of Salem, i.e., Jerusalem, and priest of "God Most High." This reflects the circumstances of the patriarchal period of the second millennium BC, in which political rule and priestly intercession with the gods had not yet been sharply differentiated. One person fulfilled both functions. Yet by the time of the kingdom, the two offices of king and priest had become differentiated such that Saul incurred divine punishment for performing a priestly function (I Sam 13), as did the later Judahite King Uzziah (II Chr 26:16–21).

13. Nicholas Ray, *Rebel Without a Cause*, Warner Brothers Pictures, 1955.

14. For Dooyeweerd's distinction between differentiated and undifferentiated societies, see *A New Critique of Theoretical Thought*, 3:346–76.

Differentiation thus means that the variety of activities undertaken by human beings in a social context come over time to be dispersed among several authoritative agents, including communities with their respective authoritative offices and the individual person with her legitimate sphere of action. Education, which previously took place in the home, comes to be undertaken in the setting of a school established for that specific purpose. Even the trend in some circles towards home-schooling has often meant, not a re-enclosure of schooling within the family, but of horizontal cooperation among several families in the education of their children. Home-schooling thus becomes cooperative schooling in which the gifts of external teachers may be brought into a somewhat less-structured classroom environment.[15]

Similarly, the family once functioned as a unit of economic production of goods and services. Husband, wife, and children were all involved in this process, as seen, for example, in *My Big Fat Greek Wedding*, where Gus, Maria, Nikos, and Toulla all work in the family's Chicago restaurant, Dancing Zorba's. A minor crisis occurs when Toulla, at age 30 and feeling her life to be less fulfilling than she would like, decides to take computer courses at a local community college, thus distancing her aspirations from that of the family as a whole. What might on one level be seen as a clash of Greek and North American cultures might on another be understood as part of the inevitable tensions that occur when activities not immediately related to family life are removed from the household and performed elsewhere. Business enterprises incorporate members from different families and are organized on a separate basis. Thus in a mature differentiated society ordinary people find themselves involved in many overlapping communities claiming their attention in some fashion. The adult person is simultaneously someone's spouse, someone's mother or father, someone's daughter or son, an employee of a business, a member of a labor union or professional association, citizen of a state, member of a church congregation, and part of a variety of other voluntary associations.

The Harvard sociologist Talcott Parsons explicitly employs the word *differentiation* to describe the growth of distinct public and private

---

15. Two of my own students were called upon to teach high-school age young people by a local home-schooling co-op in the Hamilton, Ontario, area in the first decade of the twenty-first century. This makes the very label home-schooling something of a misnomer.

realms and the plethora of communities within the latter.[16] While there is some similarity between Parsons' and Dooyeweerd's uses of the term, their meaning is not precisely identical: First, while for Dooyeweerd differentiation is an historical norm rooted in the divine intention for a dynamic creation, for Parsons it is a mere empirical phenomenon, lacking a broader normative order giving it meaning. This, of course, is hardly unusual for someone in the mainstream of secular sociological theory. Second, unlike Dooyeweerd, Parsons seems unable to relinquish the notion of society as a (political) whole with subordinate parts. No community seems, ontically-speaking, to fall outside the body politic. Yet both acknowledge in some fashion the reality of a pluriform society.

If I take a few moments to tabulate all of my own memberships and associations, I come up with a number in excess of twenty, including citizenship in two countries, membership in a local church, employment at an institution of higher learning, three alumni associations, membership in five professional associations, more than one hobby society, and, at last count, more than fifty meaningless facebook groups. Obviously not all of these are of the same importance, and some are very far indeed from the surface of my conscious loyalties. Most of these communities are organized in some fashion with duly constituted offices to which certain persons are either appointed or elected in accordance with generally-known rules. Membership is itself an office of no little significance, bearing its own form of authority. Such authority may be subordinate to another authority, e.g., to that of a president or executive body, but that does not make it any less authoritative.

Yet not every community is so organized. Marriage, family, and kinship community are examples. It is not uncommon for an older and respected member of a kinship community to be regarded as the matriarch or patriarch of the clan. No one put her in this place; she is simply accorded the respect that comes with this status. Her position as matriarch is not necessarily based on merit, although it is not unusual to expect some amount of wisdom to accompany it. When she dies, her position may be passed on to a son or daughter or other relative. This is traditional authority as defined by Weber. The community over which it presides is potentially what Dooyeweerd would label an undifferentiated society, if it exists at an early stage in the historical process, the pace of which differs from place to place.

16. Parsons, "Authority, Legitimation, and Political Action," in Friedrich, ed., *Authority (Nomos 1)*, 197–221.

Considering once again my own memberships, I am a member of all three of what might be called *natural*, as opposed to *organized*, communities. I was born into a particular birth family, one that was exceedingly close-knit during my childhood and youth. I did not choose my parents or siblings. I had to pass no tests or pay a fee to become a member. I carried no membership card. There were no elections or appointments to office. My father was simply the father of the family, and my mother the mother. As such they laid down the rules and we children were expected to follow them. I did not choose my parents; nor did they choose me. Most importantly no human being appointed them to their position. Yet that in no way derogated from their parental authority over me during my minority.

With respect to marriage, I did, of course, voluntarily choose my wife over all other women, as she also chose me over all other men. Yet my wife and I did not administer competitive examinations to each other. We courted for a time and then came to our decision based on that experience. Once we had done so, we entered into an estate called matrimony, whose contours were set long before we took our vows. We did not invent marriage to suit our purposes. It preceded us. This understanding of the stable character of marriage has been lost in many jurisdictions under the predominant influence of liberal individualism, which has attempted to reduce it to a private contract to be modified at the whim of the parties. That sexual complementarity might be intrinsic to marriage is scarcely to be admitted in a society that valorizes choice nearly for its own sake.

Furthermore, I myself am only two generations removed from arranged marriage, a practice associated with traditional societies everywhere. Here marriage is not considered a matter of personal choice based on falling in love with a prospective partner. It is certainly not a mere lifestyle choice. Rather, the entire community is involved in locating potential spouses for its young people, and this ensures the coming into existence of the next generation to whom the baton will be passed in due course. Nowadays, of course, marriage is treated as a matter of individual discretion, beginning with an increasing acceptance of love matches and perhaps culminating in the legal acceptance of so-called same-sex marriages, albeit not without considerable controversy.

Nevertheless, there is a persistent tendency for marriage and family to remain bound to tradition in a way that, on the surface at least, appears to be less true of the organized communities of, say, state, school, and business enterprise. Men and women tend to function differently within the marital community, despite the efforts of many to bring about a more egalitarian division of labor within it. There is, of course, variability within individual marriages, which may see the husband being more nurturing and domestic than the wife. Moreover, different cultures attach different expectations to the role of husband and wife in marriage. Some observers are inclined to use such evidence to deny the fixed nature of gender roles, and with respect to the specific tasks assigned to each partner they are, of course, correct. However, the same evidence indicates that the persistence of a gendered division of labor of some sort appears to be a feature of every known society, the *fully* egalitarian society being an untried, and perhaps unfeasible, ideal. This suggests, of course, that a gendered division of labor within marriage, and perhaps even in the larger society, is rooted in something deeper than mere tradition—perhaps in human nature itself.[17]

Those in the grip of Weberian analysis will be loath to admit this, due to their conviction that the historic move from traditional to legal authority occurs across the entire array of human communities. That some communities should be exempt from this trend is not easily accounted for. This is where the process of differentiation offers a plausible explanation. Many of the features that we have come to associate with the traditional society are due to the latter's being only partially differentiated. Sir Robert Filmer's valorization of the patriarchal society is an example of the erroneous assumption that hereditary monarchy, with its less differentiated understanding of the place of family and political rule, is eternally normative.[18] John Locke persuasively disputes this in his first treatise *On Civil Government*.

This relatively less differentiated character of the monarchical constitution is celebrated by some sentimental monarchists, such as members of the Monarchist League of Canada, who are dedicated to defending the country's monarchical institutions against what they see as the creeping republicanism of especially Liberal Party governments. They go so far as to favor the welfare state, so unpopular with many American conservatives of a libertarian bent, on the grounds of Canada being a kind of macro-family:

---

17. Located in southwest China, the Mosuo, or Na, are said to be a matriarchal society, yet they too are characterized by a definite gendered division of labor. See Mathieu, *A History and Anthropological Study*; and Hua, *A Society without Fathers or Husband*.

18. Filmer, *Patriarcha or the Natural Power of Kings* (1680).

> Canadians are justly proud of their health care system. It owes its origin to the welfare state that came out of British Fabianism and the sense of community fostered by the Monarchy, according to which society is perceived as a kind of extended family rather than just a corporate or social battlefield as in republican philosophy.[19]

Hereditary monarchy is a vestige of a less differentiated society in which political authority had not yet been clearly distinguished from parental authority. A respect for a country's history would argue against outright abolition of the monarchy where it still exists, particularly if it continues to play a vital role in upholding the constitution. But this hardly makes such a state an extended family. If a defense of the monarchy is to be mounted, it must be done for distinctly *political* reasons. Familial metaphors, where taken too literally, threaten to suppress these. In this respect, a constitutional monarchy must be understood, not as something *other* than a republic, but as a *monarchical republic*, where all the institutions of the state, including the monarchy, seek public justice.

To sum up, families do not need to refashion themselves as democracies or products of voluntary contracts to be historically up-to-date. Similarly, political communities should not be re-conceived as extended families, which, at this stage of history, would obstruct their central task of doing justice. Some, of course, regret differentiation, conflating it with antinormative fragmentation. In the Reformed tradition, Darryl G. Hart exemplifies this regret, assuming that, if the Bible was written in the context of a partially differentiated society, any social arrangement that moves us beyond this is not to be applauded.[20] He similarly disagrees with the assumption of tasks once performed by the family and institutional church by schools, hospitals, and governments.[21] Dooyeweerd's response is unequivocal: "The glorification of the undifferentiated medieval corporations and the depreciation of the process of differentiation and integration inherent in the disclosure of human culture show a strong influence of Romantic philosophy,"[22] which tends to glorify a supposedly more authentically human past.

Thus the larger movement from traditional to legal authority is most applicable to the organized communities insofar as they have

---

19. Bousfield and Toffoli, "The 'British' Character of Canada."
20. Hart, *Recovering Mother Kirk*, 131.
21. Ibid., 130.
22. Dooyeweerd, *A New Critique of Theoretical Thought*, 3:186.

become increasingly distinct from the natural communities of marriage and family. In the meantime, marriage and family, despite recent efforts to recast them as mere social constructions malleable at the discretion of participating individuals, tend stubbornly to resist such efforts over the long term. This Weber's followers have not adequately understood. Moreover, there is a profound sense in which even the organized communities subject to legal authority are as bound to tradition as the natural communities, as we shall see below.

Weber: Charismatic Authority

This brings us to Weber's third form of authority, viz., charismatic (*charismatische Herrschaft*), about which so much has been written over the decades. Because the word *charismatic* is subject to so many uses today, it is perhaps in order to indicate which of these we rule out here. Barack Obama may have a charismatic personality and considerable leadership gifts, but his authority rests on his occupancy of the office of the presidency, which he attained through ordinary legal means. Similarly Pope John Paul II had a certain personal charisma that his successor, Benedict XVI, seemed to lack, but both filled a position that probably best conforms to Weber's traditional authority. In Christian circles *charismatic* can also refer to the latter-day heirs of Pentecostalism, a movement that began at the start of the last century and has spread rapidly around the world. In virtually every sense of the term *charisma* is a gift of grace, with charismatics ascribing this to a special work of the Holy Spirit not generally manifested in ordinary experience.

Weber's use of the term is not unrelated to these usages, but it is not to be identified with them either. For him charisma refers to certain personal characteristics by which the possessor is popularly "considered extraordinary and treated as endowed with supernatural, superhuman, or at least specifically exceptional powers or qualities."[23] These qualities are ascribed to divine origin, with the possessor claiming a mandate from God or the gods for his leadership. Every act he performs is in response to the divine command. Weber calls attention to a paradox in the relationship between the charismatic leader and his followers. On the one hand, his leadership is dependent on the general belief within the charismatic community in its divine origin. On the other, the leader expects that his followers have a duty

---

23. Weber, *Economy and Society*, 241.

to obey him, and resistance to his authority will be treated as an abdication of this duty with coercive penalties applied to the recalcitrant.

Charismatic authority is best described by a series of negatives—by what it is not.[24] The staff of a charismatic leader is not made up of technically-trained officials. Appointment and dismissal, career and promotion have no place here, only the call of the leader himself. There is no hierarchical organization, no defined sphere of competence, and no salary scale. There is "no system of formal rules, of abstract legal principles," no systematic judicial process, and no recognition of the normative status of precedent. Each judicial decision is arrived at *de novo*, as if by a fresh oracle of the divine. Charismatic authority repudiates the past and allows no place for tradition. Ordinary economic considerations have no place either, while "'booty' and extortion" are "the typical form of charismatic provision for needs."[25] Charismatic authority is often associated with revolutionary upheaval, when polities based on one of the other two stable forms of authority has weakened or dissipated and can no longer command popular legitimacy.

Examples cited by Weber include the shaman or magician in a primitive tribal society, and Joseph Smith, who founded Mormonism through his claim to have received a divine revelation in the form of the *Book of Mormon*. Other ancient religious leaders, such as Siddhārtha Gautama (the "Buddha"), Jesus of Nazareth, and Muhammad, might be seen to conform to this pattern as well. The Buddha left his assigned station as an Indian prince, embracing a life of asceticism and the attainment of spiritual enlightenment. Jesus constantly debated the religious establishment of his day, claiming to be the fulfillment of the Law, going so far as (apparently) to break the letter of its precepts by healing on the Sabbath. Muhammad claimed to have received from God via the angel Gabriel the text of the Holy Qur'an, believed by devout Muslims to complete and correct the earlier revelations given to Moses and Jesus. Although Socrates never claimed to start a new religion, he nevertheless successfully antagonized the assembly of Athens, calling into question the old beliefs constituting the basis for civic life in the polis.

Whether Lenin and Mao might be considered charismatic leaders in the Weberian sense is subject to dispute. As heirs of Marx they were, of course, atheists and would never have claimed divine approval

---

24. Ibid., 243.
25. Ibid., 244–45.

for their programs of implementing communism in Russia and China respectively. Nevertheless, as noted in chapter 2, revolutionaries do claim for themselves a higher knowledge that confers an authority superior to the unenlightened established authorities. For Marxists this "divine mandate" is conferred on the proletariat, who are uniquely capable of taking matters into their own hands and abolishing the rule of capitalism and inaugurating the classless society. Of course, if the proletariat are not sufficiently conscious of their world historical role, Lenin's vanguard of the proletariat steps in to raise their consciousness and, if the latter remain stubbornly within their false consciousness, to implement the revolution in their behalf and possibly even at their expense. All opponents are deemed enemies of the revolution, whose imperatives take precedence over every other claimed locus of authority.

Once the revolution has occurred, of course, there is a need to consolidate its victories. By its very nature pure charisma cannot endure as such and is thus an unstable, short-term phenomenon. Over the longer term charismatic authority must become either traditional or rational, or perhaps a hybrid of the two. This is a process that Weber famously labels the routinization of charisma (*Veralltäglichung des Charisma*). Although there are a number of factors encouraging a move in this direction, Weber follows Marx in asserting that the principal motive is economic. Because the economy "is the principal continually operating force in everyday life" and not "merely a dependent variable," charismatic leadership must adapt itself to this reality or risk passing out of existence.[26] If the people are persuaded that the leader's charisma can be inherited, then authority takes on a traditional character. If the charisma is conferred on a particular office, legal authority comes into being.

Legal Tradition, Traditional Office

Moreover, unlike, say, Richard Sennett,[27] Carl Friedrich,[28] or even such greats as Plato, Aristotle, and Hobbes, Weber understands the significance of *office* as the locus of authority, at least within his category of legal authority. Nevertheless, he manages to miss the extent to which at least traditional and legal authority presuppose each other. The rule of law will

---

26. Ibid., 254.
27. Sennett, *Authority*.
28. Friedrich, *Tradition and Authority*.

almost certainly be without effect where there is no *tradition* of the rule of law, i.e., a general respect for this principle that is passed down—perhaps even *inherited!*—from one generation to another within the context of a particular polity, as Friedrich points out.[29] This underscores the reality that a pretended rational approach to law must ultimately rest on something other than reason narrowly understood. Drawing up a finely-balanced constitutional document will be insufficient where the inherited traditions of the people expected to live under it are neglected. Such a document is likely over the long term to become little more than a scrap of paper, mostly ignored by citizens and governors alike. Thus the common American belief that the country's founders were brilliant architects of a well-crafted constitution dividing sovereignty among a variety of legal offices and institutions rather misses the point. Had there not existed in the culture a prior commitment to the rule of law and representative government, efforts to create these *de novo* would likely have fallen flat.

The relationship between tradition and political order is especially well captured in the familiar concept of *political culture*, as explored in the pioneering work of Gabriel Almond and Sidney Verba,[30] Robert Putnam,[31] Seymour Martin Lipset,[32] and others. Political culture is the complex of attitudes, customs, and institutions that a people carries within itself relative to the political order. Despite attempts to quantify political culture, its contours are generally intuited in pretheoretical fashion by ordinary people, sometimes through the use of ethnic or national stereotypes.[33] Almond and Verba focused their efforts on levels of participation, the most easily quantifiable variable, in the five countries they surveyed. Putnam established the long-term durability—or perhaps stubborn persistence—of current political cultures in northern and southern regions of Italy, noting that the most vital and effective institutions exist in those northern regions where civic republics such as Venice, Genoa, and Florence flourished centuries ago. They are least effective in the south, which was subject to centuries of absolute rule by Byzantines, Normans, Bourbons, and Habsburgs. Lipset found concrete

---

29. Ibid., 90–91.
30. Almond and Verba, *The Civic Culture*, and *The Civic Culture Revisited*.
31. Putnam, *Making Democracy Work*.
32. Lipset, *Continental divide*.

33. Although stereotypes nowadays have a negative connotation, there is nothing intrinsically illegitimate about them. Indeed they may be said to be rooted in the natural human capacity to generalize and categorize the disparate data of experience.

evidence to support popular impressions of the differences between the US and Canada. This suggests that where habits of self-governance and collective initiative are lacking, no amount of institutional reform is likely to create them.

Although political culture as a concept was more than a century away from being isolated and identified, the early 19th-century conservative thinker Joseph de Maistre managed to anticipate some of its conclusions in his own writings, especially his *Essay on the Generative Principle of Political Constitutions* (1809), where he favors unwritten customary laws over written laws.[34] If a law has to be committed to paper, he sees this as evidence that it probably is no longer generally believed still to be in effect. To have to write down a law with "a pen and a little black liquid"[35] is an unmistakable sign that an institution is in irreversible decline. Although de Maistre is associated with the backwards-looking effort to restore the pre-revolutionary *status quo ante* during the tumultuous years between 1789 and 1815, he correctly understands the role of tradition in a country's living constitution: "The real English constitution is the public spirit, admirable, unique, infallible, and above praise, which leads, conserves, and protects all—what is written is nothing."[36] One need hardly go as far as he in opposing written laws, of course. Yet there is considerable truth in the recognition that a constitution is more than just a scrap of paper, and that written constitutions promulgated in the absence of supportive political traditions will almost certainly have little effect on constraining governing officials. In short, far from being opposed to tradition, legal authority is very much dependent on it.

More recently the philosophical ethicist Alasdair MacIntyre has implicitly questioned the Weberian dichotomy between tradition and reason, the latter of which Weber thought fundamental to any properly-constituted legal authority. MacIntyre argues that there is a diversity of traditions of moral enquiry, along with the conceptions of justice flowing out of them. These traditions inevitably condition the reasoning process from the outset. There is thus no such thing as justice pure and simple. There are, rather, rival justices rooted in competing rationalities. While one might repudiate a specific tradition, one cannot forgo tradition *per se*. MacIntyre recognizes that even modern liberalism, while claiming to

---

34. Maistre, *Generative Principle of Political Constitutions* 22, p. 158.
35. Ibid.
36. Ibid., 6, p. 150.

repudiate the authority of tradition, has itself become one more tradition, assuming its own authoritative status as such.[37] Clearly rival conceptions of justice are based, not on varying degrees of rationality—as though there were a single continuum extending from nonrational to fully rational—but on different traditions undergirding the reasoning process. Legal authority is thus as fully dependent on specific traditions as the authority of monarchs, bishops, and tribal chieftains.

Moreover, even an hereditary monarch, the exemplar of Weber's traditional authority, can be rightly said to occupy an *office* subject to the law, and not merely a personal *status*. At her coronation in 1953, Queen Elizabeth took a series of oaths to govern in accordance with the laws and customs of her respective realms. This was in effect an oath of office, as confirmed later in the ceremony by the Archbishop of Canterbury's prayer "that thy servant Queen ELIZABETH may be enabled to the discharge of her weighty office."[38] That the monarchy is indeed an office is especially evident since the passage of the *Act of Settlement 1701*, whereby Parliament set the terms of succession to the throne. One might also note that the election of a pope, sometimes thought to exemplify traditional authority, is governed by the very ancient code of canon law. Even in the absence of a written law, inheritance of a particular office inevitably follows a known and generally accepted rule, such as primogeniture and/or male succession. The contrast between traditional and legal authority ought not, then, to be overstated. They are quite properly to be distinguished, and Weber's doing so does help us to gain insight into the process of differentiation as it has worked itself out through many generations. In Canada and the United Kingdom, for example, it enables us to distinguish between the formal and efficient elements in their constitutions. The Queen and her Privy Councillors possess all the formal authority of hallowed tradition, yet they exercise it only on the advice of the Prime Minister and Cabinet, who are subject to regular democratic elections. Of course, the accepted convention whereby the Queen reigns but does not rule is itself rooted in a longstanding tradition of parliamentary government with deep roots in those countries following the Westminster system. There is thus a genuine interdependence between

---

37. MacIntyre, *Whose Justice? Which Rationality?* 10. See also MacIntyre, *After Virtue*, where he treats Weber as a paradigmatic figure of the modern age; and MacIntyre, *Three Rival Versions of Moral Enquiry*.

38. "The Form and Order of Service."

traditional and legal authorities that cannot be adequately accounted for by viewing them as polarities.

Authority and Legitimacy

There is good reason to question whether any of Weber's vaunted types of authority are examples of authority at all or rather three more examples of the psychological power which we treated in chapter 2. Under Weber's approach the claim of traditional, legal or charismatic leaders to possess authority is precisely that: a mere claim. Given that there can be no means of verifying such a claim, its true significance can lie only in the fact that so many people believe it to be true. In short, the leaders exert a psychological hold over their followers and it is this on which their authority is based. We call attention, once again, to Weber's use of *Herrschaft* rather than *Autorität*. If legitimacy is simply a matter of people believing in the superior position of a given leader, then it ultimately matters little whether he claims a status, an office, or a divinely-bestowed gift of grace.

There is, finally, ample reason to conclude that Weber's theory, like so many of the approaches we surveyed in chapter 2, reduces authority to some form of power, either psychological or persuasive. This suggests, once more, that if we are to find a basis for a robust notion of authority in its many manifestations, we shall have to look elsewhere. To be sure, Weber helps us in some measure to understand the phenomenon of historical differentiation and the seemingly inevitable tendency of leaders, who attain their pre-eminence during revolutionary times, to consolidate and regularize their positions through traditional or legal means.

In light of Weber's theories, we pose once again the central question of this chapter: what legitimates authority? and a related question to which we now turn: what is authority's ultimate origin? Here there can be only two basic alternatives: (1) authority is derived from human beings or (2) it comes from something or someone transcending humanity. Within each of these, however, there is more than one possible path to take. Under the first alternative, the choice is usually framed as that between *reason* and *will*, both of which are conceived as universal human faculties. If authority is held to have a basis in reason, and if rationality is the *sine qua non* of humanity, this is deemed sufficient to prevent authority's arbitrary possession and exercise. Furthermore, because the scholastic theologians and philosophers tend to identify the *imago Dei* with rationality, they might deem themselves justified in anchoring authority in something close to the second alternative, e.g., in the natural law, God's divine reason, his Word, or his created order. However, in its Kantian form the emphasis on reason need not presuppose a deity: one can be agnostic about the origin of reason while still availing oneself of its usefulness in upholding or reordering social order.

At least since Hobbes, and perhaps as early as Marsilius of Padua, philosophers have sought to understand authority in terms of the will, which need not conform to anything outside itself. According to Hobbes, man is a creature of restless desires, his happiness consisting in the continual satisfaction of those desires. Because the effort to fulfill one's desires inevitably leads to conflict, it is in everyone's interest that a single will, namely, that of the sovereign, be exalted above all others. Laws are "artificial chains" which people, "by mutual covenants, have fastened at one end to the lips of that man, or assembly, to whom they have given the sovereign power, and at the other to their own ears."[39] The content of such laws is not nearly as important as the power of the person or persons commanding them. Although Rousseau's sovereign consists of the whole assembly of the citizens of a republic, he is in fundamental agreement with Hobbes in locating the origin of law in human beings whose will is invested with supreme authority. This general will of the sovereign alone can confer legitimacy. The great American jurist, Oliver Wendell Holmes, believed "that men make their own laws; that these laws do not flow from some mysterious omnipresence in the sky, and that judges are not independent mouthpieces of the infinite. The common law is not a brooding omnipresence in the sky."[40]

This attitude is in stark contrast to virtually all ancient peoples who ascribed every manifestation of authority, whether of laws or leaders, to the gods or God. In Exodus, for example, we read that Moses mediated the Law of God to his people, principally in the Decalogue (Exod 20, Deut 5). On the advice of his father-in-law Moses delegated his (charismatic?) authority to judges, who continued to govern the Israelites until the inauguration of the monarchy under King Saul. Tellingly, however, Moses did not set up a legislative body to *make* laws, an act which would have been inconceivable in the context, not only of ancient Israel, but of the entire ancient near east. Because the law was already of God and

---

39. Hobbes, *Leviathan*, chapter XXI.
40. Biddle, *Justice Holmes*, 49, citing Holmes, "The Path of the Law," 230, 235.

because God does not change, it was believed that one cannot alter the law either. When cases arose requiring adjudication, the judges would make just rulings based on the existing laws, which were held to embody the Law of God, or Torah.

It is worth noting that, with the advent of the monarchy in Judah and Israel, appeal to the law appears to have been eclipsed by the presumed wisdom of the reigning monarch, beginning with Solomon, perhaps justifying Samuel's earlier warning against its establishment (I Sam 8:10–18). In the famous story of Solomon's judgment of the two prostitutes (I Kgs 3:16–28), we read nothing of his consulting the court legal experts or poring over the Law himself. He renders a correct decision, seemingly relying solely on his own extraordinary understanding of maternal psychology. It makes for a fitting conclusion in this case, of course, and it does much to enhance the king's reputation for wisdom. Yet his father David obviously made a snap judgment in the case of Saul's grandson Meribaal (2 Sam 16:1–5, 19:24–30), unjustly handing his property over to a slanderer—a miscarriage of justice which he never completely corrected. And Solomon himself imposed servitude on the non-Judahite tribes in apparent violation of Torah (I Kgs 5:13; Lev 25:39–55). The majority of David's and Solomon's successors in the divided kingdoms were evil kings and, with the notable exceptions of Josiah and a very few others, ignored the law, relying on their own judgment, which was all too often faulty in the extreme. This sad history would appear to vindicate Plato, Aristotle, and many others who argued that an unmixed monarchy would likely degenerate into tyranny. It also underscores the preferability of the rule of law to the rule of the ostensibly virtuous.

If authority is not anchored in presumed human wisdom, it must be established on another, firmer basis. Of course, if one is not a theist, finding such a basis becomes problematic. Though one could hardly accuse Thomas Jefferson of harboring a robust Christian faith, he was nevertheless willing to appeal to "nature and nature's God." Others, such as the ancient Greeks, were willing to stop with the reference to nature. For them nature itself becomes a normative order, to which mere human beings must conform. Whether nature might have a divine origin is an issue that can be safely put aside for the time being, as those appealing to nature will of course disagree on its provenance. Nature itself might be identified with the divine or at least personified, as seen perhaps in the popular references to *Mother* Nature. The Stoics thought it advisable to live according to nature, testifying to the strong sense they had, in contrast, e.g., to the Epicureans, that nature could be understood in terms of a moral law accessible to reason. The Stoic conception of a *natural* law would eventually be picked up by Augustine and Thomas Aquinas, from whence it passed into the larger tradition of western philosophy, as well as into our popular vocabulary in such expressions as *human nature*. Augustine and Thomas in effect christianized a notion that would eventually have a huge impact on the development of jurisprudence in the modern era. The Enlightenment thinkers took over this emphasis, preferring in many cases to speak of natural rights rather than law as such.[41]

Although in its Christian version, natural law theory points to a divine origin, Hobbes took what he termed the laws of nature in a quite different direction, identifying them, not as moral laws regulating human actions in normative fashion, but as scientific laws capable of being observed empirically by the thoughtful person trained in the scientific method. In this respect the laws governing human behavior are no different from the physical laws governing matter in motion. In his description of the various laws of nature, he assumes that, by these, human beings will act—or, better, behave—a certain way if they are strongly enough motivated to do so, primarily, of course, by the fear of a violent death. Positive law and moral precepts come about, not by gauging them against a supposed natural order accessible through reason, but through a sovereign will with the power to enforce its decisions, as we noted in chapter 2.

Weber's approach to authority is based in the first alternative mentioned above, viz., that authority's legitimacy is conferred by human beings, especially by those subject to it and whose confidence in it is required for its continued functioning. Authority, in short, is conferred, not from above, but from below. The contractarian position, as described in chapter 2, presupposes the same account of authority's origin. Rousseau's and Kant's emphasis on will as the origin of law places them, and many others, in the first category as well. One might argue that contemporary democracy, insofar as it represents an ideological creed rather than a mere form of government, presupposes this account of authority's origin from below.[42] Yet in its older form, the unifying element in this account was the universality of human reason, which would serve to guarantee a sufficient measure of human solidarity within the larger political community.

---

41. See, e.g., Finnis, *Natural Law and Natural Rights*, for a treatment of the connections between the two concepts; and D'Entrèves, *Natural Law*, esp. 48–62.

42. See, once again, this author's own *Political Visions and Illusions*, especially chapter 5.

Since the beginning of the 1960s, however, a debased version of the Hobbesian position has come to the fore, as the emphasis on reason has largely given over to a renewed focus on the will. In popular parlance the slogan "Do your own thing" and the ongoing quest for the authentic self, even at the expense of one's mundane responsibilities, have altered dramatically the cultural landscape of the west, especially North America. The most obvious manifestation of this cultural shift has come in the form of what I have elsewhere labeled the choice-enhancement state.[43] Whereas the older liberalism sought to anchor political authority within a freely-negotiated contract among the participants in political community, this latest stage of liberalism has sought to harness the power of that authority in the interest of ensuring the person's right to choose, full stop. This view of the state's task is intimately tied to the sexual revolution, an explosive trend which saw much of the west's traditional pattern of sexual mores and restraints collapse virtually overnight, as the expansive self and its desires took center stage. This development has been dressed in the superficial Kantian language of personal autonomy, although it might better be viewed as the conclusion of a process that began with Hobbes and ends with something approaching his chaotic state of nature.

Proximate Origins of Authority

To confess that God is the origin of all authority, as believing Christians, Jews, and Muslims affirm, does not answer the issue of what might be called the proximate origins of authority. The early modern west European monarchs advanced the divine right of kings. Of course this notion did not antedate the modern era and certainly had few if any medieval precedents given the untidiness of feudalism.[44] It bore some similarity to the classical Roman doctrine of imperium, which survived the fall of Rome at least nominally in the form of the two rival claimants to imperial status in Constantinople and Germany. Yet in the west the kingly realms of, e.g., the Capetian monarchs of France or the Plantagenets in England embodied highly complex and overlapping layers of patrimonial authority shared among king, nobles, and church hierarchs. For centuries the

43. Ibid., especially chapter 2.
44. See, e.g., Hogue's remarks in his *Origins of the Common Law*, 243: "Doctrines of the supremacy of law and of judicial precedents cannot thrive in the presence of a divine-right monarch claiming to be supreme lawgiver as well as supreme administrator."

effective royal powers of the French king did not extend much beyond the region around Paris. Other notables nominally under the authority of the king exercised actual control over other parts of the realm.

Beginning in the sixteenth century the Bourbon monarchs of France consolidated their own effective powers at the expense of both nobility and church, creating a highly centralized form of government which continued past the revolution of 1789 to the present. By contrast, in England parliamentary government developed almost by accident as the king came to be economically dependent on the estates of the realm for raising the revenues necessary for achieving his desired policy goals. By 1688 parliamentary supremacy over the monarchy became a reality, and England's constitutional government would become the envy of the likes of Baron Montesquieu in the following century. By the 1780s, when the American founders were putting together their own constitutional document, the separation of powers embodied in it was less than fully original and reflected generations of experience in representative government in the colonial assemblies. These in turn were patterned after English precedents taking for granted the existence of several institutions sharing political authority and counterbalancing each other in its exercise. Once again these grew out of the competing aspirations of the several estates of the realm, which effectively prevented the development of monarchical absolutism, despite the best efforts to the contrary of a succession of Tudor and Stuart occupants of the throne.

Modern democratic theory tends to eliminate all references to God, whether self-serving or not, embracing something approaching popular sovereignty, i.e., the belief that the democratic people are the source of authority for political rule. Sovereignty itself might be seen as part of an effort to locate a source of political authority and social unity in a religiously divided polity. Hobbes' reference to the sovereign as a "mortal god" is more than tongue-in-cheek, for it represents part of a much larger enterprise that dominated the modern world from the sixteenth century to the present, viz., the quest to find a God replacement. Given that west Europeans were now at odds over such crucial issues as papal authority, the sacraments, justification, sanctification, and even the number of books in the Old Testament, it seemed impossible to bring about a satisfactory settlement on the basis of generally accepted principles. Catholics and Protestants were reduced to shouting at each other across an increasingly wide abyss and, when that failed to persuade their opponents, to brandishing their swords.

If two potential antagonists believe that God has given a message to each and if these messages are mutually incompatible, one of two possible options must be chosen. Either the two appeal to a common recognized higher authority or they come to blows. In matters of faith, of course, there can be no higher authority than God. But, as Hobbes understood, God does not speak with equal clarity to everyone and it is inevitable that people will claim to have heard different things from him. Is Jesus the Son of God and second person of the Trinity? Did the angel Gabriel genuinely reveal the Qur'an to Muhammad? Did the angel Moroni really lead Joseph Smith to the golden plates containing the Book of Mormon? Christians, Muslims, and Mormons alike would answer two of these questions negatively but disagree on which two.

At this point there is a great temptation to embrace a practical atheism that would eliminate such disagreements entirely or at least to relegate them to a nonpublic realm where they become innocuous. After all, what one believes concerning the presence of Christ in the Eucharist is not obviously related in a direct way to political order. Fellow citizens may believe that the bread and wine literally become the body and blood of Christ, or they may recognize in them only a symbolic representation of Christ. Nevertheless, they continue to abide by the laws of the land, respecting their fellow citizens' lives and property. Why not agree to disagree on the matter and go on to cooperate on other issues where agreement is forthcoming? As Thomas Jefferson put it: "it does me no injury for my neighbor to say there are twenty gods or no God. It neither picks my pocket nor breaks my leg."[45]

Yet God or a god-substitute cannot be done away with quite that easily. Fr. Richard John Neuhaus famously coined the expression "naked public square" to describe the modern pursuit of a political order shorn of all "thick" accounts of meaning or, as John Rawls puts it, comprehensive doctrines.[46] However, the naked public square is structurally impossible. Human reason is an inadequate substitute for the divine, because it is always conditioned by prior commitments of an ultimate character. For the mainstream of the modern era this commitment is to sovereignty, which is ascribed to some human person or community. At the outset it is assumed that common human reason is foundational for this sovereignty, but as the centuries progress reason is slowly replaced by mere will. As

---

45. Thomas Jefferson, *Notes on the State of Virginia* (1781–1782), Query XVII.
46. Neuhaus, *The Naked Public Square*, 157.

democracy comes increasingly to be accepted, this will is the popular will, as expressed either through representatives in a parliamentary body or directly through the referendum. The popular will confers its legitimacy on authority.

However, this raises a question that various political theorists have addressed in their own distinctive ways: how do we check the arbitrariness of the popular will? Can the shifting desires of the people provide an adequate authority for law? While Rousseau believes they can if they are sufficiently general in focus, Hannah Arendt denies it. For Arendt only the mutual promises embodied in a singular past event called the act of foundation can provide this stable authority for the body politic.[47] The act whereby the body politic was constituted, e.g., the American states' claim to independence in 1776 followed by the inauguration of federal union in 1787, is of greater significance to her than a written document labeled "the Constitution." The latter is the product of making or manufacturing, while the former is a free act whose stability is grounded in the reality that past events cannot be altered. Americans' reverence for their country's eighteenth-century founders would appear to bear out Arendt's views.

Above all, Arendt is concerned to protect the freedom of action in the public realm from any ideological vision that followers might attempt to impose on it. Even the law of Moses is antipolitical in the sense that it claims the sanction of God and therefore cannot countenance the free deliberation of citizens over the direction of their polity. If God has spoken, there is no need for someone else to do so. However, the virtue of the exodus story and Moses' role in it is that, by the very act of founding the Israelite community, he himself initiated a set of events to which later judges, kings, and prophets could appeal and which constituted the narrative underpinning of the polity.

Yet one might properly question the sufficiency of an act of foundation as a substitute for belief in a transcendent God and the norms implied by this belief. Is it really the case that the people confer legitimacy on those claiming authority? Does authority flow from the bottom up? Do those subject to authority grant the latter its status? Democratic theory would say yes to these questions, but this only pushes the issue of authority's origin back to the next level. It does not address where the authority of the people *ultimately* comes from and in what capacity they exercise it. To be sure, the status of citizenship itself can be said to carry authority, which includes

---

47. Arendt, *On Revolution*, especially chapters 4 and 5.

several elements falling under the two interrelated rubrics of rights and obligations. To speak of the citizenry or the electorate implies an authoritative office bearing a certain responsibility for the makeup and direction of government. Such labels are preferable to that nebulous expression "the people," which is too undifferentiated a concept to be of any practical or theoretical use within the political sphere.

A better approach, that is, one that does justice to the fullness of human experience, would recognize that consent of the governed is a *necessary precondition* for just governance by the bearer of an authoritative office but *cannot stand at its origin*. Parental authority, for example, issues out of the reality of the biological relationship between parents and offspring. It is made necessary by the immaturity of the latter and their inability to care fully for themselves. It is supported, particularly at the outset, by the greater size and capacities of the mother and father relative to their children, but it is not, of course, reducible to this factor. The larger size and greater power of adults facilitate the exercise of discipline over the child, but these factors must be seen as means at the disposal of parental authority and not equivalent to it.

Similarly, the need for government and the laws underpinning it exists simply because we are interdependent human creatures requiring overall coordination of our activities to enable us to live together. Furthermore, because of our sinful natures and our tendency to grasp for more than that to which we are entitled, government has a divinely mandated task to punish acts of injustice. If these two functions of government are required because of who we are as fallen image of God, then consent from below is inadequate as a foundational basis for government in general. Once again we must have recourse to office, which is the proper locus of authority. We shall take up office in chapter 5.

Natural Law: Pros and Cons

It is not surprising that many philosophers have undertaken to free democracy as a form of government from the grip of Rousseau's doctrine of popular sovereignty. This is especially true of those in the Roman Catholic tradition, of which Jacques Maritain and Yves R. Simon stand out. So skittish is Maritain about employing the term *sovereignty* that he expresses a decided preference for ascribing it to God alone.[48] Other hu-

---

48. See Maritain, *Man and the State*, 28–53.

man forms of authority must be rooted, not in an untrammeled will, but in something called the natural law, which is thought to be a powerful antidote to the relativistic implications of the historicism and legal positivism that originated in the nineteenth century and all but dominated the twentieth.

Natural law has its roots in ancient stoicism, where a distinction was made between domestic human laws and a higher cosmopolitan law thought to be valid for all human beings. To some degree this approach has its roots in Plato's doctrine of the forms, which were deemed identical to ultimate reality. Truth, goodness, beauty, and justice are real while the true, good, beautiful and just things we experience in the world are only pale reflections of the former. In stoicism this higher law constitutes a standard for positive or human law and, in Cicero's words, constitutes a *vera lex*, or true law, which is as binding as positive law.[49]

Augustine picks up on this notion from the stoics, accordingly drawing a distinction between eternal law and human law.[50] Eternal law has its origins in the wisdom of God and it directs everything to its proper end. Eternal law is unchangeable: it is always and everywhere the same. It can be accessed in principle by all human beings, and it stands at the origin of order and justice. Human law imperfectly reflects the perfect eternal law. It applies the principles of the latter to specific communities living in particular times and circumstances. It necessarily differs from place to place and from time to time. Although justice is always and everywhere the same, concrete efforts at implementing it will inevitably lead to varying temporal laws.

Thomas Aquinas borrows from the stoics by way of Augustine, articulating the existence of at least four different kinds of law: eternal, natural, human, and divine, the last being further divided into the old and new laws. Eternal law is that by which God, or the "Divine Reason," governs the universe. The natural law is "the participation of the eternal law in the rational creature,"[51] or that law capable of being grasped by unaided human reason. Human law consists of "particular determinations, devised by human reason," from the natural law (Ia-IIae, q. 91, art. 3, *resp.*; q. 95, art. 3). Unlike the natural law, human laws "can be rightly changed on account of the changed condition of man" (q. 97, art. 1). Hu-

49. Cicero, *De re publica*, 3.22.33.

50. Augustine, *De Libero Arbitrio* (*On Freedom of the Will*) 1.6.

51. Thomas Aquinas, *Summa Theologica*, Ia-IIae, q. 91, art. 2, respondeo. Cf., q. 93. Subsequent quotations from this section are placed parenthetically in the text.

man laws may indeed be codified, but even longstanding custom carries the force of law (q. 97, art. 3). Finally Thomas asserts the need for a divine law guiding man to his final end. This is for four reasons: (1) because man's ultimate end is eternal happiness, which he cannot attain through his natural faculties alone; (2) because his understanding of the natural law is often faulty; (3) because human laws cannot comprehend inner motives; and (4) because human laws do not and cannot forbid all evils. These reasons call for a supplementary law that will compensate for the insufficiencies of the other kinds of laws (q. 91, art. 4). The divine law is manifested in two forms: the Old Law and the New Law, which correspond to the two covenants in scripture (q. 91, art. 5).

The natural law tradition has been carried into the modern era by a number of figures, including, in some fashion, John Calvin, Johannes Althusius,[52] Francisco Suarez, and many others. In the late nineteenth century Thomas Aquinas' approach was held up by Pope Leo XIII as the proper way to do Catholic philosophy.[53] Thus a tradition that had seemed moribund, especially after Hegel and Nietzsche's efforts, was renewed for the next century, when the crises of the two world wars, totalitarianism and the Cold War shook the then dominant school of legal positivism.

Of course, despite the apparent bankruptcy of the notion that law is whatever the sovereign says it is, not everyone, even among those professing the Christian faith, was ready to jump on the bandwagon of natural law as a theory. This was for five reasons.

First, it assumes a kind of religious neutrality in which thinking occurs independently of one's ultimate commitments. If the natural law is a law of reason, and if all human beings are possessed of reason, then all should in principle agree on the requirements of the natural law. On the surface this seems to be a plausible argument. After all, many existing polities, even those that are religiously divided, are able to uphold a common legal framework based on a general agreement on the principles of justice. Without having to come up with sophisticated theoretical rationales, most citizens can be readily brought to agreement that, say, murder and theft should be prohibited and punished. Is there not indeed a law written on the heart, as seemingly affirmed by St. Paul the Apostle?[54] At the same time and despite this apparent commonness, it is clear that

---

52. Johannes Althusius, *Dicaeologicae* (1617).
53. Leo XIII, *Aeterni patris* (1879).
54. Rom 1:18–20.

one's ultimate beliefs definitely impact the way one lives. Moreover, if an entire community is oriented around a specific set of ultimate beliefs, say, Christianity, Islam or postchristian secularism, this will inevitably influence its shared life in huge ways. Principles taken for granted in one context, e.g., equality under the law or an independent judiciary, cannot necessarily be assumed in another. Is it irrational to believe, for example, that titled nobles deserve more privileges than commoners? Does it really violate the canons of reason to hold that votes should be weighted according to property or education instead of our current principle of one-person-one-vote coupled with majority rule?

If reason is less a human faculty than the logical aspect of the totality of human experience, then it cannot bear the weight that has often been placed on it. The belief that human beings are created in God's image—are invested with authority—is nonfalsifiable according to most understandings of rationality—this despite centuries of efforts to prove or disprove God's existence. The belief that lower-caste Dalit are inferior, not only to members of the higher castes, but also to the cattle considered sacred in Hinduism, is not intrinsically irrational. Similarly, reason cannot settle the dispute between pro-life and pro-choice sides in the abortion debate, because both groups reason from within different worldview paradigms. Human beings exercise logic within the larger context set by such religiously-based worldviews. If this is true, it casts doubt upon at least the efficacy, if not the truth, of natural law as a source of common ethical precepts applicable to the whole of humanity. Empirically speaking, arguments from natural law have not done what their proponents would have them do, despite the best of efforts. The assertion, for example, that homosexual acts violate the natural law has been largely ineffective in persuading those who believe otherwise. Opponents of natural law are likely to see it as the peculiar pastime of dogmatic Roman Catholic philosophers and perhaps a few Protestants. Indeed, with some exceptions, natural law philosophers tend to understate the extent to which their own approach is anchored in the specifics of their own comprehensive doctrines, or religiously-grounded worldviews. For the larger culture, citing natural law will likely seem as quaint and sectarian as quoting revealed scripture.

Second, natural law appears not to take seriously enough the fall into sin and its effects on the noetic faculties. This is the objection one is most likely to hear from traditional Protestants, i.e., from those heirs of the Reformation who are truest to their own confessions. Such Christians would not, of course, be at all sympathetic to the antinomian tendencies of so-called mainline Protestants. If anything, they might tend to err in the direction of a biblicism that does not take into account the reality of what Abraham Kuyper and his followers labeled common grace, viz., that divine grace which does not save but nevertheless preserves God's creation from the full effects of the outworking of sin. According to such traditional Protestants, the theory of natural law posits a realm of reality which appears to be exempt from the impact of sin. Given the biblical understanding that the whole of man in all of his activities is affected by his sinful propensities, this would seem to exclude the possibility of a natural law to which all have access.

Third, natural law theory is thought to presuppose a kind of two realm conception of the cosmos in which the natural possesses a certain autonomy *vis-à-vis* God himself. This is most evident in Thomas Aquinas' account of the virtues, in which four cardinal virtues — prudence, justice, fortitude, and temperance — are deemed capable of being attained, though not necessarily to perfection, "according to the capacity of human nature," while the three theological virtues — faith, hope, and charity — must be infused in us by God "supernaturally." According to Herman Dooyeweerd the entire medieval era in western philosophy was in the grip of what he called a nature/grace groundmotive (*grondmotief*), which saw the whole of reality divided up into two dialectically-related realms of nature and grace, or nature and supernature.[55] A groundmotive is similar to what others would call a worldview, a motivating basic-heart-orientation that animates what one thinks and does. It differs from a worldview in operating at a nearly subconscious civilizational level. It is a "fundamental motivation," a "driving force," in Albert M. Wolters' words.[56] For Dooyeweerd the nature/grace groundmotive is synthetic in that it juxtaposes an earlier Greek view of nature with the biblical revelation of grace. Rather than grace restoring nature through the comprehensive redemption of creation through Jesus Christ, grace is superadded to nature, completing it but not transforming it in any meaningful sense.

The popular evangelical apologist, Francis Schaeffer, appears to pick up on Dooyeweerd's groundmotive analysis, especially in analyzing the

---

55. Dooyeweerd, *Roots of Western Culture*, 111-47.

56. Kalsbeek, *Contours of a Christian Philosophy*, 348. Wolters's glossary of terms is found on pp. 346-54 and is printed in McIntire, ed., *The Legacy of Herman Dooyeweerd*, 167-71.

historical eras of western art. Similar to Dooyeweerd, he sees various philosophers and artists being in the grip of a very few two-story conceptions of reality, including the medieval, which places spiritual matters in an upper story and an autonomous nature in the lower. Insofar as Thomas Aquinas affirmed a certain autonomy of nature—a certain independence from the realm of divine grace—this autonomy would expand, eventually eliminating grace itself in the modern era.[57] This two-story view of the universe Schaeffer holds largely responsible for the triumph of nihilism in the twentieth century arts. If one realm of the cosmos stands in no need of redemption in Christ, there is in principle no reason why others should not be similarly understood. It is no surprise that so many should give way to a general sense of despair and loss of deeper meaning in their culture-shaping activities.

Although there is something to Dooyeweerd's and Schaeffer's critiques, it is inaccurate to hold that Thomas thought there to be a natural realm altogether free from the effects of sin. According to Thomas, there is a threefold good of human nature: (1) "the principles of which nature is constituted"; (2) man's inclination to virtue; and (3) the "gift of original justice," as granted to the first human being. Of these three, the first is entirely undiminished by sin, the second is diminished by sin, while the third "was entirely destroyed through the sin of our first parent" (Ia-IIae, q. 85, a. 1, resp.). In short, Thomas affirms that nature is indeed impacted by sin, Dooyeweerd and Schaeffer's views to the contrary notwithstanding. All three admit the commonness of created good, i.e., that it rains on the just and unjust alike (Matt 5:45). Where they differ is in the two Reformed thinkers' focus on the religious worldviews undergirding, say, the Aristotelian and stoic philosophical projects, and their unwillingness, contrary to Thomas, to sum up the *imago Dei* in terms of man's possession of rationality.

Fourth, within the realm of jurisprudence natural law theory has difficulty accounting for the status of an unjust law as a genuine law. Thomas writes that a human law that "deviates from reason . . . is called an unjust law, and has the nature, not of law but of violence" (*Sum. Th.* Ia-IIae, q. 93, art. 3, reply obj. 2). In his famous "Letter from Birmingham

---

57. See Schaeffer, *Escape from Reason*, and *The God Who Is There*. Although Schaeffer gives no indication of having read Dooyeweerd, the latter's influence seems to have come via his longtime friend Hans Rookmaaker, a professor of art history at the Free University of Amsterdam, whose major written work in English is *Modern Art and the Death of a Culture*.

Jail," Dr. Martin Luther King Jr. favorably cites Augustine to the effect that "an unjust law is no law at all."[58] This he uses to defend his and his followers' disobedience of the segregationist laws of Alabama. Yet as a defense of an act of civil disobedience, this is less than fully adequate, because civil disobedience can only be to something possessing a lawful character requiring obedience. It would make better sense to recognize that the laws in question were unjust, viz., that they had got the balance wrong, but that this did not diminish the character of these laws as genuine laws. Here the legal positivists, for all their considerable flaws, have a valid point that natural law theory does not sufficiently take into account. Thomas himself nuances his own statement by admitting that "even an unjust law, in so far as it retains some appearance of law, though being framed by one who is in power, is derived from the eternal law; since all power is from the Lord God, according to Rom. Xiii. 1" (Ibid.).

We have argued above that reason must be understood, not as a faculty, still less as an entity, but as the logical aspect of human experience. Something similar can be said of justice. Over the centuries much of the western tradition has seen justice as (1) an ideal, as in Plato; (2) a virtue, as in Aristotle; (3) a set of formal procedural principles, as in Kant and Rawls; (4) a future state of affairs, usually characterized by economic equality, to be achieved through liberating struggle, as in the nineteenth- and twentieth-century revolutionary thinkers; or (5) some combination of the previous four definitions. We argue instead that justice must be understood, not as a thing at all, but as the *jural aspect of experience*, the *jural* having to do with the legal weighing of a diversity of interests. If this is so, then an unjust law is not a law that lacks the element of jural balancing, because all laws undertake this in some fashion. Rather, an unjust law is one which, in its ordinary jural functioning, has got the balance fundamentally wrong. Even ordinary parlance tells us that injustice is precisely the *miscarriage* of justice and not its *absence*. Natural law theory would appear to err in neglecting the aspectual character of the jural—conceiving it as a noun rather than an adjective.

Fifth, within the realm of theology natural law theory assumes that one can know God apart from his revelation in Jesus Christ, which is the basis of Karl Barth's objection to so-called natural theology. Barth's rejection is qualitatively different from the first four positions described above, in that he appears to be dismissing, not simply natural law as a

---

58. Augustine, *On the Free Choice of the Will* 1.5, cited in King Jr.'s "Letter from Birmingham Jail."

theory, but the very reality of which it is an account. Barth's treatment of natural law is primarily within the scope of his larger treatment of soteriology, where he is at pains to reaffirm the Reformation's understanding that salvation is by the electing grace of God alone through Christ. For Barth sin is not the violation of a law of nature: "There is no law and commandment of God inherent in the creatureliness of man as such, or written and revealed in the stars as a law of the cosmos, so that the transgression of it makes man a sinner."[59] Sin, rather, is the human negation of God's mercy manifested in Christ: "there is no other or higher law than that of the divine mercy, now revealed, established and applied in the oblation of the Lamb of God."[60]

By contrast, Dooyeweerd, Schaeffer, and others, even as they dispute natural law as a *theory* of God's common grace in nature, nevertheless affirm the reality of a creation order to which the theory points. The very name of Dooyeweerd's philosophy in Dutch is *de Wijsbegeerte der Wetsidee*, or the Philosophy of the Idea of Law, or Cosmonomic Idea, as it has been inelegantly translated into English.[61] In fact, the mainstream of the Christian church has affirmed the reality of an orderly creation subject to divine norms to which human beings are called to give effect. The various sub-traditions have labeled it differently, but no one had thought to deny it altogether until the twentieth century, with the rise of historicism within the bosom of the church and of the neo-orthodoxy championed by Barth himself.

With this affirmation of a creation order, the church from the outset has understood that we are created to live in obedience to God's norms for human life. We do not invent these norms; they are given to us by a faithful God, who upholds them by his common grace. Recent efforts to dispense with creation order founder on the rocks of two basic difficulties: (1) They are parasitical in that they depend for their very meaning on the order they claim to reject. One cannot coherently dismiss something that enables one to make a meaningful statement in the first place. (2) They are rooted in a misunderstanding of the nature of personal freedom as something standing over against authority rather than as itself a manifestation of authority. Whether natural law as *theory* adequately accounts for this order has long been and will continue to be subject to debate,

---

59. Barth, *Church Dogmatics*, 4/1, § 58, 140.

60. Ibid., 3/2, § 47, 484.

61. Dooyeweerd's magnum opus in Dutch bears this title: *De Wijsbegeerte der Wetsidee*.

but that the order itself exists can be denied only with the greatest difficulty, especially as the entire human cultural enterprise is so evidently dependent on it.

Authority: Relative to God's Sovereignty

All human authorities are subject to God's sovereignty, as the three monotheistic religions testify. Even in a democratic polity in which citizens have the authority to elect their public officeholders, the authority of both is rightly said to come from God. However, the various traditions within Christianity differ as to whether this relationship between human authority and divine sovereignty is mediated or immediate. The Roman Catholic principle of subsidiarity recognizes a plurality of authoritative agents, both communal and individual, in a hierarchically-ordered society with the institutional church at the pinnacle under God himself. Authority is mediated through the church institution, which retains the right to step in and correct the subsidiary agents if they go seriously awry in the conduct of their activities. The state is subordinate to the church institution, while it in turn presides over the lower agents, not in top-down dictatorial fashion, but always respecting the latter's distinctive responsibilities within the whole.

As articulated by more than one Pope, especially Leo XIII, Pius XI, and John Paul II, subsidiarity protects the legitimate autonomy of lower agents while providing for the possibility of temporary assistance by the higher agents if need be.[62] The relationship between higher and lower authorities is not a military-style chain-of-command; rather each level of society exercises authority on its own initiative, yet always ordered towards the larger common good. Jacques Maritain expresses what he calls the pluralist principle as follows: "everything in the body politic which can be brought about by particular organs or societies inferior in degree to the State and born out of the free initiative of the people should be brought about by those particular organs or societies."[63] This, he believes,

---

62. See Leo XIII's encyclical, *Rerum Novarum* (1891), Pius XI's *Quadragesimo Anno* (1931), and John Paul II's *Centesimus Annus* (1991), for official articulations of the principle of subsidiarity.

63. Maritain, *Man and the State*, 67.

constitutes an indirect but efficacious way for the people to maintain control over the expansive tendencies of even a democratic state.[64]

On the side of the Reformation, however, the relationship between God's sovereignty and human authority is understood to be a direct and immediate one, without other communities standing in between. This approach closely parallels the reformers' soteriology and ecclesiology, in which the priesthood of all believers plays a crucial role. The reformers, of course, affirmed the centrality of the institutional church in preaching the word and administering the sacraments, yet they also affirmed the right of believers to read scripture for themselves and to relate to God directly without the mediatorial interposition of deceased saints and living church hierarchs. Accordingly, the heirs of the Reformation conceived of society in a rather less hierarchical form, while definitely holding to the pluriformity of authorities, each of which owes its status directly to God's sovereign will. Proponents of this nonhierarchical vision of societal pluriformity include Johannes Althusius (1563–1638), Guillaume Groen van Prinsterer (1801–1876), Abraham Kuyper (1837–1920), and Herman Dooyeweerd (1894–1977).

Kuyper is generally credited with originating the term "sphere sovereignty" or "sovereignty in its own sphere" (*soevereiniteit in eigen kring*), although the translation of *soevereiniteit* as *sovereignty* in English is regrettable, primarily due to the influence of Hobbes' use of the latter in his own political philosophy, where it has troubling absolutist connotations. Nevertheless, whatever one calls it, sphere sovereignty has three implications, the last of which distinguishes it from the Catholic principle of subsidiarity: (1) ultimate sovereignty belongs only to God; (2) all earthly authorities are subordinate to and dependent upon God's sovereignty; and (3) there is no single earthly sovereignty from which other authorities are derived.[65] The implication of sphere sovereignty is that the overall health of society requires a balanced development of the various authoritative spheres, in which no single one takes on idolatrous

---

64. For a compendium of essays related to subsidiarity, see Skillen and McCarthy, ed., *Political Order and the Plural Structure of Society*.

65. Kuyper, "Sphere Sovereignty," in Bratt, ed., *Abraham Kuyper: A Centennial Reader*, 461–90. This was an address Kuyper delivered at the opening of the Free University of Amsterdam in 1880. See also Skillen and McCarthy, ed., *Political Order and the Plural Structure of Society*, for essays related to sphere sovereignty as well.

proportions. This idolatry is the source of the various *-isms*, that is, the ideologies that have so disfigured the modern world since at least 1789.[66] The differences between Roman Catholic and Reformed approaches to society developed out of a late medieval controversy over the political authority of the pope. Did the pope possess the authority to depose an apostate king and to absolve his subjects of their obligation to obey him? Or did the king receive his political authority from God in unmediated fashion? The issue found Giles of Rome (Ægidius Romanus, c. 1243-1316) on the side of papal authority and John of Paris (c. 1255-1306) and Dante Alighieri (1265-1321) supporting more of a peer relationship between institutional church and state, the authority of each coming directly from God himself.[67] While the conflict between these two positions began as an intramural one, it became an inter-ecclesial struggle in the sixteenth century with the disintegration of the western church. Nevertheless, both sides could agree that all human authority has its ultimate origin in God's sovereignty. Their unity on this central point would make for similar responses on each side to the rise of the political ideologies of the eighteenth and nineteenth centuries, all of which in some fashion declined to acknowledge it. We shall return to this issue in chapter 6 in discussing the pluriformity of authorities.

---

66. See once again this author's own *Political Visions and Illusions*, especially chapter 8, which treats at greater length the principles of subsidiarity and sphere sovereignty in their historical context.

67. See Ægidius Romanus, *De ecclesiastica potestate* (c. 1302); John of Paris, *De potestate regia et papali* (1302-3); and Dante Alighieri, *De monarchia* (c. 1308-13).

5

Office: The Key to Authority

Authority, Office and the Image of God

On Monday, 2 February 1942, the Rev. Dr. Kornelis Sietsma is arrested by the German Sicherheitsdienst *(SD) at his home in Amsterdam. Yesterday he preached a sermon on Luke 4:1–13, the account of Jesus' temptation in the wilderness, in which he emphasized the temptations that come with power. This was at his own congregation, the Schinkelkerk, which worships in a 50-year-old building in the Dutch capital city. At the offering he announced that a collection would be taken for the denomination's mission to the Jews, something that had come to the attention of the SD, whose agents had attended his church that day.*

German troops have occupied the Netherlands for not quite two years. Queen Wilhelmina and her government have taken refuge in London and the occupiers have established a pro-Nazi government in its place. All of this has occurred despite the Dutch declaration of neutrality at the beginning of the war in 1939. However, only months later Germany violated Dutch neutrality and invaded the country. Now German soldiers patrol the streets and the Jewish population has begun to receive discriminatory treatment at their hands, with much worse to come.

The Schinkelkerk is part of the Reformed Churches in the Netherlands, a denomination that began as a merger of two Reformed denominations dissenting from the established church. This union was engineered in 1892 by Abraham Kuyper, who would go on to become Prime Minister of the Netherlands shortly after the turn of the century. In his own political thought Kuyper had recovered an emphasis on something he called soevereiniteit in eigen kring, *or sovereignty in its own sphere—a principle that is in sharp contrast to state absolutism and certainly to the pretensions of any totalitarian régime.*

A week and a half earlier, Sietsma presided over the meeting of the Schinkelkerk consistory (council of pastor and elders), which was faced with two issues of political significance, viz., the status of liturgical prayers for the exiled Royal Family, and the Arbeitsdienst, *or the mandatory service imposed on young people by the Germans. These had been raised in a letter issued by the General Synod of the Reformed Churches which has been communicated to the congregations, calling them to discourage the young men from participating in the compulsory* Arbeitsdienst *(labor service) and to remember the Royal Family, especially Queen Wilhelmina, in worship services. The minutes of that meeting indicate that Sietsma commended the courage of this synodical letter which had brought joy to his heart.*

Sunday, 1 February, would mark Sietsma's final sermon. SD officials were in the congregation that day when the special collection was taken. During his prayers, Sietsma recalled the fourth birthday of Queen Wilhelmina's little granddaughter, Princess Beatrix, which had occurred on Saturday, and asked God for the safe return of the Royal Family to the Netherlands. All of this was duly noted by the visitors, who took this incriminating information back to their superiors.

Following his arrest, Sietsma is put on trial for three transgressions of SD standards: (1) provoking resistance to the governing authorities, (2) collecting funds for the Jews, and (3) praying for the royal family's return. During his trial he admits, under questioning, that the lust for power, on which he had preached, is present also in national socialism. Sietsma is held in prison until July, when he is transferred to Dachau. Two months later, at only 46 years of age, he is dead, having paid the ultimate price for his courage in the face of his persecutors.[1]

Authority is so ubiquitous that any effort even to identify it, much less to analyze it, inevitably calls for great care. At the outset we must recognize that authority, properly understood, belongs to the human world. Forests and trees cannot be said to possess authority. Neither can mountains and seas. Nor can the myriad species of animals that inhabit the earth. To be sure, each has its assigned place in the fabric of God's creation. Yet authority is uniquely granted to those created in God's image, which is the meaning of the Cultural Mandate as recorded in Genesis

---

1. A biography of Sietsma was written by Sikkel, *Een waarlijk vrije.*

1:26–29. Over the centuries various theologians have offered their own explanations of the *imago Dei*. Augustine suggests that this image entails "a soul endowed with reason and intelligence."[2] Thomas Aquinas locates this image in the human mind—in the intellect. He goes even further and asserts that this image is found *only* in the mind, suggesting that God's image is restricted to a part of the human person.[3] John Calvin does not entirely break with Thomas, arguing that "the proper seat of [God's] image is in the soul,"[4] but he does properly recognize that the image is spiritual in nature.

In the time since the Reformation a number of theologians have broken with this rationalist view, affirming instead that God's image encompasses the whole person living in response to God's call. Abraham Kuyper emphasizes the social character of this image, which includes the entire human race. Furthermore, "in creating human beings in his likeness God," according to Kuyper, "deposited an infinite number of nuclei for high human development in our nature."[5] Other Reformed theologians, including Karl Barth,[6] Emil Brunner,[7] Herman Bavinck,[8] and G. C. Berkouwer,[9] have affirmed that the image resides in the whole person and not merely in the intellect.

We here follow this august group of later theologians in affirming that God's image encompasses the total person and the entirety of humanity. It is relational and representational. It is not restricted to our capacity to think logically, although that certainly is one aspect. It is not limited merely to the mind, but extends to our bodies, which are, after all, the temple of the Holy Spirit, as St. Paul the Apostle affirms (I Cor 6:19–20).[10] When we get up in the morning, we do so as the image of God. When we begin the day's work, we do so as those created in God's image. When we spend time with our families, we do so as

---

2. Augustine, *City of God* 12.23.

3. Thomas Aquinas, *Summa Theologica*, part I, question 93, article 6.

4. Calvin, *Institutes of the Christian Religion*, I, 15, iii.

5. Kuyper, "Common Grace," in Bratt, ed., *Abraham Kuyper: A Centennial Reader*, 178.

6. Barth, *Church Dogmatics*, 3/1:201–6.

7. Brunner, *The Christian Doctrine of Creation and Redemption*, 55–61.

8. Bavinck, *Reformed Dogmatics*, 2:530–62.

9. Berkouwer, *Man: the Image of God*, especially 67–118.

10. It is possible that in referring to the body (σῶμα) in the singular, Paul is alluding as well to the corporate nature of the body of Christ as the temple of the Holy Spirit.

image-bearing creatures. Everything we do in the fullness of our lives is inevitably impacted by our creation in God's image, even if that image is broken and defaced by sin.

During and after the Enlightenment many thinkers have reversed this relationship, arguing instead that man creates God in *his* own image. Karl Marx famously borrowed this notion from the German philosopher Ludwig Feuerbach and incorporated it into his own philosophy of history, where it became the bedrock of his atheism. Many contemporary biblical scholars and philosophers of religion, though they may not trumpet outright atheism and may in fact value their connection with a Christian church, nevertheless accept something along these lines—that when scripture speaks of the "mighty hand and outstretched arm" of God (Deut 4:34, &c), or his regret in creating man (Gen 6:6), or the possibility of seeing his "face" (Ps 17:15), it reflects, not God's revelation of himself, but the efforts of the ancient Israelites to grasp or perhaps even to *invent* the Divine. This, it is often thought, is part of a larger effort to make sense of lives filled with suffering, especially at the hands of their pagan neighbors. Within this perspective God does not reveal himself to us; rather we can do no more than to grope and stumble our way towards—what? Something or Someone we conceive to stand at the point of origin of the cosmos. Perhaps a Supreme Being or a Platonic idea—something which we have personified, to whom we attribute human characteristics, albeit magnified and perfected.

Prior to the outbreak of the Second World War, Kornelis Sietsma wrote a book called *Ambtsgedachte*, published posthumously and translated half a century later as *The Idea of Office*.[11] In this brief volume the author ties the exercise of authority to the possession of office. Office is not a static position that certain persons happen to occupy within a large impersonal bureaucracy. It is a commission, an assignment, or calling given by God to specific persons for the fulfillment of specific tasks. Office is not *self*-serving but is *other*-serving, oriented towards God and our fellow human beings, especially within a communal context for which the assigned tasks are relevant. Surveying the biblical data, Sietsma notes the connection of office with *service*. Although only the office of deacon (διάκονος) carries an obvious etymological link with service (διακονία), "the general class term for all the offices is 'servant,' or 'servanthood,' and

---

11. See bibliographic entries for full information.

the general task is 'serving.'"[12] Office is not static; it is active, because it is always connected to a specific task to be performed. Yet office is stable in that it functions within generally known limits and possesses a certain solidity and reliability. Most important of all, office is intrinsically connected to authority. To have authority is to exercise an office.

From the outset Sietsma undertakes to cut through the distinctively modern notion that authority is entirely conventional, or, as more recent philosophers would put it, socially constructed. Once more, Rousseau argues that "no man has a natural authority over his fellow" and that all such relations based on authority and subordination must be rooted in generally agreed-upon conventions. Sietsma, by contrast, argues that "office is the only justification and the proper limitation of any human exercise of power and authority." Apart from office, there simply is no obligation to obey another person. There is no natural right for one person to rule over someone else.[13] Whether the German SD ever saw this book is unknown, but if they had, they could not have failed to recognize the implications of Sietsma's approach for the Nazi claim to Aryan racial superiority over other peoples. Only office can confer authority, not some form of power, however the latter be defined. Thus authority's exercise is not dependent "on the condition or power of an organization or institution, nor on the gifts or stature of a given person." It is instead dependent "on the appointment to an office, or the giving of a commission, and on the acknowledgment and acceptance of that office and commission."[14]

Sietsma is correct, we believe, in focusing on office, which is key to understanding the meaning of authority. Max Weber, as noted in the previous chapter, properly recognizes the place of office and even the differentiation of offices, which we shall take up in chapter 6. Yet his own definition of office is too narrow, excluding hereditary offices and resting on the uncertain foundation of a subjective popular sense of legitimacy. He also unduly restricts office to the various forms of dominion over others, whereas office in its more encompassing sense covers both authority *over* and authority *under*, as we shall see in the next section.

The most basic office we hold is indeed that of divine image. Respect for authority must begin with this authoritative office, in which all the other offices find their focus and point of origin. This indeed is the grain

---

12. Sietsma, *Office*, 20.
13. Ibid., 15.
14. Ibid., 16.

of truth to be found in the contemporary ideology of human rights, as manifested in both practical jurisprudence and popular culture. In the absence of a robust belief in a creating and redeeming God, the prevailing trend setters have exalted the status of the expansive self and its subjective aspirations. Another way of putting this is that the image of God has been mistaken for God himself. Yet, as we noted in chapter 3, this focus on the self makes for a very insecure status for the human person. By contrast, to recognize that human beings are created in God's image is to acknowledge at once their *limited and dependent yet pivotal position* over the rest of God's creation.

It is telling that, with a loss of belief in God, and with it the image of God, people have been increasingly driven to seek out substitutes. Otherwise they have difficulty knowing why there should be laws undertaking to protect human beings from theft, murder, rape, and a host of other criminal offenses. Immanuel Kant once again argued that human beings must be treated as ends and not as means. This has become one of the foundations of modern human rights jurisprudence, as embodied in the Universal Declaration of Human Rights and the many domestic bills of rights such as Canada's Charter of Rights and Freedoms. Divorced from her relationship to God, the human person becomes an end in herself, a quasi-divine being whose status is simply presupposed. Through exercising her reason she becomes the arbiter of right and wrong, and of just and unjust. She is the supreme legislator, and all political authority must defer to this exalted status.

On a popular level, the purveyors of self-esteem offer yet another substitute for the image of God. Self-esteem is heralded as the panacea for a variety of personal and social ills: if people can be made to feel good about themselves, all things will be well. There is, of course, something proper in the emphasis on self-esteem, especially where people lack ordinary self-confidence to go out and live productive lives. Furthermore, given that some abuse their bodies through drugs, alcohol, and sexual and eating disorders, lack of respect for the image of God in oneself is hardly to be commended. God's creation, even his human creation, is good because a good God brought it into being and pronounced it such (Gen 1:31).

Yet on its own and isolated from an awareness of God's creation, self-esteem is paper thin and offers an exceedingly poor substitute for this image, in part because it fails to differentiate between the goodness of creation and its deformation due to sin. We cannot and should not feel good about our sinfulness, the very thing that mars God's image in us. If, through various psychological techniques, we are brought to the point of feeling good about ourselves when at the same time we continue to abuse alcohol, cheat on our taxes, loaf on the job, and generally treat people poorly, then we are in grave danger of losing the very conscience that might otherwise cause us to sorrow and prompt us to amend our lives. Feelings of guilt ought not be diminished when the guilt is real and needs to be addressed as such.

According to Sietsma, the fall into sin entails a fall from our divinely-appointed office. The unbeliever is an office-breaker, even when she tries to do what she believes to be good.[15] Do human beings then forfeit their office? Do they cease to be God's image? Sietsma does not say this in so many words and is somewhat ambiguous on the point, stating simply that "man fell from his official position of responsibility in the service of God and ended up under the tyranny of the evil one."[16] Yet Sietsma admits that "the image of God did not completely disappear, for man did not cease to be man."[17] For this reason we would argue that breaking office cannot imply giving it up altogether. To be sure, our office as image of God needs to be restored in Jesus Christ, and this restoration is promised to those actively believing in his saving grace. Nevertheless, through his common grace God upholds and is faithful to his creation despite our sin. Or as Sietsma puts it, "The Lord sees to it that the thoughts of the human mind, the affections of the human heart, and the works of the human hand still manifest His glory and the rich qualities of His creation."[18] This common grace in creation does not itself save in the absence of faith; yet it does declare the glory of God, as Psalm 19 expresses it.

Authority Over and Authority Under

There is a persistent tendency, owing perhaps to the conflation of authority and power, to assume that all authority is *authority over* someone, which is not the case. To be sure, all authority is over some*thing* that has been given us as image-bearing stewards of God's creation, as affirmed in Psalm 8.[19] Nevertheless, when we think of authoritative offices, we

---

15. Ibid., 29.
16. Ibid., 27.
17. Ibid., 26.
18. Ibid., 27.
19. See also Sirach 17:1–14, which reiterates the Cultural Mandate given in Genesis

generally think of those issuing commands to people under them, e.g., kings, prime ministers, presidents, chair persons, employers, parents, bishops, pastors, teachers, administrators, and managers. As children we were generally taught to obey those in authority. This precept is correct as far as it goes, but it misses what seems to us to be a crucial element of authority: while it is always set over something, it encompasses *every human activity, including that of obedience itself*. Thus citizens, members of an organization or association, employees, minor children, parishioners, students, and other subordinates can themselves be said to possess an authoritative office deserving of respect. Such respect may not call for obedience as such, yet it does call for honor. A university professor presiding over a classroom bears an important office, entailing a teaching authority. Yet so also do his students bear an office. Each of these offices is authoritative in its own way, even if the authority of each is not identical and one is set over the other in that context.

The professor sets the terms of the course in the syllabus at the outset, and his students are subject to them. To receive a passing mark they must complete the tests and examinations, write the assigned papers, attend class, and contribute intelligently to the discussions therein. One might say that the professor bears a certain metaphorical "power of the sword" in the form of the coercive power of the grade book. In assessing his students' performance throughout the term, he properly assigns marks to each component, which will then go into the final mark at term's end. If a student disagrees with the mark assigned by the professor, she may, of course, attempt to persuade him of its unfairness, with which he may or may not agree. If he does not and if she remains persuaded that an injustice has been done, she may perhaps appeal the mark to the department chair or whoever immediately supervises the professor's performance. The latter may or may not uphold the professor's judgment. In any event, such appeal procedures underscore the fact that the professor must respect the authoritative office of the student as well. Professor and student do not have the *same* authority; it is not reciprocal or egalitarian in that sense. Nevertheless, both occupy an authoritative office worthy of respect.

Recognizing that even subordinate offices are authoritative follows from the general acknowledgement that *all human authority is authority under*, that is, it is derivative from a higher authority, ultimately that of God himself. As Victor Lee Austin puts it, "To be an authority is to be

---

1 and Psalm 8. Catholics and Orthodox consider Sirach (Ecclesiasticus) deuterocanonical scripture, while Protestants group it with the Apocrypha.

authorized by someone or something beyond oneself."[20] One possesses authority because one is under authority. St. Paul the Apostle once more tells us that "there is no authority except from God, and those that exist have been instituted by God" (Rom 13:1). This should not be read as a blanket endorsement of the overstated claims of the Roman emperor, who fancied himself divine. Nearly all of the original apostles died as martyrs for refusing to accede to the godlike claims of the emperor and confessing instead that Jesus is Lord. It is, however, a recognition that political rulers have their own legitimate sphere of authority alongside other authorities. In fact, Paul's statement could be said to apply to *any* form of authority, whether it be authority *over* or authority *under*.

Some observers have tried to soften the biblical commands to honor those in authority by emphasizing an egalitarian mutuality among Christians.[21] To be sure, any focus on treating others with kindness and forbearance is to be welcomed. Moreover, any hint of authoritarian*ism*, i.e., the abuse of authority, should definitely be ruled out, especially among believers. Yet consideration of each other's interests need hardly rule out authoritative office. Indeed, it is in the very conduct of office that office-bearers need to be reminded of the responsibilities and obligations that come with it. These obligations may not be identical or symmetrical, yet they are indeed mutual: everyone is called to an authoritative office—to multiple offices in fact—and everyone is similarly called to respect these offices. In Ephesians 5, for example, Paul calls the recipients of his letter to respect the offices of husband, wife, parent, offspring, master, and servant in the course of fulfilling their own offices. He is not subverting these offices, as some might argue; he is, rather, calling for their proper exercise.[22]

---

20. Austin, *Up With Authority*, 19.

21. See, e.g., Keener, *Paul, Women & Wives*, especially 157–83, where he treats "Mutual Submission in Ephesians 5:18–33."

22. It is, of course, hotly disputed in Christian circles whether husbandly authority requires wifely obedience as a trans-temporal norm for marriage. I will not weigh in on this issue except to note that not all authority is executive authority calling for obedience. Yet all authority calls for respect. See chapter 6 for a discussion of Richard de George's systematic theory of authority. As for the master-servant relationship, it is often said that this no longer has relevance after slavery's abolition. Yet chattel slavery, in which one person was held to own another person in totalistic fashion on a par with inanimate property or livestock, could be seen as a deformation of the legitimate relationship of *authority over and authority under*. As such it could apply to virtually any organized communal context.

This focus on the proper use of authority is too frequently obscured, even by the translators of these biblical texts. For example, Matthew 20:20-28 recounts the episode in which the mother of James and John, apparently at their instigation, approaches Jesus requesting that her sons be granted viceregal positions in his forthcoming kingdom. This elicits protests from the other disciples, and Jesus himself alerts them to the perils that come with the lust for power. This is how the New International Version recounts it:

Jesus called them together and said, "You know that the rulers of the Gentiles lord it over them, and their high officials *exercise authority over them*. Not so with you. Instead, whoever wants to become great among you must be your servant, and whoever wants to be first must be your slave — just as the Son of Man did not come to be served, but to serve, and to give his life as a ransom for many" (verses 25-28, emphasis mine). The majority of English translations generally agree that Jesus, somewhat incongruously, is commanding his disciples *not* to exercise authority over others. This is true of the King James Version, the Revised Standard Version and the English Standard Version, in addition to the NIV.

However, the Greek verb translated as "exercise authority" may have a different connotation as captured in some of the more paraphrastic versions of the Bible. The clue to the meaning of κατεξουσιάζουσιν (κατεξουσιάζω), an otherwise rare word, is found in more closely examining its construction. The prefix κατα- is added to εξουσιάζω, the latter of which means simply to exercise authority. The use of this prefix, especially when the object of the verb is rendered in the genitive case (αὐτῶν), may imply that the compound verb has a negative connotation.[23] This is certainly true of the immediately preceding verb, κατακυριεύουσιν (κατακυριεύω), which the NIV translates as "lord it over" and which is followed again by the genitive plural pronoun αὐτῶν. Thus it may be that the New Revised Standard Version best translates the passage as follows: "You know that the rulers of the Gentiles lord it over them, and their great ones are tyrants over them." This interpretation is picked up as well by *The Message* and the New Living Translation.[24]

---

23. This reading of the word was suggested to the author by biblical scholar Albert M. Wolters in an email dated 11 March 2008, and was subsequently confirmed by the author's father, a native speaker of modern Greek who has also studied Koine. See also O. O'Donovan's discussion of the parallel Markan passage (10:35-44) in *Desire of the Nations*, 106.

24. *The Message*: "'You've observed how godless rulers throw their weight around, how quickly a little power goes to their heads.'" The New Living Translation: "'You

Far from being incompatible with servanthood, the rightful exercise of authority requires it. This is confirmed in ordinary parlance wherein government employees are frequently referred to collectively as the public service.[25] Public servants precisely serve the public in the conduct of their offices. In many English-speaking Commonwealth countries, members of cabinet are called *ministers*, i.e., servants, of the Crown, though they are effectively responsible to Parliament. St. Paul refers to governing authorities as both "God's servant for your good" and "ministers of God," employing the Greek words διάκονος and λειτουργοί, which are also used to describe deacons and ministers presiding at the liturgy (λειτουργία) in the institutional or gathered church (Rom 13:4, 6). The positive role for government envisioned in this passage forms the basis for John Calvin's assertion that government's "function among men is no less than that of bread, water, sun, and air; indeed, its place of honor is far more excellent."[26] Something similar could be said of all forms of authority found in human society. One is tempted to assert that, without authority, society in all its complexity would founder and degenerate into chaos. There can be no such thing as a society lacking authority in some fashion. Indeed it is necessary to human flourishing, as Yves R. Simon, Victor Lee Austin and many others correctly understand. Where authoritative offices are regularly subject to derision and where such offices lose the power to function adequately, mere power will come—authoritatively!—to be thought a sufficient substitute. Revolutionary action rarely accomplishes a net gain for justice, despite the best of intentions. It tends rather to substitute one form of abuse for another, in effect asserting its perpetrators' own highly disputable claim to authority in opposition to that of the predecessor régime.

The Limits to Authority

It should hardly require saying that all authority, like everything else in God's creation, normatively functions within limits of different kinds. Weber understood this in observing that an office is subject to norms

---

know that the rulers in this world lord it over their people, and officials flaunt their authority over those under them.'"

25. This label is used in Canada more than in the United States, where its counterpart is known as the civil service.

26. Calvin, *Institutes*, IV.20.3.

appropriate to its peculiar setting. Someone occupying an office is subject to a higher office only in the conduct of the first office and not in his personal life. A central feature of the various tyrannical and totalitarian régimes that marred especially the twentieth century is the pretense that nothing falls outside their sphere of competence. Such régimes claim total jurisdiction over all human activities of any sort. It is by no means accidental that such régimes are typically inclined to embrace atheism insofar as they themselves effectively assume godlike capacities and cannot bring themselves to acknowledge any authority outside themselves. That said, totalitarian rulers often claim to act on the basis of a superior understanding of the workings of the historical process, so in this sense they might be said implicitly to acknowledge authority—namely, the authority of history and their own interpretation of it.

Even the claims to *sovereignty* asserted by kings, states, nations, and democratic peoples represent a certain unwillingness to acknowledge the limits that God has placed on all authorities. Here it would be best to soften sovereignty to *supreme political authority within a designated territory*. This is more compatible with a biblical understanding of created limits. Only God is sovereign in the full sense. All human authority derives from God's sovereignty, either immediately or mediately, or both.

In recent years the term *inclusivity* has come into use in some circles, particularly those influenced by postmodernism. The assumption is that communities are somehow more salutary and just as they become increasingly inclusive of greater numbers of people. The fact that communities seem necessarily to exclude those who do not conform to the criteria for membership is deemed scandalous. Once again this protest is rooted in a failure to acknowledge that everything God has created is bounded by limits. To be sure, one might rightly protest the drawing of *unjust* and *improper* boundaries, e.g., those excluding black Americans from the body politic prior to the 1960s or women prior to the 1920s. But this can hardly be an argument against boundaries as such. To eliminate boundaries would be to eliminate community. The current use of *inclusivity* tends to ignore this reality.

Furthermore, a focus on inclusivity neglects the legitimate pluriformity of human communities. Families come in different sizes, ranging from childless couples to those with large numbers of children. Nevertheless, whatever the family's size, parents necessarily and quite properly care for their *own* children rather than for those who are not their own. Similarly, marriages can consist only of two opposite-sex partners (although a number of jurisdictions now legally deny this reality) and necessarily exclude everyone else on earth. Marital fidelity is obviously incompatible with an emphasis on boundless inclusivity. The state as a political community is necessarily limited to those born within its jurisdictional boundaries or who have acquired citizenship through naturalization, though without discrimination on ethnic, religious, ideological, racial, and other grounds. Yet it necessarily excludes noncitizens. Families, marriages, and states are distinct communities, whose boundaries are drawn differently but in ways appropriate to the internal character of those communities. The emphasis on inclusivity is strikingly similar to the longstanding liberal effort to recast all communal formations as voluntary associations. Both would effectively blur the legitimate differences among the various kinds of communities, yet in different ways. The push to include ever greater numbers of people into every community, however commendable it may seem superficially, would, if followed to its logical conclusion, render community itself impossible. Nevertheless, communities continue to exist, because they are rooted inexorably in human nature.

The single exception to this necessarily limited nature of human communities is the *corpus Christi*, the (mystical) body of Christ, which in principle includes all of God's image-bearers in all of their overlapping temporal offices. Churches properly undertake to evangelize throughout the world so as to bring as many people as they can into the fold. Yet even here those who will not accept the claims of Christ in their own lives necessarily exclude themselves from the ecclesial community.[27] All communities are limited, as are the authoritative offices required for their continued existence. These offices are limited in the following ways.

Spatial/numerical limits. Although it is theoretically possible to imagine an authority limited in other ways extending over all human beings everywhere, as in, e.g., the Roman Catholic Church's claim in principle to universality or catholicity, in the real world all human authoritative offices are limited in their jurisdiction to those obviously subject to them. The authority of the federal government of the United States extends in a primary sense over those who are citizens of that country and secondarily over all persons living within its borders irrespective of citizenship. The authority of parents covers only their own minor children and not their neighbors' children. The authority of a platoon commander extends only over the soldiers in his or her platoon. The

---

27. This, of course, brings up the doctrine of election, which, though it has relevance, is probably best left to the theologians.

professor's authority applies only to the students in her class, although students in other classes are likely to pay respect to her professorial authority. Others appropriately respect an authoritative office, even when they themselves are not subject to it.

To be sure, we sometimes speak of the *human* community or the *international* community, but in general the more expansively a community is defined, the more abstract and less concrete it becomes. The more abstract a community becomes, the less able it is to command the loyalty of its members and to become a focus of communal identity. Furthermore, so broadly defined a community can hardly be a responsible agent, which would require some form of authority set over it. But there is, of course, no king of the world or universal emperor, Dante's *De Monarchia* to the contrary notwithstanding. If a group of people, however defined, has no office set over it to exercise communal coordinative authority, then this group can probably not, after all, be defined as a community. At most it is a society or association composed of a network of interactions among people and communities but which is not itself a responsible agent.

Substantive limits. Even if there were a human community with effective jurisdiction over all human beings, it would still be limited to those matters falling within its sphere of competence. This is what might be called the substantive limits on authority, insofar as it concerns the substantive content, or subject matter, of authority's jurisdiction. For example, the authority of political leaders extends only to political matters and not directly to, say, matters more properly within the jurisdiction of church institutions, families, schools, labor unions, etc. Bishops' authority is over matters related to the church institution, including confessions of faith, liturgies, preaching the word, and administering the sacraments. They properly do not instruct political leaders how they should fulfill the demands of their peculiar offices, unless the latter are violating biblical principles in egregious fashion. Similarly parliaments do not formulate binding confessions of faith, despite the precedent set by the Long Parliament in 1646 appointing the Westminster Assembly to reform the Church of England. A professor's authority extends to assigning readings, essays and examinations within the classroom context; he does not tell his students what to eat for dinner that evening or whom and when to marry.

Instrumental limits. The various authoritative offices have recourse to different *means* appropriate to a particular community. Political authority is said to possess the power of the sword, i.e., the power of life and death over those subject to it, but it cannot bar them from receiving the sacraments in their church community. Ecclesiastical authority cannot incarcerate those who will not heed its directives, but it can withhold the sacraments or, as a last resort, excommunicate them from their church communion. Parents properly discipline their children by, e.g., spanking them, sending them to their room, or withholding a privilege for a time. An employer may dock an employee's pay or terminate her employment. Voluntary associations may suspend or expel someone from membership. If an authority attempts to employ an improper means to enforce obedience to its otherwise proper commands, we intuitively understand that something is seriously amiss.

Temporal limits. All authority exists within temporal limits, due partly to the limited lifespans of the human bearers of authoritative offices and partly to the general conviction that the tasks of office are best fulfilled when its holders alternate on a regular basis. A man and woman are husband and wife "until death do us part," as traditional wedding liturgies put it. The parental office endures in an active form only until the children reach maturity and thereafter continues in honorific form until the death of the parent. In those countries with hereditary constitutional monarchies, with the exception of the Netherlands and now Belgium, the monarch generally occupies the throne until death. Similarly, in the Roman Catholic Church the occupant of the papacy almost always serves for life, although other bishops retire at age 75. Yet Benedict XVI arguably set a different precedent for even the papacy by effectively retiring at age 85.

Most organized communities are led by authoritative office-bearers serving for limited terms. After the term expires, the holder of the office stands down and relinquishes the reins to his or her successor. The length of the term and the number of terms one is allowed to serve will naturally differ from one organization to the next, but after the maximum period has elapsed, the occupant hands over the office to someone else, who has in the meantime been elected or appointed to replace him or her. Retirement from office due to age is another manifestation of this temporally limited character of authority. In Canada from 1867 until 1965, Senators, i.e., members of the upper chamber of Parliament, were permitted to serve for life, though after the latter date a retirement age of 75 became mandatory. In 1997 the General Assembly of the Presbyterian Church in Canada permitted congregations to establish terms of service for elders rather than the life-time appointments to which they are still called in most congregations.[28]

Despite the alternation of personnel in specific offices, the offices themselves are frequently much more long-lived. The papacy, e.g., has endured for at least a millennium, and perhaps the better part of two, depending on whose history we read. The presidency of the United States has existed since 1789. The office of prime minister in Canada has existed since 1867. Yet such offices can almost always be traced to temporal beginnings and, although they may continue to exist for the time being, will not of course last forever. So even the offices themselves, and not only their occupants, are subject to temporal limitations.

The pluriformity of authority. Over the course of human history the general office of divine image has dispersed and manifested itself in an increasing number of specific offices related to particular communities. As a consequence of this historical process of differentiation, one authoritative office is limited by other such offices, each of which exercises an authority directly dependent on God. This has two implications for the authority of the state. First, the state's authority is limited by that of other adjacent states. New Zealand's parliament cannot legislate for Australia and vice versa. Second, the state's authority is limited by the pluriform authorities even within its political jurisdiction, such as the family, the school, the business enterprise, and the labor union. Parental authority is not delegated by government. It exists by right—or more properly it is given by God himself within the context of the family, whose status might be said in some sense to be anterior to that of the state. We shall take up this subject in greater detail in chapter 6.

The Forfeiture of Authority

Given the human propensity for evil, the *abuse of authority* remains an ever-present possibility and, in many cases, a tragic reality. The very notion of abuse presupposes a normative conception of authority and of the offices to which it is attached. Of course, identifying such abuse is not always a simple matter, because not everyone will necessarily agree on what constitutes abuse in specific cases. This is further complicated by the contemporary tendency to overextend the definition of *oppression* to cover virtually any external standard or communal expectation

---

28. Henderson and Muir, "Term Service For Elders," 12.

countering or at least impinging on one's own will. Thus a community's refusal to affirm a member's chosen way of life is deemed to be on a par with being imprisoned for one's political convictions. Nevertheless, there are certain unmistakable signs that authority is being abused. A principal one is the failure of office-bearers to recognize the very limits to authority described above. Outright usurpation of office is an obvious abuse, but so is the effort to extend the office's competence beyond its proper boundaries. Self-aggrandizement at the expense of other authoritative agents, whether communal or individual, amounts to what the ancient Greeks and Romans called tyranny.

Another sign of abuse is evident when an office-bearer comes to depend too heavily on the various means described in chapter 2. The excessive presence of the military or police forces in a polity—that is, the proverbial police state—may indicate that a ruler's perceived authority is fragile and dangerously overextended. The media become tools of psychological manipulation for the régime, which can no longer trust the people's loyalty. The rule of law is replaced by personal caprice. Tyrants focus too heavily on the symbolism of authority, expending excessive time and energy on fancy uniforms, presidential palaces, and the like. A misplaced epaulette, badge, or medal becomes an occasion for crisis, virtually on a par with an attempted assassination or foreign invasion. The dictator-for-life, sporting foppish military dress and an oversized officer's cap with silly-looking plumage, is a stable fixture in the repertoire of political cartoonists and satirists. In the gathered church as well, those clergy who specialize in the minutiae of liturgical garb while neglecting the message of the gospel may be trying rather too hard to impress upon the faithful the authoritative character of their ecclesiastical office.

How is such abuse to be addressed and, one hopes, corrected? To begin with, the general office of image is one that is marred by sin, as recorded initially in Genesis 3. The ultimate remedy for this sin is, of course, the death and resurrection of the unique Son of God incarnate, Jesus Christ. Yet short of this complete redemption, God's conserving or common grace operates so as to restrain the full outworking of sin. Once again the general office of image cannot ultimately be forfeited in this life. Sin may distort the image, but it can never efface it altogether. Evil perverts but does not destroy our humanity.

When human beings come to occupy more specific offices attached to the various communal contexts, abuse of authority is best dealt with through legal mechanisms internal to the communities themselves. The church's canon law or church order might contain provisions for deposing a member of the clergy for official malfeasance. The bylaws of a fraternal society might provide for the removal of the society's president through, e.g., a vote of the majority of members or perhaps a vote of the executive. A country's chief constitutional document may allow for the impeachment of a president or of judges by the legislature. In a Westminster-style parliamentary system, the convention of responsible government permits the lower chamber of Parliament to defeat a sitting government on a vote of nonconfidence. All of these are potential ways of dealing with authority's abuse.

In the absence of constitutional and legal mechanisms, however, might there come a time when abuse of authority becomes so egregious that those subject to it are absolved altogether of their obligation to obey? Thomas Hobbes clearly thought such an occasion could arise when and if the sovereign makes war on his subjects, thereby threatening their fundamental right to self-preservation. John Locke believed that a government's failure to protect private property could justify what he euphemistically called an appeal to heaven, i.e., revolution. Whether or not they are correct in their judgments, it is undeniable that certain situations ensue in which a person formally occupying an authoritative office is simply no longer obeyed, his or her position having been effectively taken over by someone else. In a time of civil strife, for example, a country's leader may find himself losing control over its territory as various local warlords become the effective masters of portions of it.

Mustafa Kemal ("Atatürk")'s abolition of the Ottoman sultanate in 1922 came at the end of a period of civil unrest in which the nationalists expanded their power base at the expense of the formally-reigning sultan through force of arms. After February 1917 Russia's provisional government found it increasingly difficult to exercise effective political authority in the face of the rival power of local workers and soldiers' councils, or *soviets*. The authority of these soviets bore some of the characteristics of Weber's charismatic authority, as described in chapter 4 above.

In similar fashion, a legitimate government may be overthrown by a military junta without that government ever officially relinquishing its claim to political authority. Something along these lines occurred in 1967 when the young King Constantine of Greece lost his throne in all but name at the time the colonels assumed effective political power. Where does legitimate authority lie under such conditions? To whom is obedience owed? Citizens of a number of European countries were faced with this dilemma when their countries were overrun by Germany and their governments forced into exile during the Second World War. The dilemma facing foreign governments may be less immediately dangerous than to the citizens of such a country, but these governments too must decide who is the legitimate representative of a country having recently undergone an apparently unconstitutional régime change.

There is no easy way to resolve such dilemmas, and it is no simple matter to formulate a general rule to deal with them. It is worth noting, however, that these are extraordinary circumstances often accompanied by actual violence or its threat—something which virtually everyone agrees ought as much as possible to be avoided. Revolutionary uprisings are intrinsically problematic at the very least, not only because people are claiming to be free from the obligation to obey a specific authoritative office, but because they are acting in such a way that is not clearly related to their own offices. If "the people" can be said to have a general, natural right to remove their own government irrespective of the provisions of the positive law, in what capacity can they be said to act in this fashion? Who are these *people*? Which office(s) do they occupy? Who authorizes them so to act? If the law clearly provides for *citizens* to *vote* their rulers out of office on a periodic basis, then it is evidently in their capacity *as citizens* that they are so acting, and they do so legitimately. If it does not, the legitimacy of such actions is thrown into doubt.

The problem of political tyranny has been addressed by such thinkers as Thomas Aquinas, John Calvin and Johannes Althusius. While Thomas asserts as a general rule that Christians are to obey the secular power (*ST*, II-II, q. 104, a. 6) and to avoid the vice of sedition (*ST*, II-II, q. 42), he nevertheless holds that a tyrannical ruler is himself guilty of sedition by disturbing the common weal and sowing discord among his subjects (Ibid., a. 2, ad. 3). Yet the right to remedy such a situation lies, not with "the private judgment of individuals," but with a duly constituted public authority.[29] Calvin similarly counsels obedience to rulers—even to tyrants, whom God may have seen fit to raise up to punish their subjects (*Inst.* IV, 20, § 23–26). Nevertheless, like Thomas, Calvin is not without advice as to remedial action. He agrees in prohibiting private individuals from undertaking to depose a tyrant, favoring instead a constitutional solution in which "magistrates of the people," corresponding to the *ephors* of ancient Sparta or the three estates of the

---

29. Thomas Aquinas, *On Princely Government*, 31–32.

realms common in the sixteenth century, are authorized "to restrain the willfulness of kings."[30] Althusius, like his predecessors, calls upon the ephors, or optimates of the realm, to resist tyranny on behalf of the community they represent,[31] citing the Dutch revolt against Spain as an historical example.[32] None of these can be seen to support a general right of revolution; they are at pains, in fact, to affirm a *constitutional* remedy for tyranny, in which those undertaking to oppose tyrannical rule do so *as occupants of a specifically authorized office*.

On Revolution

Are *extra*constitutional remedies ever justified? Can revolution ever be right? Christians are divided on this issue, with Americans often coming down on the affirmative side, given their historical memory of revolt against British rule in the late eighteenth century. If a right to revolution be admitted, severe qualifications must be placed around this right, and wherever possible duly constituted authorities, such as the Continental Congress in the American colonies, must be set up to supervise the attendant military activities if events should come to this. If there is to be something even approximating a just revolution, it must be conducted along the lines of a just war, as set forth in the writings of Augustine, Thomas Aquinas and others. All the same, serious questions are inevitably raised, due to the heavy burden this places on ordinary individuals to decide between the rival claims of two conflicting authorities. All of this underscores the need for a polity to provide for constitutional remedies for the abuse of authoritative office.

Although both French and American Revolutions bear the same revolutionary label in common parlance, they are better seen as two qualitatively different phenomena rooted in sharply divergent understandings of society and politics. In fact, if one were to categorize the revolutions of the modern era, one would be justified in coming up with the following two classifications:

- Political revolution: The Dutch revolt against Spain (1568–1648), the English "Glorious" Revolution (1688–1690), the American (1775–1783), the revolt of the American Confederacy (1861–1865).

30. Calvin, *Institutes*. IV.20, § 31, 1518–19.
31. Althusius, *Politics*, XVIII and XXXVIII, 87–114, 185–94.
32. Ibid., XVIII, 101.

- Social revolution: France (1789 and following), Russia (1917), China (1949 and following), Iran (1979 and following).

The very term *revolution* obviously implies a *turning* of some sort. At its most modest, the political revolution simply turns out one ruler or group of rulers and replaces them with another. The political constitution and the legal system remain fundamentally the same. Most of the public offices continue to be filled with the same personnel, with only that of the chief magistrate being replaced. Successively more ambitious revolutions may aim at replacing an entire leadership team, reorganizing the internal arrangement of offices or even inaugurating a new constitution altogether. Yet the goal remains purely political. There is no effort to change society and its mores as a whole, which are generally understood to be and remain beyond the legitimate jurisdiction of government. Most significantly for our purposes there is no general attack on the principle of authority or on the authority of the public offices themselves. Some laws may be changed, but most remain as before. Moreover, no one would think of questioning the principle of the rule of law which undergirds constitutional government.

Such revolutions often claim conservative goals, usually to protect ancient rights that have only recently been violated by the chief magistrate. Spain's Philip II was deemed to have violated the historic autonomy of the seventeen Netherlandic provinces and imposed harsh taxation on their people. England's James II attempted to impose absolute royal rule on England and Scotland, and he threatened to return the by-then Protestant kingdoms to Roman Catholicism. The thirteen American colonies objected to being taxed by a parliament in which they were not represented. The southern states of the United States, although the justice of their cause was compromised by their commitment to the continuation of chattel slavery, believed that the federal government in Washington was undertaking to abrogate the sovereign rights of the component states of the union as set out in the Constitution of 1787.[33]

In all such cases duly constituted political authorities mounted the rebellion against the central government or king. This is not to say that extralegal and overtly illegal activities did not take place in the larger

---

33. See, e.g., DeRosa, *The Confederate Constitution of 1861*, in which the author argues that the southern secessionists were attempting to recover a more decentralist vision of American polity as articulated by the eighteenth-century antifederalists, as reflected in their own short-lived constitutional document, which corrected the perceived defects of the 1787 Constitution.

effort to throw off tyranny. Yet on the whole it was an organized body or several bodies that launched and coordinated the endeavor. In the case of the Netherlands, the stadtholders and the provincial estates actively opposed the usurpation of the king. In England it was Parliament that unseated King James and called his daughter and son-in-law to replace him. The Americans had their own representative legislative bodies in the colonies, and the leaders of these governments formed a Continental Congress to fight the trespassing pretensions of the government in London. Similarly, the southern states believed they had the authority to withdraw from a union they had voluntarily entered three-quarters of a century earlier. None of these revolts was a matter of unorganized masses of people rising up spontaneously against a sitting government. Each believed it was following and defending the rule of law against tyrannical abrogation of previously enjoyed rights.

One might well question whether the political revolution can be called a revolution at all. Certainly warfare was the consequence of these "revolutions," although it was not necessarily intended by those attempting to check the apparent tyranny. We noted above that Althusius classified the Dutch revolt as falling within the bounds of his proposed constitutional remedy for tyranny. Similarly, the American Revolution might better be described as the War for American Independence, in recognition that existing bodies politic were attempting, not to overthrow a political system and certainly not an entire social order, but to sever their links to the British Crown. Although one might wish that Kuyper had avoided the revolutionary label in these cases, he nevertheless plausibly argues that the "three great revolutions [*sic*] in the Calvinistic world left untouched the glory of God, nay, they even proceeded from the acknowledgment of his majesty."[34] While one might charge Kuyper with rhetorical excess, there is precedent for his assessment.

A social revolution is fundamentally different from the political variety in lacking a concrete and achievable *political* aim. To be sure its goals have definite political ramifications, but they are much more ambitious and encompassing: namely, the complete reordering of society in all its complexity by use of political means. Private activities cannot be allowed to remain private, and nothing can be out of bounds for the revolutionary régime bent on wholesale social change. The term *totalitarian* has been appropriately coined to apply to such forms of (mis)government.

34. Kuyper, *Lectures on Calvinism*, 73. Kuyper's reference is to the Dutch, English and American revolutions.

Such régimes typically claim to speak for an undifferentiated mass of people abstracted from the network of relationships and communities of which they are part. No authoritative offices are called to take charge. If authority enters the picture at all, it takes on Weber's charismatic character and is based, not on a legally-delimited office, but on a particular leader or régime's successful use of various forms of power, especially the psychological, over those finding themselves subject to it. The régime may indeed establish governing offices, but their continued existence is precarious at best and certainly subject to the whims of the régime itself, which will subordinate them to the imperatives of the regnant ideology rather than to the stability of the rule of law.

The French Revolution may have begun innocently enough with Louis XVI's convocation of the Estates General in 1789. But it soon developed into something much more pernicious, as the Third Estate abolished the first two estates and declared itself *l'Assemblée nationale*, claiming supreme legislative power on behalf of the ostensibly sovereign people. Edmund Burke was the first observer to comprehend fully the spirit of the developments across the English Channel. Already in 1790, only months after the Revolution started, Burke was prescient enough to foresee its likely end, including the rise of another monarch whose untempered power would likely be more arbitrary and destructive than that of the Bourbons.[35] Whereas the English Revolution of 1688 was a matter merely of settling succession to the Crown under the law and improving an existing constitution, the French Revolutionaries sought instead to abolish ancient usages *in toto* and replace them with an airy abstraction, viz., the rights of man, which became a tool in their hands to remake the customs and mores to which people were long accustomed. In seventeenth-century England, at the time of the Restoration (1660) and Revolution, statesmen had never thought to "dissolve the whole fabric" of the nation; rather "they regenerated the deficient part of the old constitution through the parts which were not impaired." They thus followed "the two principles of conservation and correction."[36] Better to reform a functioning constitution, thereby incrementally redressing its flaws, than to upend it in the vain hope of constructing something better from scratch. Better real inherited liberties, however imperfect, than ostensibly perfect rights of man existing only on paper.

---

35. Burke, *Reflections on the Revolution in France*, 318.
36. Ibid., 161.

Nearly six decades later the Dutch Christian statesman, Guillaume Groen van Prinsterer, an archivist for the Royal House of Orange, analyzed the French Revolution in similar fashion, just ahead of the second great wave of revolutions that swept Europe in 1848.[37] Groen distinguished between the Dutch revolt and the American revolution on the one hand and the French Revolution on the other, the latter being "a *social* revolution, whose nature is directed against every government and against every religion."[38] The French Revolution was rooted in nothing less than unbelief—in a deliberate rejection of God and of authority in general. Groen's protégé and successor, Abraham Kuyper, took similar pains to distinguish between these two types of revolution, ascribing the Dutch revolt, the English revolution and the American revolution to Calvin's system of secondary powers or lesser magistrates,[39] while the French revolution was born of a spirit that sought to impose the uniformity of liberty, equality and fraternity on the diverse peoples of the world and their ways.[40]

Other successive revolutions have followed the French pattern, including the October 1917 revolution in Russia. The February revolution had occurred in the midst of a general crisis of authority, leading to the abdication of the Tsar. Nevertheless, the provisional government had made a concerted effort to follow recognized procedures in governing what was rapidly becoming an ungovernable country in the midst of civil and international conflict. By contrast, Lenin and the Bolsheviks seized power illegally, dissolving the fledgling Constituent Assembly in January 1918 after elections did not go their way. Much as the Reign of Terror had seen the revolution in France "consume its own children," so also did Stalin's purges in the 1930s eliminate many of the old Bolsheviks who had fought for communism two decades earlier. Technical means enabled the Soviet state to foment its own reign of terror that made its earlier French counterpart pale by comparison. Nearly two decades after Mao Zedong took control of the whole of China in 1949, he similarly launched a Great Cultural Revolution that lasted ten years until his death in 1976. In 1979

37. Prinsterer, "Unbelief and Revolution," in Van Dyke, *Groen van Prinsterer's Lectures.*

38. Ibid., Lecture XI, p. 262.

39. Kuyper, "Calvinism: Source and Stronghold of Our Constitutional Liberties," in Bratt, ed., *Abraham Kuyper: A Centennial Reader*, 279–322, especially 305–6.

40. Kuyper, "Uniformity: The Curse of Modern Life," in Bratt, ed., *Abraham Kuyper: A Centennial Reader*, 19–44, especially 24–25.

Iranians supporting the Ayatollah Ruhollah Khomeini took control of their country's government from Shah Mohammad Reza Pahlavi, establishing an Islamic republic in place of the previous secular constitution. The new régime undertook to transform the whole of Iranian society in accordance with Shiite Islamic norms, notoriously requiring women to wear modest garb, segregating the sexes and prohibiting women from engaging in activities reserved for men, especially those connected to public life.

The social revolution is very nearly compelled to employ terror to implement its goals, which are dangerously disconnected from the normative patterns of life in the real world and are based on the erroneous assumption that human nature is infinitely malleable. Laws are potential obstacles to this grand transformative effort, and thus arbitrariness often accompanies the régime it spawns. By contrast, the political revolution is generally characterized by a concerted attempt to remain within the confines of the law, even if some people engage in extralegal activities in the course of the ensuing conflict.

Forfeiting Authority in Nonstate Communities

If a well-functioning political constitution provides mechanisms for redressing the abuse of authoritative office, the same can be said of nonstate organized communities as well. Such communities have their own internal laws, sometimes called bylaws, which have as much genuine legal status as the public law of the state. Although some communities, such as loosely-structured hobby associations, have little in the way of formal organization, such communities as business enterprises, labor unions, charitable foundations, schools, universities, museums, etc., generally have sophisticated organizational structures with carefully-worded and laid-out rules of governance providing for accountability to either a membership or a board or both. The existence of a board, with members drawn from outside the organization, is a proven, if not infallible, remedy for the abuse of office within the organization. Although management and labor—in the case of a large corporation—might be represented on the board, the board itself must be removed from its day-to-day operations so as to prevent possible conflict of interest, itself an abuse of office. If internal mechanisms fail to function properly, then and only then would the public law of the state, either criminal or civil or both, be brought in to rectify or adjudicate the issue.

The forfeiture of authority has implications also for marriage and family. Divorce not only legally ends a marriage, but terminates the two authoritative offices of husband and wife. It does not, however, terminate the offices of mother and father when children are involved, although either may become a noncustodial parent. However, it is possible for a parent to forfeit parental authority altogether by, e.g., voluntarily giving up a biological child for adoption, or having a child legally removed from one's custody due to some form of abuse. It is worth noting that such forfeiture of office of necessity involves the public law of the state, which must intervene in the event of marital or family breakdown. Yet that does not mean that marriage and family are creatures of the state. We will explore further the implications of this legal pluriformity in chapter 6.

6

The Pluriformity of Authority

A Multiplicity of Offices

It is June 2010 and the Québec Superior Court has handed down a long-awaited ruling in the case of Loyola High School v. Courchesne. In 2007 the provincial Ministry of Education, Recreation and Sport adopted an Ethics and Religious Culture (ERC) program to be taught in the province's schools. This was the culmination of a lengthy process of deconfessionalizing the schools, which had previously been divided into majority Catholic and minority Protestant systems. The enactment of Bill 95 by the Québec National Assembly deprived parents of the right to choose between Catholic and Protestant moral and religious instruction for their children. Linguistic school boards replaced the former religious school boards, and the "Québec State" assumed responsibility for all schools. In place of the parallel confessional schools, the Ministry decided to adopt ERC for all schools, ostensibly in recognition of the pluralistic character of Québec society. The program aims "to help students develop a spirit of openness and discernment with regard to the phenomenon of religion and to enable students to acquire the ability to act and to evolve intelligently and with maturity in a society that reflects a diversity of beliefs."[1]

Loyola High School is a private educational institution serving the English-speaking Catholic community of Montréal, Québec, since 1896, though its origins go as far back as 1848. Loyola requested an exemption from the Ministry's requirement that it teach ERC on the grounds that the latter's "normative pluralist" approach, viz., its relativistic approach to religious cultures, conflicts with the school's Catholic principles. Although

---

1. Seath, "Canadian Supreme Court Rules against Exemption."

some schools retain only a nominal affiliation with a church body, Loyola remains committed to "full growth of the human person which leads both to reflection and to action, suffused with the spirit and presence of Jesus Christ, the Man-for-Others." The intent is that the school "must be clearly Christian in all its aspects," following the Jesuit tradition of its namesake, St. Ignatius of Loyola.[2] Loyola argued that it offered an equivalent world religions program but taught from a Roman Catholic perspective.

The Minister, Michelle Courchesne, denied Loyola's request, arguing that ERC does not violate the school's religious freedom, but, "even if such an infringement occurred, it is warranted in a free and democratic society."[3] Loyola appealed the Minister's decision, and the Québec Superior Court has now upheld the appeal, arguing that the Minister does not possess the competence to determine whether Loyola's program is equivalent to ERC. According to Justice Gérard Dugré, in her ministerial capacity Mme. Courchesnes may not legislate the criteria for judging equivalence between the two programs; she may only judge under current law. Furthermore, she is not authorized to judge the manner in which world religions are taught at Loyola. The minister may mandate that a public school teach ERC from a secular perspective, but she may not require a private confessional school to do so. Justice Dugré's Epilogue is outspoken in its critique of the Minister: "the obligation imposed on Loyola to teach the ECR material in a secular way reveals a totalitarian character essentially equivalent to the Inquisition's order to Galileo to renounce Copernican cosmology."[4]

The provincial government of Premier Jean Charest has promised to appeal the Superior Court's ruling.[5]

⁂

A crisis arises and someone says, usually in frustration, "Something must be done!" The use of the passive voice may tempt us to avoid the issue of who or what should be taking action in this particular instance. In the case of Canada's only predominantly French-speaking province, Charest's Liberal government was exercising political authority over a society that was once overwhelmingly Roman Catholic. Even the young

---

2. Loyola High School (website).
3. *Loyola High School v. Courchesnes*, Summary of the Judgment.
4. *Loyola High School v. Courchesnes*. The quoted passage is translated from the French: "[L]'obligation imposée à Loyola d'enseigner la matière ÉCR de façon laïque revêt un caractère totalitaire qui équivaut, essentiellement, à l'ordre donné à Galilée par l'Inquisition de renier la cosmologie de Copernic."
5. As of this writing, the case has not yet been settled.

Pierre Trudeau, who would later embrace liberal individualism and reject the nationalistic vision of his separatist foes, was once a convinced follower of the Catholic social vision of his teachers at Montréal's Collège Jean-de-Brébeuf.[6] Under Québec's *ancien régime*, the Roman Catholic Church hierarchy assumed responsibility for a variety of social institutions and communal enterprises, ranging from schools, hospitals, and orphanages to labor unions and political organizations. The old Québec looked askance on France, its original motherland, as having apostatized during the Revolution of 1789. Québec stood alone as a shining light of Christian civilization in a largely Protestant North America.

After 1960 the *Révolution tranquille*—the Quiet Revolution—effected a sea change in that province, as the institutional church withdrew from its extra-ecclesiastical responsibilities. However, rather than the people themselves picking up responsibility through a variety of communal initiatives, the "Québec state", that is, the provincial government, moved in to assume responsibility instead. The state replaced the church, bringing with it a new nationalistic faith to supplant a now declining Christianity. Yet is either institution—church or state—competent to undertake all of these initiatives? Or might society be healthier with a variety of different authorities working independently of, albeit cooperatively with, either or both?

Where there is a robust recognition of the legitimate pluriformity of authorities, totalistic rule will find it difficult to flourish. The establishment in Poland of the independent labor union Solidarity saw the beginning of the end of Communist Party hegemony, not only in that country but virtually everywhere else as well. From an historical perspective, it seems that dominance of society by a single institution is difficult to maintain over the long term, although it may well succeed for a time in dampening independent initiatives in the people, thereby changing a culture for the worse. Thus it is hardly surprising that totalitarian régimes have often been replaced, not by constitutional democracies with vibrant civil societies, but by authoritarian régimes of the sort seen in Vladimir Putin's and Dmitri Medvedev's early twenty-first-century Russia. Such régimes do not merely quash the human spirit, as some might put it. They suppress people's ability to live out their central office of divine image in its pluriform manifestations.

---

6. See Nemni and Nemni, *Young Trudeau*.

We have been arguing throughout this essay that a grant of authority is implied in the biblical notion of the image of God. Insofar as we are created in God's image, we have been invested with an office giving us a special place in his creation, as affirmed in Genesis 1:26–29 and Psalm 8.[7] This office entails a stewardship over creation, a certain representative role in which we are called to develop further the potentialities God has implanted in his creation. As we go about our task of shaping culture, we do so, not in haphazard fashion, but in organized ways requiring the cooperation of many persons for this purpose. This further requires a division of labor in which each person performs his or her role in its fulfillment. Each person brings a unique combination of gifts and skills to the task, all of which together call for some way of coordinating the whole.

Although at first glance one is tempted to argue that this need for coordination underscores the necessity for authority, it would be more correct, as we see it, to note that any attempt at human action—individual or communal—already presupposes the authority God has granted to human beings at the outset. A better approach would be to recognize that common endeavors call, not so much for authority *per se*, which is already present, but for a differentiation of authoritative offices branching out, as it were, from this central office of divine image-bearer. Such offices will necessarily be context-specific, as indicated in the following diagram:

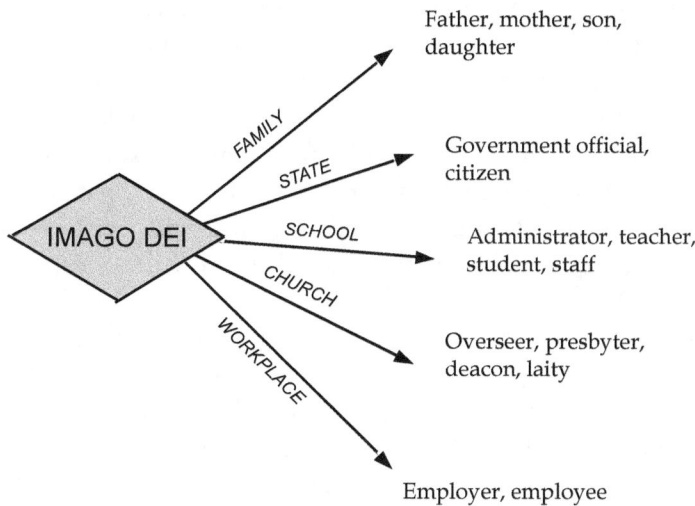

Figure 6.1. Differentiation of authoritative offices

7. See also once again Sirach 17:1–14.

All authoritative offices find their point of origin in the foundational office of the divine image. This points to the reality that all human authority, in every one of its manifestations, is *derived* authority and that underived autonomy, particularly in its Kantian sense, is no more possible than a snowstorm in the tropics. We always answer to another, even if we claim to be expressing our own wills. After all, our likes and dislikes are formed from birth by a variety of influences—genetic, environmental, social, and otherwise. Julia's love of poetry was acquired in school from an enthusiastic teacher of literature. Tom's decision to study law rather than dentistry comes of his mother being a practicing lawyer—or a dentist! Loretta's choice to holiday in Majorca stems from a friend's love of Catalan cuisine. There is no such thing as a purely rational action divorced from the web of authorities which give us our identity as culture-shaping persons created in God's image.

This *pluriformity of authoritative offices* stands in marked contrast to the classic modern notion of sovereignty which has preoccupied political theorizing for the past five centuries. With the decline of feudalism and the rise of the early modern absolute monarchies, a number of philosophers, most notably Jean Bodin (c.1530–1596) and Thomas Hobbes, came up with a God-substitute to address two sources of disunity: (1) the residual fractiousness of feudal institutions, which had proved a poor substitute for the defunct Roman imperium, were incapable of integrating a public-legal community, and could not guarantee an equitable rule of law; and (2) the sundering of western Christendom at the time of the Reformation in the sixteenth century. The hope for a politically unified Europe died with Emperor Charles V's abdication, while the national kings, Francis I, Henry VIII and, eventually, Philip II, struggled to consolidate sovereignty within their respective realms. This focus on uncontested sovereignty constituted the mainstream of the western political tradition after 1500, culminating in the failed totalitarian experiments of the twentieth century.

Yet there has always been a minority of political and social philosophers willing to recognize the legitimate pluriformity of society who felt no urge to find an office or institution possessing the final say or last word over everything under its jurisdiction. This includes Luther and Calvin in the sixteenth century and Johannes Althusius in the seventeenth. The eighteenth-century philosopher, Baron Montesquieu, might also be placed in this category, at least insofar as he is willing to divide sovereignty among legislative, executive, and judicial bodies as a guarantor of liberty.[8] The fact that particularly Calvin and Althusius acknowledged the sovereignty of God over a pluriform creation freed them from the felt need of their contemporaries to seek out a God-substitute within the creation itself. Politically-speaking, this meant that they were willing to recognize that a society composed of divine image-bearers could not only countenance but even support and encourage a pluriformity of communal formations without assuming that one of these must possess ultimate sovereignty over the others. This pluriformity of society has often been labeled civil society, for which recent social and political theorists have undertaken to account. We will explore four of these below:

A Taxonomy of Authority: Richard T. De George

Because there are so many misunderstandings surrounding authority, before one can begin to correct these, it is necessary to come up with a method of doing so. We believe this is best done by distinguishing among different *kinds* of authority, as this issue is intimately related to the centrality of office, which we have been arguing thus far. In the next four sections we will survey four distinct approaches to recognizing and accounting for these kinds, amounting to an acknowledgement of the pluriformity of authority. In order we will explore the ideas of (1) Richard T. De George, who, despite his Kantian orientation, affirms pluriformity by distinguishing between executive and nonexecutive forms of authority, and, within these categories, imperative, performatory, epistemic and exemplary authorities; (2) Yves R. Simon, who, from within an Aristotelian/Thomist framework, differentiates among authority's functions; (3) Oliver O'Donovan and Victor Lee Austin, who work from a theological understanding of authority rooted in the Anglican tradition; and (4) Abraham Kuyper and Herman Dooyeweerd, who affirm the pluriformity of authority from a neocalvinist framework. Each of these in its own way has contributed to a greater comprehension of the different kinds of authority characterizing an ordinary society of image-bearing human beings.

Of course *kinds* can be understood differently, depending on the criteria used for distinguishing among them. In Richard T. De George's masterful taxonomy of authority, the author does this principally by

---

8. See Montesquieu, *Ésprit des lois* 11.

asking what authority does and does not do.[9] De George's taxonomy can be visualized in the following diagram:

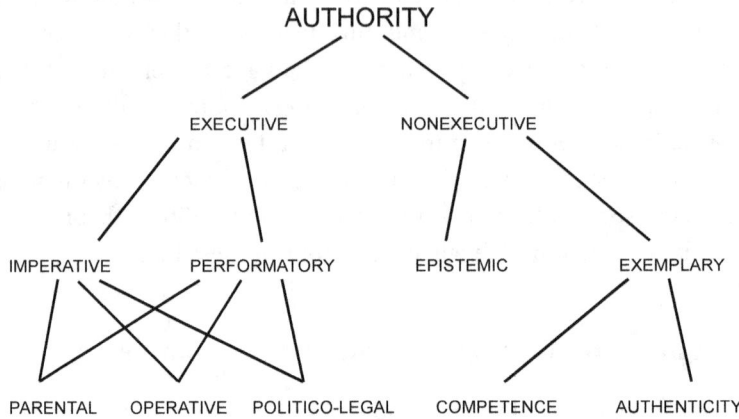

Figure 6.2. De George's Texonomy of authority

De George begins by making an initial and basic distinction between executive and nonexecutive authority. *Executive authority* "has the right or power to act for or on someone else" (p. 22). Executive authority issues in action, while nonexecutive authority does not. Executive authority is further divided into imperative and performative varieties. *Imperative authority* "involves the right or the power of some bearer (X) to command someone who is subject to authority (Y) to act or to forbear from acting in certain ways."[10] This is the stereotypical exercise of authority that comes to most people's minds when they hear the word authority. Someone commands someone else to do something with the expectation of being obeyed. This is the type of authority Milgram investigated in his notorious Yale experiments. It is most obviously manifested in political and military contexts, but also has relevance to virtually any organization requiring common action for specific purposes. Even voluntary associations such as a little league team or an amateur choral society are structured in such a way as to require authoritative direction. As long as one remains a member of such an association, one is bound by its bylaws and its governing executive. Within the family context non-adult children are expected to obey their parents, although this is related only in part to the need for central coordination of the family's activities. Parental authority

9. De George, *The Nature and Limits of Authority*.
10. Ibid., 63.

is also needed to substitute for the children's as yet undeveloped maturity, as we shall see in the next section.

By *performative authority* one person acts on behalf of another person or a community of persons. It is "the right or power of X to perform some action, sometimes on or for another person (Y)."[11] A diplomat is authorized by his government to negotiate a treaty with a foreign state. Parents authorize a teacher to act *in loco parentis* over their children during school hours or on field trips. In a corporation certain officials have the authority—or the "power," as it is often said—to sign for purchases from a supplier. In common law jurisdictions the concept of *power of attorney* covers De George's notion. A power of attorney may be granted to person A to negotiate on behalf of person B if she has been incapacitated due to illness or injury. Performative authority differs from imperative authority in that performative authority need not issue commands as such. The person granting someone performative authority is not herself subject to this authority in an immediate sense, unless she explicitly agrees to be bound by its decisions, as, e.g., when an agent agrees to terms with a negotiating partner on her behalf.

De George perceptively notes that executive authority is context-driven, that is, it functions differently in different communal contexts. What is appropriate in one setting may not be so in another. A chief financial officer has authority to sign on budgetary matters directly related to the organization for which she works, but not for the local Scout troop or the Methodist church down the road. Nor does she have the authority to hire and fire employees in her own workplace, which lies outside her official internal competence. Although De George makes little of the concept of office itself, one might perhaps detect its implicit presence in the fact that he recognizes limits to its proper field of jurisdiction and repudiates the overheated claims of totalitarian rulers to unlimited authority.[12]

Executive authority can be further grouped into three types based on context, viz., *parental*, *operative* and *political*. All three manifest imperative and performative authority. *Parental authority* belongs, of course, to mother and father, is multifaceted, and extends to the raising and protection of children until they reach maturity, after which time it no longer functions in the immediate sense.[13] It is both imperative and

---

11. Ibid.
12. Ibid., 64.
13. Ibid., 72–80.

performative insofar as parents command their children and act in their behalf *vis-à-vis* others outside the family. The disciplinary element connected to parental authority is especially significant, as the immaturity of the child requires parental correction and overall guidance. The exercise of imperative authority properly diminishes with time as the child gradually assumes more and more adult responsibilities. Legally speaking, performative authority continues until the child reaches the age of majority, though in the exercise of these newly assumed responsibilities, he increasingly speaks in his own behalf. As he reaches for maturity, fewer commands need be issued and fewer actions performed in his place.

Operative authority is exercised within "freely formed groups, societies, or organizations"[14] or what might be called voluntary associations. Executive authority is found in most such organizations, and it exists in both imperative and performative forms. The setting for operative authority is significant, once again. De George cites as example a group of First-Nighters who are attending the performance of a play. They have perhaps delegated one of their number to purchase tickets on their behalf, but beyond that there may be no formal organization.

Politico-legal authority "is exercised by a state or a government, and ... preeminently by the leaders of a state.... It reinforces and adds legal weight to some other types of authority."[15] It has four salient characteristics that distinguish it from the two others: (1) It is exercised permanently over its subjects, quite unlike parental authority, which is only temporary in duration. (2) It claims "a monopoly of force within the area and over the people who are subject to it."[16] This monopoly is unique to political authority and cannot be attributed to another authority within the same territory. (3) It claims sovereignty, or the right to ultimate authority, within the territory over which it has jurisdiction. Finally (4), it seems to be all-pervasive in ways that other authorities are not. "It enters our lives from the moment of birth; it infuses all the important aspects of life from education to marriage, to family rearing, to business activities; it commits us to paying taxes and fighting wars; and it decides what constitutes death."[17]

---

14. Ibid., 80.
15. Ibid., 90.
16. Ibid., 91.
17. Ibid., 92.

Politico-legal authority also acts in imperative and performative ways. In a representative democracy members of congress or parliament may be said to possess performative authority in that the voters have given them the right to make laws. At a further remove, Congress or Parliament may delegate its legislative authority to a regulatory agency or, in the case of Canada and Great Britain, to the Cabinet, which is then authorized to issue Orders-in-Council. However, statutes and Orders-in-Council alike bear some of the characteristics of both performative and imperative authority, because their content is binding on legal subjects within their jurisdiction. Therefore, in an election citizens invest their representatives with performative authority but are also bound to obey the policies these representatives issue in accordance with the latter's possession of imperative authority. A similar phenomenon can be found in virtually any organization whose members take a participatory role in choosing its executive but are also bound by the latter's policies.

So much for executive authority. *Nonexecutive authority* does not issue commands or act on behalf of someone else. Although it is distinct from executive authority as such, its possession "is frequently the basis for conferring executive authority on an individual,"[18] as when an authority in zoology (nonexecutive) is awarded an academic position authorizing her to teach and to conduct research (executive) in a university setting. Nonexecutive authority is in turn divided into epistemic and exemplary authority. *Epistemic authority* belongs to someone who is an authority in a particular field of knowledge. Much of what we claim to know comes from the testimony of others. We trust their claim to knowledge and on that basis make a similar claim to the same knowledge. The fact that people believe what other people tell them makes the latter epistemic authorities. Epistemic authority is substitutional in that it substitutes for the lack of knowledge in those accepting its testimony.[19]

A second variety of nonexecutive authority is *exemplary authority*, which is further subdivided into the authority of competence and authenticity. Exemplary authority is communicated by example, not by overt verbal communication of knowledge and certainly not by issuing commands. It exists when one person imitates or follows the example of another person, who becomes an authority for the former person. The communication of this authority is mostly tacit and need not be

18. Ibid., 26.
19. Ibid., 36.

expressed in written or spoken words. *Competence* in a particular field, say medicine, is communicated through observed practice. Much of what children learn from their parents is acquired through observation and not only verbally. Apprenticeship involves both teaching and role-modeling. Thus the master's authority consists of both epistemic and exemplary authority in its shaping of the apprentice.

In his articulation of the meaning of the *authority of authenticity*, De George clearly displays his Kantian proclivities: "An authentic person is the author of his own life style and not the follower of another's. He is master of his craft who sets his own style or trend. He dominates his material. He is a master of himself, and he realizes values to a preeminent degree. *His actions become correct because he does them*."[20] Accordingly, De George manifests a largely negative attitude towards the claims of *executive* moral authority over others. If morality consists of norms and rules incorporating worthy goods and values,[21] then such authority can be properly possessed only by the person legislating for herself and not for others. Consequently, the role of authority in the moral realm must be limited to epistemic and exemplary authority to the exclusion of executive authority.

No form of nonexecutive authority confers the right to command another. If it attempts to do so, it risks becoming authoritarian, i.e., abusing authority. Epistemic authority, in particular, elicits belief but does not call for obedience. Once again, the possession of epistemic authority may become the grounds for giving the possessor some form of executive authority, yet the two remain logically distinct and ought not to be conflated. Nor does epistemic authority involve a *right* to be believed.[22] The mere possession of knowledge does not confer on someone a right to speak or be heard.

What is significant for our purposes is that De George, in articulating his taxonomy of authority, has put forth a plausible basis for recognizing and accounting for the pluriformity of authorities characteristic of the mature differentiated society. Although he does not recognize the centrality of office, as we believe he ought to, and although he is too enamored of a Kantian ethic, despite the defects we noted in chapter 3, his taxonomy is nevertheless a significant contribution to our understanding of authority. The final sentence in his book is very nearly worth the price

20. Ibid., 45; emphasis mine.
21. Ibid., 188.
22. Ibid., 59.

of the book itself: "The enemy, however, is not authority but the abuse of authority."[23] Exactly right!

Authority's Functions: Yves René Simon

In some fashion Yves R. Simon has been present from the outset of this study, because, perhaps better than anyone else writing on the subject, he has persuasively argued for the positive role authority plays in human flourishing. This he has done out of the Aristotelian and Thomistic traditions, although his fundamental insights are not necessarily dependent for their validity on those traditions. As we noted in chapter 1, Simon was at pains to recover authority's reputation a century and a half after the French Revolution had called it into question. Out of this grew two subsidiary aims, one practical and the other theoretical. The practical aim was to encourage his fellow Roman Catholics to appreciate democratic institutions independent of their typical Rousseauan defense, as found, for instance, in the French Declaration of the Rights of Man and of the Citizen.[24] During the 1920s and '30s traditional Catholics in France were generally hostile towards democracy, reflecting church teaching up to the end of the nineteenth century. This often translated into a sympathy for the fascism of Benito Mussolini, Francisco Franco and Philippe Pétain.

Simon's more theoretical aim was to refute the widespread assumption that authority is needed solely because of human deficiencies. He was convinced he could do so by focusing on authority's several functions, only three of which were necessarily related to deficiencies. Simon envisions three *substitutional* functions of authority: (1) to communicate theoretical truth, of which the witness and the teacher are examples, in that they communicate the truth to those not already possessing it;[25] (2) to guide deficient or immature persons to their proper good, in which case authority's function is paternal and is required because of an inability of those in its charge, e.g., children, to seek their own proper good; and (3) to unify action where the means are uniquely determined., i.e., where there ought to be unanimity but there is not, due to ill will or ignorance.[26] This might well be labeled corrective or restraining authority, though

---

23. Ibid., 291.
24. See especially articles 1, 3, and 6.
25. Simon, *General Theory*, 81–131.
26. Simon, *Democratic Government*, 7–19.

Simon himself does not use these terms. In all three cases, it is possible to envision a different, improved state of affairs in which authority is no longer required because the defects for which it must compensate have been removed. According to Simon there has long been a tendency to assume that all authority belongs in this category. We saw this in chapter 2 where, e.g., Carl Friedrich and David Easton thought it desirable for persuasion eventually to supplant authority, as traditionally understood in its mandatory sense.

Nevertheless, Simon believes that authority's functions are not only substitutional and paternal but are also *essential* to the functioning of any society—even of one from which all defects have been banished, if that were possible. Authority is essential to unify action towards a given end when there are multiple legitimate means to reach that end. Here it is impossible that everyone should go his own way; all must take the same route or the end will not be accomplished. Public safety (the end) requires that everyone drive on the *same* side of the road, but *which* side (the means) is a matter of legitimate disagreement among otherwise good persons desiring the common good. Authority, even if it consists only of a vote of the majority, must determine this for safety's sake. In most of the world, the laws decree that drivers drive on the right side of the road. In other countries, such as the United Kingdom, Australia and other Commonwealth members, automobiles are driven on the left side. It matters little for the common good which side is chosen, but only one side can be chosen, and this choice must be binding on all.

Something similar can be said of an enterprise to produce electric motorcars, which calls for overall coordination of individual efforts towards this end. Parts must be complementary and follow quite specific measurements. The voltage of the battery and the method of recharging, the upholstery on the seats, the size and material of the frame, axle, wheels, tires, etc., are all matters on which one cannot expect spontaneous unanimity among even ideally virtuous human beings willing the common good. The production of automobiles, or virtually any composite product, requires an authoritative determination on all these matters and more, due to the sheer variety of possible means available to this one agreed-upon end. Indeed, building on Simon's general theory of authority, Victor Lee Austin correctly understands that, as our society becomes increasingly complex with the numbers of means to a given end continually proliferating rather than narrowing, our need for authority increases accordingly.[27]

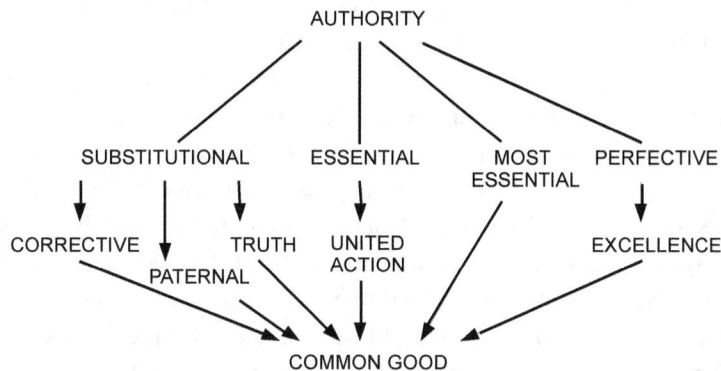

Figure 6.3. Yves R. Simon's functions of authority

Authority is needed, not only to narrow down the choice of means employed by society to reach the common good, but also to determine the substantive content of the common good. Simon once again assumes a society of ideally virtuous human beings, who, because they are virtuous, do not need coercion or the substitutional functions of authority. The question of the plurality of means may be put aside, yet authority is still required by the nature of the end, i.e., the common good itself. All virtuous persons formally will that the common good be done, recognizing that it is in the nature of the community to pursue the common good. They support it in this task accordingly, even if they themselves do not yet know what the common good will require of them, materially speaking. As Simon puts it, they will only the *form,* but not the *matter,* of the common good. They do so, not out of lack of virtue, but out of lack of sufficient knowledge, due to their own finite capacities.

The need for authority in this case stems from the reality that particular goods are no less good than the common good, the latter of which actually requires that particular agents pursue particular goods. The common good demands that parents love and care for their own children, that wives love their own husbands, and that property-owners care for their own property. The objects of these acts of love and care are no less good for not being common to the entire community. Yet the common good must take priority over these particular goods when the two come into conflict; otherwise the community would fragment fatally.

27. Austin, *Up With Authority,* 26.

Consequently, authority must necessarily determine precisely what the common good requires in each case. Virtue and good intentions may suffice for ensuring the willingness to cooperate, but they cannot provide the substantive content of that cooperative effort.

There may be general agreement in principle that the common good requires that a bridge be built to facilitate movement of persons, goods and services across a waterway. Of course, there is no such thing as a bridge "in principle." There are only particular bridges crossing waterways at specific locations. The citizens of such a community can be expected to disagree concerning the particulars of this bridge, e.g., what materials it should be made of, how it should be constructed, and where it should be built. An engineering firm might be able to resolve the first two issues through superior technical competence. But the third will continue to be divisive for the simple reason that building the bridge will impinge upon the particular interests of particular parties. A baker on Elm Street might wish to see the bridge built at Elm to facilitate an increase in her business. A restaurateur on Fifth Avenue might prefer to see it built on *his* street so as to bring more customers into his establishment from across the waterway. A homeowner on that same street might want to see the bridge built elsewhere to keep traffic away from her neighborhood. All three parties are seeking the good of their own interests, each of which in its own way contributes to the common good of all. There is nothing amiss in this seeking of particular goods. Yet it does point to the need for an authoritative determination of a common good transcending the particular goods and the agents pursuing them. This could be done in one of two ways: by majority vote or by the decision of distinct governing personnel. For Simon the former quite adequately satisfies this most essential function of authority. In this sense authority might be said to precede leadership.

Nevertheless, authority also has a *perfective function* that goes beyond its essential functions and aims at the communication of excellence. In so doing, it aims at the further development and greater perfection of a community that is already virtuous.[28] The perfective function entails the achievement of the classical aristocratic régime, or the rule of the best. It presupposes the existence of distinct governing personnel which authority *per se* does not require. Authority as such demands only that a rule of action be binding upon all; it does not aim at greater perfection in the

---

28. Simon, *General Theory*, 136n6.

community.[29] Once more, a decision taken by the community as a whole through the exercise of a direct vote of the majority satisfies the criterion of authority in its essential and most essential functions. This said, Simon also believes that a community is incomparably better off under the rule of those who possess the virtue of the statesman, that is, prudence or practical wisdom. To will and intend formally that the common good be done requires virtue in general, but no special virtue. To determine, on the other hand, what the common good requires, i.e., to determine its matter, demands more than that virtue possessed by all persons of good will. To want to do the right thing is virtuous, but to know what that right thing is requires the specialized virtue of prudence.

To illustrate this perfective function of authority, Simon sets up the following example.[30] Once more he assumes a hypothetical society made up of virtuous people who are free from deficiency in order to demonstrate that authority has functions unrelated to deficiency. Because of certain changes in that society, e.g., an industrial revolution effectively altering its structure, the ways in which wealth has been distributed in the past are no longer adequate to these new conditions. Despite the virtue of the population, it cannot be assumed that everyone is equally aware of the changed situation and its effects. Nor are people equally competent in areas of economics, history, sociology and other disciplines that would provide a key to understanding such changes. Clearly there is a need for some person or persons who will be able to decide on an appropriate course of action on the basis, not of their own expertise in these areas, but of their own judgment in selecting those who are expert and choosing among the alternatives presented by them.

Practical wisdom is not a purely intellectual virtue. It is not a matter of expertise in a technical area, but consists in *the right use of the available expertise*. An act of prudence proceeds "by way of righteous inclination"[31] and is "ultimately determined by the obscure forces of the appetite,"[32] or will. It cannot be reduced to an exercise of the intellect. Since prudence deals with the contingent and not with the necessary, it must inescapably operate within a realm of risks and uncertainties where the grounds for a particular judgment are incapable of demonstration.

29. Ibid., 48.
30. Ibid., 145–47.
31. Ibid., 146.
32. Simon, *Democratic Government*, 24.

The person possessing a greater degree of prudence is the more capable of assuming the role of political leader. Such a person is far from being Plato's philosopher-king, who requires extraordinary virtue rooted in exact knowledge of the good political order. But he does develop his leadership capacities such that the community at large will almost certainly benefit under his authority. This is Simon's argument for distinct persons assuming authoritative offices. In this respect, Simon appears to have anticipated the revival of virtue ethics occurring some twenty years after his death in the writings of such figures as Alasdair MacIntyre and Stanley Hauerwas.

In addition to distinguishing among authority's functions, Simon, following Aristotle, makes a further distinction between the *political* and *despotic* régime. A political régime may or may not be democratic in the strict sense of permitting a wide franchise among the citizens. Although democracy is undoubtedly a desirable mechanism for selecting rulers, of more importance is the relationship between state and civil society, or the plethora of nonstate institutions and activities requiring a certain legal space to flourish. In Simon's words, a political system "gives the governed a legal power of resistance,"[33] though not in the sense of an overt right to rebel or revolt. Rather, it recognizes the pluriformity of authoritative offices throughout society and makes no pretense of assimilating these into an all-encompassing state sovereignty. In a political regime the people in their various communal settings retain authority against the imperialistic tendency of especially state authority.

By contrast, the despotic régime is one that governs the body politic as though it were a private household. Aristotle makes much of the distinction between the household and the polity, the latter of which must be governed constitutionally, that is, in a way fundamentally different from the household, whose members, including women, children and slaves, are more obviously subject to the head-of-household.[34] Similarly, Hannah Arendt is at pains to distinguish between the free participatory character of genuine politics, and economics, the latter of which is subject to the technical norms of labor and fabricating work and can only be imposed on subjects from above.[35] Sir Bernard Crick likewise distinguishes between politics, which he defines as the peaceful conciliation of diversity, and the

---

33. Ibid., 74
34. Aristotle, *Politics*, III.
35. Arendt, *The Human Condition*, esp. 28–37.

various anti-political trends that would subsume the public realm under technique, ideology and even democracy itself.[36] Simon, Crick and even Arendt are in their own fashion heirs of Aristotle, who openly combated Plato's monistic tendencies as manifested in *The Republic* while not entirely breaking with the Greek assumptions undergirding them.[37]

Although Simon does not mention in so many words the *principle of subsidiarity* which has been a central feature of Roman Catholic social teachings since at least 1931 and perhaps even 1891,[38] its presence is nevertheless felt in his articulation of the two complementary principles of authority and autonomy. The principle of authority requires that "Wherever the welfare of a community requires a common action, the unity of that common action must be assured by the higher organs of that community."[39] The principle of autonomy states that "Wherever a task can be satisfactorily achieved by the initiative of the individual or that of small social units, the fulfillment of that task must be left to the initiative of the individual or to that of small social units."[40] Working together, these principles serve to ensure that the multiple communal formations develop in a healthy, balanced fashion, without succumbing to either a statist collectivism or a (ultimately statist!) liberal individualism.

From our perspective, that which Simon labels *autonomy* should be understood, not as something different from authority, but as a recognition of the legitimate space occupied by the authoritative offices resident in the variety of nonstate communal formations found in the mature differentiated society. Once again, Simon's notion of autonomy is not to be understood in the Kantian sense of authoring one's own morality without reference to external authority. Quite the contrary, Simon defines autonomy as the internalization of authority, as manifested in the natural law, by which the person makes its precepts a part of herself.[41] To the extent that someone willingly conforms her being and actions to the law, to that same extent she can be said to possess autonomy. This applies as much to

36. See Crick, *In Defence of Politics*.

37. Aristotle, *Politics*, II.

38. See Leo XIII, *Rerum Novarum* (On Capital and Labour, 1891) and Pius XI, *Quadragesimo Anno* (On Reconstruction of the Social Order, 1931). The term *subsidiarity* originates in one of the translations of the latter encyclical, while the principle covered by the term is found in both.

39. Simon, *Nature and Functions of Authority*, 45.

40. Ibid.

41. Simon, *Freedom and Community*, 96.

communities as to individual persons. Autonomy in this sense is not in tension with authority, even less a repudiation of it; it is rather an affirmation of the diversity of authoritative offices, each of which is obligated to respect the legitimate spheres of the others.

The difficulty with the notion of subsidiarity, as with Aristotle's vaunted political pluralism, is that it does not go far enough in accounting for the *distinctive* character of offices resident in these communal and individual agents, relying instead on a prudential principle to mitigate the potential for autocracy within a hierarchical understanding of society. Here we would follow Jonathan Chaplin's proposal for a "horizontal conception of subsidiarity" in which the help (*subsidium*) extended by one social agent to another goes not only "downwards" but "looks both ways."[42] It is not simply the state that intervenes to put things aright in, say, a business that pollutes the environment or abuses its employees. Nor is it a matter of the church institution calling government to its task of seeking the common good. Rather "every community . . . can be seen to provide for others—perhaps every other—a distinctive kind of aid."[43] Families, just by being families, contribute to the state by inculcating the virtues of citizenship in those raised to maturity within their context. Where labor unions function according to the norms proper to the labor union, they contribute to businesses, families, churches and states the virtues of solidarity, loyalty, hard work and perseverance, without which a society cannot enjoy good health. We agree with Chaplin that reconceptualizing subsidiarity along horizontal lines holds great promise for a recovery and recognition of genuine authority in its pluriform manifestations.

A Theology of Authority: Oliver O'Donovan and Victor Lee Austin

The British theological ethicist Oliver O'Donovan brings to his notion of authority a deep familiarity with the western historical narrative and its impact on the development of political thought and practice within the context of Christendom.[44] Although the concept of Christendom has a bad reputation nowadays, due in part to the negative assessment of such Anabaptist-leaning theologians as John Howard Yoder and Stanley

---

42. Chaplin, *Herman Dooyeweerd*, 137–38.
43. Ibid., 138.
44. See O'Donovan, *From Irenaeus to Grotius*.

Hauerwas, the notion that a civilization's ultimate religious commitments must necessarily impact its social and political life is hardly an unusual proposition—one readily comprehensible even outside the Christian world. Indeed it has deep biblical roots, especially in the Old Testament. Recognizing this, O'Donovan situates his discussion of authority within the larger framework of God's creation and man's unique place within it. This has yielded a unique political theology prompting reflection and debate from a number of quarters.[45]

For O'Donovan there is an intimate connection between authority and freedom: "Where authority is, freedom is; and where authority is lost, freedom is lost."[46] Because the individual person is limited in her knowledge and capacities, she is less free if she is forced to rely only on herself to accomplish a given good. By contrast, because authority enables cooperation, and because cooperative activities achieve more than individual acts, authority effectively expands the range of freedom. This produces what is commonly thought to be a paradox: "To be under authority is to be freer than to be independent."[47] In his earlier work, *Resurrection and Moral Order*, O'Donovan wrote of the natural authorities of beauty, age, community and strength, which possess the ability "to inspire and order our actions in distinctive ways."[48] In so doing, he appeared to identify authority with power, something against which we have been arguing here. However, in his later book, *The Ways of Judgment*, he questioned in part his earlier conflation of the two, arguing instead that the goods constituting the grounds of action must be mediated by some agent, that is, by someone bearing authority.[49]

The story recorded in Matthew 8:5–13 of Jesus' encounter with the Roman centurion illustrates for O'Donovan the intimate connection between having authority and being under authority. Jesus commends the faith of this God-fearer, who believed in Jesus' authority over disease because he himself understood what it means to be authorized to act authoritatively in the conduct of his own office as centurion. To have authority is to be under authority. To be under authority is to be given

---

45. See, e.g., Wolterstorff, *Justice: Rights and Wrongs*, in which the author disagrees with O'Donovan's emphasis on right order as a foundation for justice, preferring instead the intrinsic worth of human beings.

46. O'Donovan, *Ways of Judgment*, 132.

47. Ibid.

48. O'Donovan, *Resurrection and Moral Order*, 124.

49. O'Donovan, *Ways of Judgment*, 132.

the freedom to act, i.e., to exercise authority. O'Donovan recognizes that authority manifests itself in both political authority and "a multitude of non-political authorities" that oblige us in a variety of ways, including "doctors, teachers, parents, employers, all of whom the catechism called our 'pastors and masters.'"[50] All of these are obvious examples of the assortment of offices which touch our lives on an ongoing basis, making overlapping claims on us.

Building on both Simon and O'Donovan, Victor Lee Austin distinguishes among four basic kinds of authority: social, epistemic, political, and ecclesiastical. For Austin, authority is a "performative concept" and is never static. It is always in play and resides in persons exercising it. Even the authority of the law or of Scripture is mediated by persons invested with authority in this active sense: "without the living authority of persons doing what authorities do, there is no authority."[51] The apparent authority of a text, coupled with the dilemmas of interpretation, requires that it "be read with a rational mind."[52] In this respect, authority can never be adequately located in documents and institutions. At best such authority is "latent or potential,"[53] needing to be drawn out by an authoritative interpreter.

Social authority is based on the reality that human beings are social by nature, i.e., they live with their fellow human beings with whom they are interdependent. They undertake myriad cooperative endeavors whose successful accomplishment requires overall coordination. Hence, with Simon, Austin believes that authority is required for united action.[54] The need for social authority underscores the reality that human beings are members of a multitude of "mini-societies" covering different facets of their lives and various endeavors. The members of a symphony orchestra, for example, will also belong to families, churches, neighborhood associations and charitable organizations, each of which effectively limits the authority of the others.

Austin argues that authority, far from opposing freedom, enhances it. As the amount of music available to the orchestra's repertoire

---

50. Ibid., 130. The reference is, of course, to the Catechism in the Book of Common Prayer: "*Question*. What is thy dutye toward thy neighbour? Aunswere . . . To submitte my selfe to al my governours, teachers, spiritual Pastours and Maisters."

51. Austin, *Up With Authority*, 37.

52. Ibid.

53. Ibid.

54. Ibid., 15–39.

expands, the conductor's authority is increasingly needed to enable the members of the orchestra to master this music. No trombonist can play Beethoven's *Eroica* by himself, but by acknowledging the conductor's authority within the context of the ensemble as a whole, he can do so in concert with the other instrumentalists.[55] "Authority, I say, is held by a person or persons who lead humans to a fuller exercise of their freedom to accomplish human tasks."[56]

We have already encountered *epistemic authority* in both De George and Simon, and Austin too treats this, identifying it as a second type. If social authority aims at united action, epistemic authority aims at the truth, which is as necessary to human flourishing as social authority. Yet whereas De George and Simon regard epistemic authority as substitutional, Austin, following Michael Polanyi, disagrees, viewing it as essential, in that the acquisition of knowledge, even under the best of circumstances, requires a social context facilitated only by authority. Personal knowledge comes with the mastery of skills of knowing that are ineffable and are communicated only by example. The fabric of knowing is a complex one requiring a period of apprenticeship. "As human nature is social, so is human knowing. And as the achievements of our social nature require authority, so does human knowledge."[57]

Epistemic authority applies in virtually any context in which knowledge is handed on to others, which is to say: everywhere! We all recognize the stereotypical bookworm who spends his time alone absorbing knowledge from the stacks of books on his shelves. Such a person makes the acquisition of knowledge appear to be a nonsocial—perhaps even *anti*-social—process. Yet apart from the obvious fact that the publication of books is itself a cooperative endeavor, most of our knowledge of how to function as human beings we gain, not by filling our heads with information, but by observing how others function and patterning ourselves—consciously or unconsciously—after them. Few, if any, words are necessarily uttered in the course of this process. If parents are athletically inclined and actively participate in amateur sport, the likelihood of the children picking up this interest is rather great, even if the parents never verbally express to them its health and social benefits. The same can be

---

55. Ibid., 17–18. The example is purely hypothetical, as there is no part for trombone in *Eroica*.

56. Ibid., 21.

57. Ibid., 51.

said for learning a trade or some other skill for which a period of apprenticeship is in order.

This brings us to *political authority*, which is "social authority at its most extensive."[58] Following O'Donovan, Austin distinguishes between political authority *per se* and political authority in between the times. Political authority as such consists of three constitutive elements: wielding power, exercising judgment and perpetuating tradition, all of which have characterized political authority throughout history. However, in the period following the coming of Christ, who is at once prophet, priest and king, political authority is limited to the more modest and chastened task of protecting the right. Austin makes four observations concerning political authority. First, "this authority has no (human) social authority beyond itself." Second, it has at its disposal coercive means, which are needed because of human sin. Third, if there were no sin in the world, political authority would still be needed, but it would not have to enforce obedience. And fourth, despite the existence of coercive means at its disposal, for the most part it functions on the basis of assent, the threat of coercion normally remaining in the background.[59] In all of these political authority is unique.

After the advent of Christ, the power of earthly rulers has been relativized and superseded by his higher authority. Christ's kingship has irrevocably altered the claims of secular political authorities, especially those related to "salvation," "military victory or survival." In this "secular" era, that is, the era "pertaining to this age (only)," political authority cannot be ordered by transcendent purposes that once characterized it before the coming of Christ. It is no longer properly taken up with self-defense, law-making or maintaining social identity, none of which can justify its existence. Instead, "all the functions of government can be, and should be, re-conceived as the exercise of judgment."[60] Such judgments are always imperfect and provisional, stopping well short of rendering final justice or even of fashioning a just society.

The relationship between authority and power is a complex one. We have noted above that Austin sees coercion as unique to political authority. Other authorities can only exclude; they do not coerce as such.[61] Coer-

58. Ibid., 71.
59. Ibid.
60. Ibid., 81–82.
61. Ibid., 71. This is, of course, open to question. The teacher may be said to possess the coercive power of the gradebook; parents punish their errant children through

cion would not, of course, be needed in a sinless society, and even now authority's directives are generally followed without the appeal to force. We reflexively defer to the police officer in uniform when we see her in the street or elsewhere. We do not evaluate each of her directives to see whether they measure up to, say, the categorical imperative. Nor do we assess her personal virtues or lack thereof. We simply recognize the authority of her office and act accordingly, believing it to be the right thing to do. Austin concludes that we obey authority's commands because we intuitively understand at a pretheoretical level that authority communicates to us a good that would not be ours without it.[62] In short, we defer to authority simply because it *is* authority and we recognize it to be such.

Finally Austin treats *ecclesial authority*. Austin believes there is a paradoxical quality to any discussion of the authority of the church, because the church is not just another "mini-society" or voluntary association among other such associations. Yet neither is it an "umbrella" society presiding over everything else. It defies any attempt to categorize it. "The church is not a political society and will never be one, but its mission is to point to one peculiar and ultimate political society: a kingdom of citizens who freely obey and follow their King, who live in a city of which their Lord is the light."[63] We suggest that the apparent paradox can be resolved by distinguishing between the church as a specific differentiated institution in a complex society and the church as *corpus Christi* or body of Christ. As an institution the church is not one more voluntary association; it is not simply a collectivity of Christian persons joining themselves together for self-chosen purposes, even if those purposes are good and salutary, e.g, worshiping God and preaching the gospel. Rather the church as an institution is a covenant community called into existence by God himself for the purposes of preaching the Word, administering the sacraments and maintaining discipline. Its members are those who have been called by God into this community through baptism.

But this differentiated community is not the whole of life, even as it calls its members to live for Christ in the full array of their life's activities. They do so as members of the *corpus Christi*, which normatively manifests itself not only in the institutional church, but within every communal setting, including marriage, family, state, business, labor, the arts,

---

either corporal punishment or withholding privileges; and employers may dock an employee's pay. These actions fall well short of outright exclusion.

62. Ibid., 83.
63. Ibid., 95.

etc. The *corpus Christi* encompasses all Christians everywhere, in every time and in everything they do. Nothing takes place outside the church understood in this comprehensive way. The *corpus Christi* is not to be identified with any particular church institution. In this respect there is some similarity to the traditional Protestant distinction between the visible and invisible churches, although they are not precisely the same.

Once more Austin emphasizes that authority is always personal. It resides in persons and not in things. Despite a seemingly robust institutional ecclesiology, he nevertheless affirms that "authority resides in the individual believer."[64] The church cannot exist without its individual members and their confession of faith in Jesus Christ. The church quite properly has its offices, creeds, traditions and, above all, the Scriptures. Yet authority in the full sense is to be found in none of these by itself: "Authority resides in the individual believer who, inspired by the Holy Spirit, proclaims faithfully her allegiance to the suffering Jesus, and thus to her Lord, and thus to the Triune Reality that is the source of all authority in heaven and earth."[65] Yet, for Austin, the individual's confession of faith is dependent on the larger community which authorizes her to make this confession.

In both O'Donovan and Austin there is a recognition that political authority must take its place alongside a variety of legitimate authorities with their own spheres of responsibility. Although neither explicitly emphasizes *office* to the extent that we believe is warranted, their focus on the pluriformity of authority, each manifestation of which normatively functions within proper limits specific to context, might be seen to imply it.

Sovereignty in Its Own Sphere: Kuyper and Dooyeweerd

We have thus far surveyed three efforts at supporting a robust concept of the pluriformity of authorities issuing from the Kantian, the Aristotelian-Thomist and Anglican traditions. We turn now to a fourth such effort growing out of the continental Reformed or European Calvinist tradition, namely, that associated with the Dutch theologian and statesman Abraham Kuyper and philosopher Herman Dooyeweerd. Since the sixteenth century it has been a hallmark of the Reformed tradition that it has focused, not solely on doctrine, but on articulating a worldview encompassing in principle the whole of life. In so doing it has repudiated the strategy of

64. Ibid., 100.
65. Ibid.

those Christians positing dichotomies within the created order between, say, sacred and secular, soul and body, spiritual and temporal, gospel and law, and the like. All of these in some fashion confuse the central confessional affirmation of the Christian faith, namely, that God is fundamentally distinct from his creation. Under the influence of neoplatonism, many Christian philosophers and theologians posit an order of being characterized by an ontological hierarchy, with God at the pinnacle and everything else arrayed on rungs or levels extending below him. Each entity is located in the hierarchy relative to its participation in the divine or lack thereof. God is the ground of all being with lesser entities partaking of this being to a decreasing extent as one descends the hierarchy.

The central difficulty with this conception is that it blurs the distinction between Creator and creation, making God one element—albeit the highest—within a larger category called "being." This masks the reality that God's mode of existence is fundamentally different from that of the things he has created. God's existence is that of *sui generis*, nondependent being. By contrast, everything else constituting the created order exists only in dependent fashion, radically dependent on God's creative and sustaining activity. Even to assert that God lives, as scripture does, must be qualified so as not to conflate God's mode of living with that of the biological organisms he has brought into being by his grace. Accordingly, the task of the theologian must be articulated modestly so as not inadvertently (1) to treat God as a specimen to be examined under a microscope; (2) to treat creatures as if they shared certain divine attributes in pantheistic or panentheistic fashion; and (3) to deny God the worship due only him.

In the Reformed tradition, perhaps more overtly than in other Christian traditions, the principal sin from which all others stem is idolatry, i.e., esteeming something within the creation as divine. Our first parents in the garden were tempted to sin with the promise that, in eating the forbidden fruit, they would become like God (Gen 3:4). Since then human beings have been pretending to take God's place in any number of ways with a variety of means. Above all, as we have explored throughout this essay, this pretense entails a denial of authority and our utter dependence thereon, asserting instead our right to order our own lives and affections as we see fit. St. Augustine famously averred that a commonwealth is defined by common agreement on things loved.[66] The

---

66. Augustine, *De Civitate Dei* 19.24.

City of God is ordered above all by the love of God, while the City of this world is defined by the love of self. As James K. A. Smith has persuasively argued, these loves are shaped by the cultural liturgies in which we are caught up, such as those of the shopping mall, the modern higher educational enterprise and so forth.[67] Because the rituals of the larger culture play a formative role in fashioning our affections, it must be recognized that idolatry is not merely an individual sin but is embedded in the very patterns of civilizations where they take on a systemic character. This is perhaps the moment of truth in those who assign such labels as *empire*, *technique* and *capitalism* as descriptors of entire systems seemingly operating apart from our individual wills.

Within the Reformed tradition there has been a heightened awareness of the role of idolatry in the outworking of the political ideologies spawned by modernity in general and by the French Revolution in particular. We have already noted in chapters 4 and 5 the respective roles of G. Groen van Prinsterer and Abraham Kuyper in articulating the principle of sovereignty in its own sphere in recognition of societal pluriformity. In the twentieth century Herman Dooyeweerd, whom we have already met above, worked out this Kuyperian principle with a greater degree of philosophical sophistication than found in his two predecessors. Indeed Dooyeweerd's social philosophy is probably the best-known element of his larger theoretical systematics, with profound political implications for a proper understanding of the relationship between state and civil society.

Dooyeweerd begins by distinguishing two horizons of experience, namely, the modal horizon and the plastic horizon. The modal horizon corresponds to the "how," as opposed to the "what," of reality. The "what" embraces the things or entities we experience, while the "how" encompasses the multiple ways in which we experience such things. The entire created cosmos, or meaning, is dispersed in a variety of modal aspects, much as sunlight "is refracted by a prism in a rich diversity of colors."[68] Dooyeweerd has provisionally isolated fifteen modes. Each of the modes is characterized by a "modal kernel" or "nuclear moment" which defines in broad intuitive fashion the content of that particular modal sphere, as shown in the following list:

- *pistical*—faith, certainty
- *ethical*—love in temporal relations

67. See Smith, *Desiring the Kingdom*.
68. Dooyeweerd, *In the Twilight of Western Thought*, 7.

- *jural*—retribution, justice
- *aesthetic*—harmony, beautiful proportion
- *economic*—thrift, frugality
- *social*—social intercourse
- *lingual*—language, symbolic signification
- *historical*—cultural formation, power
- *analytical*—logic, cognition, theory
- *psychical*—sensation, feeling
- *biotic*—organic life
- *physical*—energy, physico-chemical
- *kinematic*—motion, extensive movement
- *spatial*—continuous extension
- *arithmetic*—numerical, numerable, calculable

For Dooyeweerd the primary meaning of sphere sovereignty is closer to what might better be called modal irreducibility. Each mode follows its own law and none can be reduced to any other. The jural cannot be reduced to the economic, notwithstanding the views of Marx and his followers to the contrary. The aesthetic cannot be reduced to mere feeling, though some nevertheless undertake to subjectivize all aesthetic judgments ("I know what I like"; "beauty is in the eye of the beholder"). Similarly, faith in God or the lack thereof cannot be reduced to psychological motives.

The modes cohere in a definite order by what Dooyeweerd calls "cosmic time" (*kosmische tijd*), which constitutes, as it were, the "glue" that maintains the modes in their place. More encompassing than the conventional notion of time as the physical movement from past to present to future, cosmic time has to do with succession in general, manifesting itself in different ways according to the respective structures of the modal spheres. For example, arithmetic or numerical time is something different from (though related to) cultural time. What we think of as clock-time is but a manifestation of cosmic time in the kinematic aspect.

Cosmic time also arranges the modes themselves in an irreversible order whereby certain of them fall "earlier" or "later" in the modal scale. The earlier modes are foundational for the later modes, which cannot exist without a basis in the former. There cannot be economic transactions, for example, without the existence of prior historical-cultural patterns enabling such activity. Similarly, human culture cannot exist without the foundational conditions of biological life; life in turn presupposes certain physico-chemical properties; and so forth.

Although the modal spheres are irreducible, each one is nevertheless reflected in every other. The modal kernel of the historical, for example, is cultural formation or "the controlling manner of moulding the social process."[69] This is a distinct aspect of meaning that cannot be reduced to another modal sphere and vice versa. Yet one can detect modal analogies of the other fourteen modes within the historical. For example, it is possible to speak of cultural economy whereby the formative power of culture is exercised in a conserving manner that does not attempt to overextend itself. This is the economic analogy within the historical mode. Or one can speak of cultural harmony whereby cultural formation occurs in a balanced and proportionate manner. This is the aesthetic analogy within the historical mode. The economic and aesthetic are *anticipatory* analogies in that they fall later than the historical in the modal scale. The psychical analogy (i.e., cultural feeling or sensation) is a *retrocipatory* analogy within the historical mode because it comes earlier in the modal scale.

The second dimension of experience is what Dooyeweerd calls the "plastic horizon" of the structures of individuality (*individualiteitsstructuur*). It is the dimension in which we experience the concrete entities of created meaning. If the modal horizon concerns the *how* of reality, the plastic horizon concerns the *what* of reality. The modal horizon is foundational for the plastic horizon.[70] The structures of individuality function in all the modal aspects and are capable of being analyzed with respect to the various modes. Yet they cannot be reduced to an aggregate of modal functions. The unity and identity of the former are guaranteed by the order of cosmic time. An understanding of how an entity functions modally is essential to an understanding of the internal structural principle of the entity. Different types of entities are distinguished from each other according to their inner nature by their placement and configuration within the modal scale.

---

69. Dooyeweerd, *A New Critique of Theoretical Thought*, 1:195.
70. Ibid., 3:77.

Every entity functions in all the modes as either a subject or an object.[71] For example, a person functions subjectively in the economic mode in that he is able to act in obedience to economic norms as a subject. He is able to exercise thrift with respect to the economic resources at his disposal. A coin, on the other hand, functions objectively in the economic mode in that it is an object of economic intercourse. But not all the modes are equally important in determining the inner structure of an entity. Two modal functions in particular play the principal role in determining the inner nature of an entity. These are the foundational and qualifying or leading functions. The qualifying function is "the ultimate functional point of reference for the entire internal structural coherence of the individual whole in the typical groupage of its aspects."[72] In other words, it is that function which most specifically characterizes the unique structure of a distinctive entity.

Dooyeweerd does not explicitly define foundational function, but L. Kalsbeek describes it as the "lower of the two modalities which characterize . . . structural wholes."[73] The foundational function may also be defined as that modal aspect at which point an entity begins to take on its unique character as a particular entity—or perhaps the modal point at which something begins to be differentiated from other entities.[74] The category of entities possessing the same foundational function is considerably larger than that of entities sharing the same qualifying function. The former category includes a number of the latter categories. Not every entity has both a foundational and a qualifying function, as can be seen in the case of undifferentiated communities.[75] Dooyeweerd's modal analysis of communities can be illustrated as follows:

---

71. Clouser terms these "active" and "passive" functions. See Clouser, *Myth of Religious Neutrality*, 250–54.

72. Dooyeweerd, *A New Critique of Theoretical Thought*, 3:58.

73. Kalsbeek, *Contours of a Christian philosophy*, 348. Chaplin believes that Dooyeweerd's modal analysis would quite adequately function without the notion of a founding function. See Chaplin, *Herman Dooyeweerd*.

74. Clouser further distinguishes between two kinds of foundational functions in human artifacts, namely, that characterizing the natural material from which the artifact is fashioned and that characterizing the process by which the artifact came into existence. See Clouser, *Myth of Religious Neutrality*, 263–68.

75. Undifferentiated communities are what some might refer to as tribal communities in which institutional differentiation has not yet occurred. In such communities, educational, parental, political, ecclesiastical, and other functions are performed by the same persons in their all-encompassing leadership capacity and

190   We Answer to Another

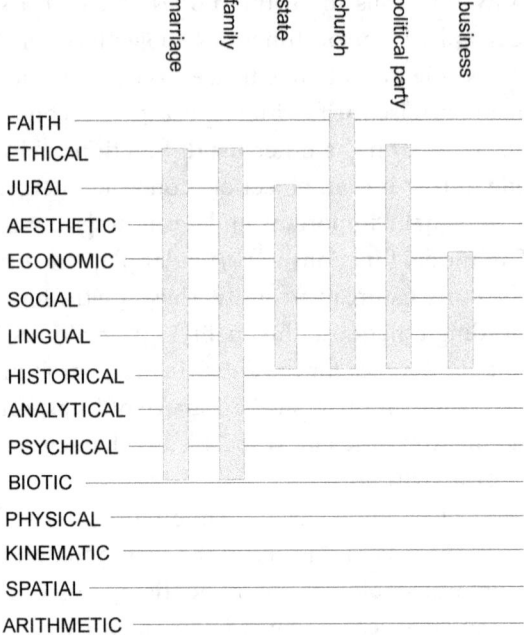

Figure 6.4. Dooyeweerd's Modal Analysis

Dooyeweerd's modal analysis in turn yields the following social categories, which are illustrated in the diagram immediately below:

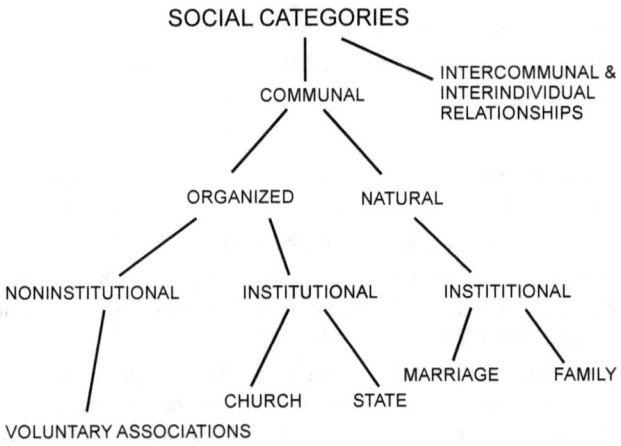

Figure 6.5. Dooeyweerd's social categories

---

are not assigned to the distinct communities of school, family, state, church, etc. See Dooyeweerd, *A New Critique of Theoretical Thought*, 3:346ff.

The first distinction Dooyeweerd makes is between the *individual* and the *community*. Individuals and communities are both alike authoritative agents, although there is a persistent tendency to assume reductively that one is derivative from the other. Liberal individualism assumes that communities are nothing more than the aggregate of individuals, with all of their particular concerns and idiosyncratic preferences. Accordingly any authority exercised within a communal context must in some fashion be derivative from the sum total of individual wills. An ontic collectivism, by contrast, derives individual responsibility from an ostensibly more encompassing collectivity, such as state, nation, class or gender. Both approaches err in failing to discern both individual and community as legitimate and immediate holders of authoritative agency.

With respect to the *individual*, authority and responsible agency coincide within a single person. Plato famously draws an analogy between the *polis* and the individual human being—an analogy which forms the basis of his central argument in *The Republic*. Although Aristotle is correct to be wary of this facile identification, its truth lies in the fact that both community and individual are responsible, authority-bearing agents. However, the principal difference between the two is that a *community* requires a specialized authoritative office primarily to fulfill a communal coordinative function. Otherwise the community as such cannot be an active, responsible agent. Thus, within the community, the locus of authority must lie with either a single person, a small group of persons constituting an executive body, or a majority of the whole. Theoretically, it could also lie with the entire community itself, but since this would require a highly unlikely unanimity, this must remain a mere theoretical option rather than a lived reality.

According to Dooyeweerd, most durable communities are necessarily characterized by an internal "*societal relation of authority and subordination.*"[76] This includes the organized communities of state and institutional church and the "natural" communities of marriage and family, but it does not include the extended kinship community or the neighborhood. Organized communities are founded in the historical modality, that is, in the aspect of power formation. This activity of power formation requires an office or offices, as we would put it, authorized to exercise this power within the context of the community as a whole. This is not just an empirical phenomenon, from Dooyeweerd's perspective, but a normative

---

76. Ibid., 3:180.

one, in which particular human persons, answering God's multifaceted call, assume authority within the context of communal formative activities.

Inter-individual relationships range from transitory commercial transactions to enduring friendships. They do not require any sort of relationship of authority and subordination, although one can say that authority in its broad sense of *imago Dei* is certainly present. In a mentor/protégé relationship, executive (imperative) authority, once present in the context of an educational (teacher/student) or work (master/apprentice) community, is now replaced by a more appropriate exemplary authority in one of the parties to this relationship. The authority present is no longer executive (imperative) authority but a nonreciprocal exemplary authority similar to that between parents and their adult offspring. Such a relationship approaches that of the friendship, yet lacks much of the character of a reciprocal comradeship between peers.

Intercommunal relationships come into play when two communities, whether of the same type or a different type, relate to each other in some fashion, e.g., two or more states, the state and a political party, business and labor union, businesses and chambers of commerce, families and schools, neighboring universities, competing business enterprises, publishing company and book seller, etc. Once again such relationships might be transitory or they might be relatively lasting, as, e.g., in a long-term contract between a publisher and a bookstore chain.

When such relationships are looked at in the aggregate, one often speaks of *society*. Society as such is not a responsible agent but consists rather of the larger pattern of interactions and interrelationships among numerous individuals and communal agents. Thus society does not possess an authoritative office unique to its status as society. Even government does not preside over society, however much one might speak of, say, American society. Government presides simply over the political side of that society, insofar as its members are citizens of the state over which it exercises authority. British Prime Minister Margaret Thatcher famously said that "there is no such thing as society," responding to those who would blame "society" for various social ills and call on "society" (read: "government") to solve them.[77] Although one might well dispute Thatcher's libertarian economic philosophy, Dooyeweerd would agree with her judgment that society lacks the authoritative agency of the organized or natural community.

---

77. Thatcher, Interview by Douglas Keay.

Natural and *organized communities*. In our societies virtually the only examples of *natural communities* are *marriage* and *family*, with the *extended kinship community* in an undifferentiated society providing another. Natural communities, although they are certainly affected by the peculiar characteristics of the culture in which they find themselves, are not basically cultural entities arising in history. They are intrinsic to humanity from the outset. Consequently authority in these contexts is likely to be based on ascriptive characteristics almost altogether unrelated to the merits of the person holding the office. Parental authority belongs to a man and a woman solely by virtue of their having begotten children, a biological fact of life. Similarly within the marital community sex differences are all-important, notwithstanding current efforts in some jurisdictions to deny this reality legally. Only a man can be a husband and only a woman can be a wife. The two offices are not interchangeable.

In an undifferentiated society, or what some might label a primitive or tribal society, a patriarchal figure takes on a variety of functions, solely based on his status as, say, the senior male ancestor or collateral ancestor in a clan. To some degree, hereditary monarchy in an otherwise differentiated society, such as Sweden and Belgium, might be seen as a vestige of this clan arrangement at an earlier stage in the differentiation process. In constitutional monarchies the status of the monarch has become largely honorific and symbolic, with effective political authority being exercised by offices more characteristic of an organized community.

Organized communities arise within the historical process. As their name suggests, they are established intentionally to fulfill a particular cultural task as that task has come to be differentiated from other, possibly related tasks. Thus the task of educating children, while properly belonging to the parents, comes to be delegated to the school. Virtually every community that is not based on blood or sexual relationship is an organized community. This includes state, institutional church, business enterprise, publishing house, museum, chamber of commerce, professional society, hospital, labor union, political party, private foundation, dance troupe, etc., etc. Within organized communities, exercise of authority will be more closely tied to merit while biological and gender differences typically play much less of a role. Furthermore, within organized communities there are likely to be temporal limits placed on a term of office, as noted above.

Institutional and *noninstitutional communities*. Institutional communities are those communities in which membership is not ultimately traceable to the will of the members and whose bonds of obligation are lifelong. One may be born to membership in such a community, or, if one has entered it willingly, one cannot simply quit such a community on a whim. Institutional communities include family, marriage, state and institutional church. Three of these one is born into. One does not choose one's birth family, including parents and siblings. One is born into a particular family and one's obligations to this family inhere irrespective of one's personal decision. The same can be said of the state, of which one is generally born a citizen. True, it is possible to move to another country and assume that country's citizenship through naturalization. But that may not absolve one of one's duties as a citizen to the country of birth, including the responsibility to vote, to perform jury duty, to be subject to military conscription, to obey the laws, etc.

As for the institutional church, those communions practicing infant baptism may more obviously fit into the category of institutional community. If I was baptized in a Presbyterian Church congregation as a small child, it could be argued that my membership in this body exists apart from my deliberate choice. Yet even if I had been born in a congregation practicing adult baptism only, it is likely that this congregation would have had a rite of dedication of infants conferring on me a kind of provisional membership to be nurtured through parental upbringing. In either case I did not choose in which church, or even in which faith, I would be raised. For a variety of reasons, including the fragmentation of the institutional church over the centuries, increasing geographic mobility, and the weakening of the churches themselves, Christians may not in fact stay within a particular ecclesial communion. This has tended to compromise the disciplinary function of ecclesiastical authority over its members.

Marriage is different from these other three communities in that one is not born to it. It is something entered into when one is of age and finds a suitable partner. But once one has entered into it, the marriage normatively lasts for as long as one of the partners lives. Prior to the modern era, of course, marriages were generally arranged by the parents, and in some parts of the world this is still the practice. It may be that this practice emphasized better than the current one the binding, institutional character of marriage. The legal provision for divorce in most jurisdictions is based on the recognition that marriages occasionally break down, thereby requiring intervention by the larger communities of which the partners are members. Yet the fact that spouses cannot simply go their separate ways without attending to its consequences for others, especially their children, only underscores the institutional character of marriage, whose enduring character is taken as the norm.

In the case of all four institutional communities there is a tendency among those in the grip of especially liberal ideology to re-envision these along the lines of noninstitutional communities, and particularly voluntary associations. With respect to the state, this began already centuries ago with the rise of social contract theory in Hobbes, Locke, Rousseau, etc. Whatever the differences between early and late liberals, all are agreed in viewing political community as a voluntary association. With respect to the institutional church a similar tendency to view it as a voluntary association can be traced to Enlightenment thought, reinforced by certain trends arising within the churches themselves.[78] This voluntaristic conception of the church has probably gone furthest in the United States, where denominationalism has made a mockery of any effort by the church to act authoritatively. This has likely been exacerbated by the rise of congregations independent of any larger ecclesial fellowship.

With respect to marriage, the rise of no-fault divorce dangerously attenuated this institution, eviscerating its enduring character and facilitating a sharp rise in marital dissolutions. Current legal efforts to play down sexual complementarity are a further concession to the tendency to reshape marriage into a mere private contract, whose terms are deemed alterable at the discretion of the partners—or possibly only one of the partners. Although the predominant view of marriage nowadays is partner-centered and contractarian, there has long been recognition among those less enamored of the liberal vision that it is essential to the health of society, not only as a means of taming and containing sexual behavior, but as the best context for raising children, given the possible alternatives of promiscuity and single parenthood.

Noninstitutional communities, taken individually, are less evidently crucial than the institutional communities to societal flourishing, yet as a whole they fulfill a significant role for which the state is not an adequate substitute. Consider the role of the independent Polish trade union movement, Solidarity, in the demise of communism in the 1980s. Trade unions are obviously not as central to social wellbeing as marriage, family, state, and church. Nevertheless, where a single agent undertakes to monopolize

---

78. See, e.g., Locke, *A Letter Concerning Toleration* (1689), in which the author states: "A church, then, I take to be a voluntary society of men, joining themselves together of their own accord in order to the public worshipping of God in such manner as they judge acceptable to Him, and effectual to the salvation of their souls" (4).

those activities typically undertaken by voluntary associations and organizations, a society will tend to become needlessly bureaucratic and hierarchical. People will tend to lapse into passivity and fail to take the initiative in multiple fields of endeavor. Members freely enter and quit noninstitutional communities, whose sheer variety matches the breadth of the human imagination.

As do the institutional communities, the noninstitutional communities also contain offices based on authority and subordination, as Dooyeweerd expresses it. A business enterprise is likely to be governed by a board of directors, with an executive and other officers, including the chairman. Under the board come a number of administrative positions collectively known as management, capped by a president and perhaps more than one vice president. If this is a manufacturing enterprise, beneath the management level we will find those employees most immediately responsible for the production of the goods to be offered in the open market. In a service-oriented firm, the lower level is occupied by those directly providing that service to the public.

What Dooyeweerd's phrase "authority and subordination" fails to take into account, however, is the existence of authoritative offices throughout the structure of an organization. Assembly line workers in an automobile-manufacturing plant do not lack authority for being subordinate to the plant supervisor. In this respect *communities are suffused with authority, resident in offices that relate to each other in different ways, depending on context*. Indeed authority and subordination are not opposites, any more than authority and freedom are. All human authority is derived authority, subject to norms appropriate to the office at issue.

The affirmation of authority's pluriformity is not, of course, restricted to the four approaches explored immediately above. Writing in the wake of Watergate and the Vietnam debacle in the United States, Robert Nisbet lamented the twilight of authority and the concomitant tendency for the state to move into the breach left by the failure of other institutions.[79] Nisbet saw a great need to restore the precarious balance "between political-military power on the one hand and the structure of authority that lies in human groups such as neighborhood, family, labor union, profession, and voluntary association."[80] We would do better, he argued, to abandon the monistic legacy of Plato, Hobbes, Rousseau, Bentham, and others in

---

79. See Nisbet, *Twilight of Authority*.
80. Ibid., 276.

favor of the more pluralistic tradition of Aristotle, Cicero, Thomas Aquinas, Althusius, Burke, Tocqueville, and Proudhon.[81] In similar fashion, Catholic philosopher Thomas Molnar, while not focusing on office as such, nevertheless acknowledges the pluriformity of authority in the various social spheres, including family, school, church, the courts, workshop, literature and art, state, and international relations. This recognition requires a firm awareness of the limits of authority, which secular utopians ignore to their—and everyone's—peril. The various authorities are so interlinked that the "collapse of authority within one institution, let us say the courts, is soon accompanied by the weakening of authority elsewhere: in church, family, army, and so on."[82] A properly structured society requires that authority be respected in each setting within which it is appropriately exercised. "Authority," argues Molnar, "is the guarantee that man is not totally subordinated to authority," or, better, to a single overreaching authority that would extinguish all others.[83]

Authority in Practice: Case Studies

What difference does all this make? Are there practical implications for our theory of authority and office? Will it help us to live better lives or to govern our communities better? Will families thrive and economies flourish? We believe there is much to be said for using the language of authority and office in the policy debates surrounding a number of significant issues. We shall look at four issues below, hoping thereby to illustrate how we might move beyond the sterile arguments of the past, affected as they are by the various political visions and illusions that have impacted the world over the past two or more centuries. We begin with the nuclear family consisting of parents and underage children.

Parents' and Children's Authority

In 1989 the United Nations General Assembly adopted the Convention on the Rights of the Child (CRC), which was subsequently signed by representatives of 140 countries and ratified or accepted by 193, with

---

81. Ibid., 245. Somewhat oddly, Nisbet includes Jean Bodin in the second group, despite the usual attribution to him of a monistic view of sovereignty.

82. Molnar, *Authority and Its Enemies*, 29.

83. Ibid., 131.

the notable exceptions of Somalia, South Sudan and the United States.[84] This was not the first time that obligations towards children had been expressed in terms of rights; an earlier Geneva Declaration of the Rights of the Child had been adopted by the League of Nations in 1924, although in its five brief points it never once used the word "rights," speaking instead the language of duty: the child "must be fed," "must be sheltered and succored," "must be protected against every form of exploitation," etc.[85] The 1959 UN Declaration of the Rights of the Child is similarly spare in using the language of rights, mentioning them twice under Principle 1 and not at all in Principles 2 through 10.[86] By contrast, the CRC consists of 54 articles in which "rights" are referred to 26 times and the obligations of "States Parties" mentioned 110 times.

These differences between the CRC and the two earlier documents are significant in that they appear to represent an historic shift which Michael Ignatieff has described as the "Rights Revolution," Francis Fukuyama as the Great Disruption, and the present author as the dawn of the "choice-enhancement state," as we saw in previous chapters.[87] It is worth noting that, especially in the US, the CRC is controversial because it would seem to bring the state too far into the legitimate sphere of family intimacy. Such reservations have thus far successfully prevented the US from ratifying the Convention. Even among the signatories, several states, including the Vatican, have explicitly qualified their acceptance for various reasons. Indeed it is not altogether clear that recasting parental or societal obligations towards children as rights represents genuine progress in ensuring the latter's well-being, especially if the tendency to view all rights as adjudicable by the courts is not sufficiently curtailed. In one sense, of course, no one can doubt that children have the right to be loved and cared for by their parents. Yet the primary agents for fulfilling this responsibility are the parents themselves, and not the "states parties" which have signed the document, though the latter certainly have an obligation towards both parents and their children under their general mandate to do public justice. It is worth noting that the word *authority* appears only three times in the text of the Convention and each time refers to legal or

---

84. Convention on the Rights of the Child. Somalia indicated its intention to ratify the CRC, but had not yet done so as this was being written.

85. Geneva Declaration of the Rights of the Child.

86. Declaration of the Rights of the Child.

87. See Ignatieff, *The Rights Revolution*; Fukuyama, *The Great Disruption*; and the present author's own *Political Visions and Illusions*.

judicial authority. When used in the plural form, *authorities* always denotes political authorities. Noticeably absent from all three documents is a recognition of the primacy of *parental* authority in nurturing the child towards maturity.

To be sure, the CRC does recognize "that the family, as the fundamental group of society and the natural environment for the growth and well-being of all its members and particularly children, should be afforded the necessary protection and assistance so that it can fully assume its responsibilities within the community" (Preamble). It also calls upon states parties to "respect the responsibilities, rights and duties of parents" (Article 5), referring twice more to parental "responsibilities" (Article 18) and twice more to their "rights and duties" (Articles 3 & 14). In many respects, the CRC is a salutary document, whose drafters enshrined in its provisions their hopes for the betterment of the world's children. However, the language of parental *authority* is missing from the document, thereby at least potentially skewing the balance between state and parental authority.

What will a shift to the language of authority gain for us? We believe it will enable us better to account for the full complexity of the relationship between parents and minor children—necessarily an ever-changing relationship as the children grow to maturity. At the birth of a child, the parents' authority over her is virtually total: among living creatures, the human child is uniquely helpless, unable to walk, talk, feed herself and so forth. Her parents must care for her in an especially intensive way. Created in God's image from conception, her own *active* authority as image-bearer is largely latent at this point, her well-being closely bound up especially with her mother, but also with her father. However, as she grows, she gradually assumes new capacities, her parents' authority over her slowly receding until she attains full maturity and the limited authority over the course of her own life that accompanies it. Even before she reaches this point, direct parental authority over her recedes before other authorities, including those of child-care workers, teachers, pastors, and other so-called agents of socialization. This begins when the child starts school around age 5, if not earlier. Yet parental authority properly remains primary throughout. The authority of teachers supports parental authority and should never be supposed to supplant or override it.

Education offers an issue in which clashing visions of authority come to the fore. It is one thing to claim that a child has a right to receive an education, as does Article 28 of the CRC. It is quite another to recognize that one agent or another has a unique authority to educate a child. The CRC obligates its signatory states to facilitate the education of their children without actually mandating them directly to do so through a unified public school system. However, it does call upon the states to inculcate in them certain values conducive to a free society, including tolerance of diversity, friendship among all peoples, respect for the physical environment and respect for parents (Article 29). This would seem to imply that the states parties must assert some control over the educational process, including an effort to override parental and cultural values when these conflict with those of the Convention. The historic theoretical basis for such an approach can be seen in both Plato and Aristotle, who argued that the *polis* must educate its young in those virtues most conducive to the welfare of the community.

A better option would be to recognize the primary authority of parents over their children's education, while nevertheless acknowledging that other communities, including the state, have a legitimate interest in ensuring that children are educated and prepared for membership therein. This comes of recognizing that children themselves occupy an office—or, better, an increasing diversity of offices—that require adult support and supervision, especially at the outset. The oft-quoted African proverb that it takes a village to raise a child might be improved and updated by observing that a diversity of authoritative agents is required to raise a child, with parents holding clear primacy. While the update lacks the pithiness of the original, it arguably better accounts for reality in a mature, differentiated society.

The interconnection among these various offices might be seen with respect to the means of discipline, which wise parents will see fit to adjust to the increasing age and maturity of the child. What might begin with direct physical punishment, such as spanking, properly progresses to the withholding of privileges as the child is better able to comprehend the latter with increasing years. Although in past times teachers also administered corporal punishments to their pupils, now, at least in North America, they are more likely to impose a detention or something more evidently related to the assessment of overall performance, such as a lower mark. Controversy is inevitably raised in cases where a government undertakes to enact a law proscribing spanking, as many people believe it is thereby transgressing the legitimate sphere of parental authority. However, few would deny that government, in carrying out its mandate to do public justice, must prohibit adults from exercising *undue* force on the child, e.g., through the use of objects that bruise or batter. If parents abuse their own children, the state has an obligation to step in and rectify this abuse. In so doing, however, it is not overriding parental authority, as if the latter functions within a hierarchy with the state at the top. It is in fact protecting the office of the child from those parents failing to respect it. It is worth noting, however, that the state itself does not attempt to raise the child; it places him in a home with foster parents who will properly care for him. By this the state continues to recognize the primacy of parental authority, which is not derived from the supposedly "higher" authority of the state. To put it in overtly confessional terms, God confers parental authority directly on the parents and not by way of a mediating institution such as state or church. In this way, the child grows to maturity, slowly coming into the full array of authoritative offices possessed by the mature image-bearer of God.

Once the children have grown and are out of the parental home, the familial offices of mother, father, son and daughter continue, albeit in different form, as we have noted above. To express it in De George's and Simon's terms, the executive (imperative) authority of the parents, which is substitutional in character, has been rendered obsolete by the maturity of the son or daughter. However, the offices of mother and father retain a certain exemplary authority, while the offices of son or daughter will eventually take on performative and perhaps even imperative authority as the parents age and become less able to care for themselves. The offices continue, although the precise nature of the authority possessed by each changes along with the stages in life of the person occupying it.

Church and State: Ecclesial and Political Authorities

So much has been written on church-state relations over the decades that all we can do here is to survey the landscape, as it were, and to attempt to reconfigure the debate in accordance with what we believe is a better account of authority and office. There is a widespread myth that, prior to the modern age, throne and altar were locked together in a dark alliance to thwart all progressive ideas and innovations. Only with the coming of the Enlightenment did westerners finally succeed in breaking this bond and separating church and state for good. The First Amendment to the US Constitution was the culmination of this trend insofar as it guaranteed religious freedom and prohibited a Church-of-England-style ecclesiastical establishment. Other progressive nations have followed suit in the ensuing two centuries.

This narrative ignores the historical reality of the often intense competition among the various estates of the realms in the pre-modern medieval constitutions. One need only recall the tense relations between Henry II and Thomas Becket, King of England and Archbishop of Canterbury respectively, culminating in Thomas' murder by Henry's agents. Or the dramatic investiture controversy between Holy Roman Emperor Henry IV and Pope Gregory VII, climaxing in the Emperor's legendary—and perhaps overstated—barefoot penance in the snows at Canossa. King and bishop were competitors as often as not, as monarchs undertook to consolidate their own sovereignty within their realms, increasingly unwilling to share authority with nobles and churchmen alike. Only in the eastern half of Europe, in the Byzantine and Russian empires, did the throne and altar alliance come close to reality, though even here it frequently came about when such rulers as Peter the Great succeeded in forcibly subordinating the institutional church to their own political ends.[88] It would be a mistake to assume that political and ecclesiastical leaders had been at one in an ostensibly bygone dark or, as some would have it, golden age.

Nevertheless, it is true that the boundaries between political and ecclesiastical authorities were once more fluid than they are now, with "secular" authorities routinely called upon to enforce orthodoxy as judged by their "spiritual" counterparts. The history of the Inquisition in Spain and elsewhere is familiar enough not to warrant further mention here. Moreover, the Reformed confessions of the sixteenth and seventeenth centuries generally granted a role to the civil magistrate in supporting the task of the church. However, by the beginning of the nineteenth century increasing numbers of Christians began to see that this cozy relationship put the civil authorities in the uneasy position of having to judge which church institution best embodied the true faith, an assessment taking the state well beyond its own resources and competence. Even those less evidently loyal to the faith preferred to see the state restrict itself to those matters on which general agreement was forthcoming, leaving disputable matters to the private conscience of individuals.

At this point the Enlightenment project took two different directions in different places. In the English-speaking countries it took on a more

---

88. See, e.g., Muller, ed., *The Spiritual Regulation of Peter the Great*.

moderate form. Although England and Scotland retained their established churches, by the mid-nineteenth century the British government had already allowed for toleration of nonconformists (1689), Catholic emancipation (1828), and Jewish emancipation (by 1858). In the United States once again the First Amendment provided that "Congress shall make no law respecting an establishment of religion, or prohibiting the free exercise thereof," thereby putting an historically divisive issue under the broader rubric of freedom of religion, guaranteed alongside other individual liberties, such as speech, press, and association. The net effect of these was, not only to protect the freedom of individuals to worship as they saw fit, but to allow the gathered church communities themselves to function with minimal government interference and even with tax-exempt status.

In much of the European continent, by contrast, the loosening of ecclesiastical establishments led to their replacement by an establishment of something approaching an official secularism, or *laïcité*, as the French euphemistically call it. The French Law of 1905 separating the churches and the state claimed to respect liberty of conscience and the free exercise of religion. Although the Concordat of 1801 provided for state funding for the Roman Catholic Church in France, the 1905 law rescinded this arrangement and, more controversially, made church buildings property of the republic, the departments, and the municipalities, which worshipers were nevertheless permitted to use provided they met certain conditions (Title III, article 13). Thus a law claiming to separate church and state effectively placed the institutional churches, both Catholic and Reformed, under the supervision of the state, which dictated that worship must be their sole aim (Title IV, article 19). Much as Rousseau had viewed traditional religious believers as potentially divisive of the general will and sought to tame them with his proposed civil religion, so the Third Republic put the churches on notice that they had better behave themselves . . . or else. While the Third Republic died at the hands of the Nazis and Marshal Pétain in 1940, the 1905 law survived into the Fourth and Fifth Republics and has practically attained something approaching constitutional status in France.

Since the end of the Second World War, American jurisprudence has brought the religious freedom issue closer to the continental model, as the no-establishment clause has in many respects come to assume priority over the free-exercise clause. This approach has been encouraged by such groups as the American Civil Liberties Union and Americans United for Separation of Church and State. Although the courts have not taken the logic of this position as far, some have argued that the First Amendment separates religion and politics, as though it were possible to prevent citizens from acting politically on their ultimate convictions. If so, the focus is less on maintaining a distinction between institutions as on privileging a certain worldview which holds, in the face of considerable opposition, that religion is a mere private predilection with no legitimate political implications. In short, a particular religious view concerning the nature of religion has become the received orthodoxy among many who would have it enforced by the state apparatus.

All the same, the belief that institutional church and state are distinct agents possessing their own unique spheres of authority is a sound one. If the state should undertake to appoint church officials or if the church should try to encourage the state to impose a church-membership test on would-be public office-holders, each exceeds its legitimate range of authority. Abraham Kuyper even persuaded the Synod of Utrecht of the Reformed Churches in the Netherlands to alter Article 36 of the Belgic Confession, which accords government a role in supporting the true faith and suppressing false religion, a move subsequently followed in 1958 by the Synod of the Christian Reformed Church in North America. This was in recognition that church and state normatively have their own distinct spheres which ought not to be usurped by the other. This is not exactly tantamount to Thomas Jefferson's famous "wall of separation," but it does acknowledge that, under most circumstances, parliaments ought not to formulate ecclesiastical confessions and churches ought not to set concrete political agendas. This is less a matter of religious freedom, as conventionally conceived, as of admitting that all human authoritative institutions function within proper limits.

Inside Church and State: Multiple Authoritative Offices

Like every community, institutional church and state are characterized by a series of internal offices playing crucial roles in their proper functioning. Depending on which manifestation we are treating, these have different names and responsibilities attached to them. In a US-style presidential system, such offices include the President, cabinet secretaries, Senators, Representatives, Supreme Court Justices, federal court judges, civil servants and, of course, the citizens themselves. In a Westminster-style parliamentary-cabinet system these offices would be the Queen, the Prime Minister, Senators (or Lords), Members of Parliament, court judges, public servants, and, once again, citizens. No member of the state lacks an office relevant to its central task of doing justice. In a democratic constitution the citizens play a crucial role in holding the other offices accountable for their conduct. They do so obviously during formal elections, but they also do so in other ways, for example, by means of the press publicizing the activities of the elected officials. Citizenship is an office held by all members of the political community, with the possible exception of an hereditary monarch, who may have responsibilities over more than one country. In the United Kingdom a cabinet minister is also a Member of Parliament and a citizen, the former offices building on the latter. In the United States a cabinet secretary cannot also be a member of Congress, but he or she must be an American citizen.

The institutional church too consists of offices, sometimes called Holy Orders in the older ecclesial communions. Traditionally there is a three-fold conception of office, including bishop (ἐπίσκοπος), priest or presbyter (πρεσβύτερος), and deacon (διάκονος). These are rooted in the usage of the early church, as recorded in the New Testament (e.g., 1 Tim 3:1-7, Acts 14:23, Acts 6:1-6, Phil 1:1, 1 Tim 3:8-13), and are maintained in hierarchical form in the Roman Catholic, Orthodox and Anglican communions. In the Reformed and Presbyterian churches this three-fold order is maintained in less hierarchical fashion in the offices of pastor, elder, and deacon. In addition there are synodical assemblies bringing together these office-holders whose collective decisions have authoritative status for an entire communion of churches.

Recently, however, it has come to be recognized that this three-fold understanding of office must be supplemented by a fourth, namely, that of the laity. The sixteenth-century reformers famously emphasized the priesthood of all believers, rejecting the notion of a sacerdotal priesthood mediating God's saving grace to the people. The role of the laity was never entirely forgotten by Rome and Constantinople. In fact, in the latter case the laity of Constantinople effectively nullified the reunion of eastern and western churches negotiated at the Council of Florence in 1439. Although properly delegated officials were authorized to sign the agreement to heal the schism of 1054, the Orthodox faithful declined to accept this agreement, which in effect became null and void. The Orthodox recognize only Seven Ecumenical Councils, although more councils were certainly held during the early Christian centuries.[89] Despite the latter following established procedures and being negotiated and approved by legitimate church hierarchs, the laity have effectively exercised something approaching a right of veto over those decisions. This lay veto is all but unknown in official Roman doctrine and polity, although it has been asserted by some, mostly dissenting, Catholic theologians. Nevertheless, the position of the laity has been brought to the fore especially in the wake of the Second Vatican Council of 1962–65.[90]

The offices in both church and state are intimately tied to what might be called the structural principle of the two communities. Bishops, presbyters, and deacons govern the institutional or gathered church in ways appropriate to its inner nature, recognizing that the latter is a faith community, and not a political, artistic, or familial community. The *raison d'être* of the gathered church is to worship God, to celebrate salvation in Jesus Christ and to preach the gospel. Where these purposes are forgotten or neglected, ecclesiastical officials will tend to exercise their authority in inappropriate ways, for example, by making pronouncements on political and other matters properly lying outside their field of competence. A perusal of the websites of the major Protestant denominations in North America will illustrate this phenomenon in action.

This is not to say that pastors should ignore such issues in their preaching or pretend they are of no significance for the Christian community. It is not a call for Christians piously to put aside the concerns of the larger communities of which they are part and focus solely on preaching a gospel irrelevant to real life in a real world. This would be to preach half a gospel in which Jesus saves us only in our spiritual lives, with our other extra-ecclesiastical activities relegated to an ostensibly neutral realm under the authority of pure reason—or worse. Church office-holders and even synodical assemblies are right to call their members to live the life in Christ, including political life. However, if they elevate prudential judgments concerning concrete and contestable policy options to the level of confessional truth, they misuse their authority. There will always be disagreement among serious Christians on, say, the proper minimum wage or even whether mandating a minimum wage at

---

89. Most notably the Iconoclast Council, held at Hieria in 754, is not considered a genuine ecumenical council and was later repudiated by the second Council of Nicaea in 787. See Ware, *The Orthodox Church*, esp. 248–54, for a discussion of what makes a council genuinely ecumenical.

90. See, e.g., the Vatican II document, *Lumen Gentium*.

all might be counterproductive and exacerbate unemployment. In such contexts, church denominations are ill-advised to intervene in such debates beyond calling attention to the biblical mandate to care for the poor.

In the newly independent Cyprus Republic in 1960, the head of the Church of Cyprus, Archbishop Makarios III, *né* Michael Mouskos (1913–1977), was elected President of the Republic by the Cypriot electorate. In many respects the spiritual integrity of the church had already been compromised by the ethnic nationalist role it had played in the guerrilla war of the late 1950s in support of *enosis*, or union of the island with Greece. This goal was unpalatable to the ethnic Turkish minority, who feared for their lives and livelihoods in an enlarged Greek kingdom. Although President Makarios abandoned the goal of *enosis* and articulated a non-aligned role for the republic, the fact of his ecclesiastical leadership made it difficult for him to pursue policies that might have reconciled the two ethnic communities in the face of opposition from subordinate hierarchs in the institutional church. Makarios' role as ethnarch over the Greek Orthodox community in Cyprus had deep roots in Ottoman practice, while a clearer differentiation between church and state might have better enabled the government to exercise distinctly *political* authority for the well-being of all Cypriot citizens, whatever their religion or ethnicity.[91] After Markarios' death in 1977 the top ecclesiastical and political offices were quite sensibly separated, going to Archbishop Chrysostomos and Spyros Kyprianou respectively.

Similarly, the authority of political officials is limited by the jural character of the political community, whose very task it is to balance the legitimate interests found within its jurisdiction, that is, to do public justice. Within the state the various elements of this central jural task are properly distributed among the offices for two reasons. First, a division of labor increases the opportunity for doing a job well. Second, and more important, the political task has long been recognized to consist of legislative, executive, bureaucratic, and judicial functions, which are best fulfilled by specialized bodies within the whole designated for these purposes. When one of these attempts to usurp the task of the other, many people rightly sense that an injustice is being done.

---

91. For an accessible history of Cyprus, see Hunt, ed., *Footprints in Cyprus*. See especially chapter 10, "The Turkish Period: 1571–1878" (226–54), for a description of the Ottoman practice of granting civil powers to the religious leaders of the non-Muslim communities.

We have noted above that the First Amendment to the US Constitution guarantees several liberties to its citizens, primarily by prohibiting the federal government from interfering with them. Yet we would suggest that, by protecting freedom of religion, speech, press, assembly, and the right "to petition the Government for a redress of grievances," it is in fact recognizing that these are necessary for the citizen to exercise properly her political authority. During elections voters must have the authority to debate and weigh the merits of candidates and policy alternatives if they are to vote intelligently and responsibly. The recent substitution of "freedom of *expression*" for "freedom of speech" tends to obscure the relationship of this fundamental freedom to the exercise of the office of citizen, as well as to other responsibilities. It does so by focusing on the expansive desire of the individual for self-disclosure rather than on his responsibilities to a larger community.

Although the different church communions disagree with respect to the hierarchical character of their ecclesiastical offices, there is no getting round the reality of hierarchy within the state. Legislatures make laws binding on all residents within their jurisdictions. Executives make decisions binding on other political actors, especially within the realms of foreign and defense policies. Court judges hand down rulings binding on legislators and executives alike. Bureaucrats make administrative rulings within their formal areas of competence. Legislatures, executives, bureaucrats, and judges have limited authority over citizens in specific fields. Yet insofar as the latter are citizens, they also possess authority over the elected officials who govern them. In short, the hierarchy is not exclusively a top-down relationship. It is less accurate to speak of the state as a grand hierarchical system and closer to the mark to recognize it as a complex of smaller, context-specific hierarchies relating to each other in ways that are themselves not necessarily hierarchical.

The American founders in particular understood this in dividing sovereignty (read: supreme political authority) among the branches of government as well as between federal and state governments. If the federal government is supreme in the field of, say, minting currency and setting foreign policy, the state governments are superior to the federal in those areas not granted the federal, such as education and most of the criminal and civil law. In this respect one cannot say in unqualified fashion that the federal government is superior to state governments. This is why the organic vision of society, so popular with early nineteenth-century European conservatives, is in error: it mistakenly envisions society as a single, undifferentiated whole characterized by a unified hierarchy of superiors and inferiors. By contrast, a mature differentiated society finds people relating to each other in a multitude of overlapping ways, some of which are hierarchical but many of which are not.

Authority in the Workplace: Labor and Management

The nineteenth century saw the dawn of a new form of economic productive activity, which came on the heels of the industrial revolution. In the early modern era most people were involved in agrarian pursuits, either as landed or landless peasants. But towards the end of the eighteenth century in England many people began to flock to the cities where the new factories offered them manufacturing jobs. The factory system brought together large numbers of people under the authority of a plant manager who set the terms of employment. Under the economic laws of supply and demand, the larger the numbers seeking factory work, the more wages were driven down for those fortunate enough to secure such work. This enhanced the power of the employer over its workers, making it more difficult for employees to receive a living wage and to work under satisfactory conditions. We need not rehearse the abuses of the factory system, which are familiar to anyone with knowledge of the history of industrial relations. The rise of trade unions came about in response to these abuses as a way of enhancing the bargaining power of employees, who were otherwise at a distinct disadvantage in the workplace. The National Labor Relations Act of 1935, also known as the Wagner Act, solidified the role of labor unions in the American workplace, giving them the authority to bargain on behalf of workers which employers were obligated to respect.

This development was, of course, controversial, and not everyone accepted the legitimacy of unions. Followers of the older classical liberalism argued that they violated the individual's right to enter freely into contractual relations and thus distorted the market. They could appeal to the negative example of the medieval guilds, which they held to have stifled economic growth and innovation. By contrast, management objected, not necessarily on principled grounds, but out of concern that acceding to union demands might hamper their competitiveness in the marketplace, where they might be at a disadvantage relative to nonunionized companies. If they were forced to pay higher wages to their own employees, labor costs would constitute a larger proportion of their total expenditures, forcing them to raise prices. Raising prices could encourage consumers to purchase from a neighboring business for which labor costs were lower, thereby enabling them to keep their prices low. This could put the first company out of business.

Furthermore, the unions' tactic of striking, that is, of refusing to work unless their demands were met, was problematic for more than one reason. First, if resorted to too quickly, the strike could damage the viability of the targeted company, thereby cutting the ground out from under the workers themselves. At the start of 1951 members of the AFL Brotherhood of Telegraphers, Switchmen and Clerks went on strike against the Chicago Aurora & Elgin Railroad, a small electric line founded in 1902 connecting Chicago with its western suburbs. Forced to suspend operations during the work stoppage, the company lost passengers to parallel rail lines and failed within a decade.[92] Similarly, at the beginning of 1962 a United Auto Workers strike at the Studebaker automobile plant in South Bend, Indiana, further crippled an already struggling company and alienated actual and potential customers, thereby contributing to the plant's closure in December of the following year. An effort to protect workers thus backfired. It is not unusual to hear people blame the unions for the decline in the manufacturing sector in North America after the mid-1960s. Whether such a charge is fair, it nevertheless underscores the disaffection from the labor union movement in some segments of the public in recent decades.

Second, to strike would seem to involve violating a contract between employer and employee, whereby employer agrees to pay employee for providing work. If the employees withhold their labor, they could be seen to be breaking their agreement with the employer. This, of course, assumes that employer and employee have entered their contract *as individuals*, bound only by their own signatures and by the public law of the state and not by the sorts of collective agreements whose legitimacy would come only with the general acceptance of the right of collective bargaining. Nowadays the collective bargaining agreement can be said to be authoritative for both parties, but this was not always so.

Third, if one were to take an exclusively hierarchical view of a business enterprise, one might hold there to be an unqualified relationship

---

92. Plachno, *Sunset Lines*, 379–80. In fairness to the unions, the CA&E's continued viability was also compromised by the building of the Congress (later Eisenhower) Expressway and the resultant loss of its one-seat service into downtown Chicago.

of superiority and subordination between management and workers, whereby workers are obligated to obey management. This would mean that management decides the nature of the work, hours, wages, etc., and workers are obligated to accept these as a condition of their employment. To go against management is to disobey a legitimately-constituted authority. To strike is then a deliberate act of disobedience, sedition, and disloyalty. By this account the formation of a labor union is a revolutionary act aimed in effect at denying or at least qualifying management's authority. This is the position taken by the small Calvinist denomination, the Protestant Reformed Churches, whose regions of strength are the Chicago and Grand Rapids, Michigan, areas. In fact, on two occasions the denomination's synod wrote to Presidents Roosevelt and Truman, asking them not to support the closed union shop, and calling unionism a "great evil in the sight of God."[93] According to the Rev. David Engelsma, representing the PRC, God has conferred the authority to govern a business on its owner and given the worker the duty to obey. Therefore, labor unions "are guilty of rebellion against lawful authority, just as is the case with a rebellious child, or a revolutionary against the state."[94] Workers are bound by the biblical injunctions that servants obey their masters (e.g., Eph 6:5–8, Col 3:22–25).

While one should not minimize the empirical abuses and corruption of actual trade unions, these should not be assumed to delegitimate them in principle. To begin with, the assumption that ownership uniquely confers authoritative office is based on too narrow an understanding of office. Indeed a business enterprise is composed of various offices related to the specific contributions made by each member. A modern limited-liability corporation may see its capital—its physical productive resources—owned by investors who expect a fair return on their investment. Yet their practical authority may extend over only the capital itself and not necessarily over the direction of the enterprise as a whole. They may play a role in electing the board of directors, but the latter again may play a minimal role beyond ensuring that current management is capable of turning a profit so as to ensure a fair return to stockholders. The day-to-day running of the enterprise may effectively belong to management, that is, to officers hired specifically for this purpose. These managers cannot be said to own the enterprise as such, yet they possess undoubted authority.

---

93. Engelsma, "Labor Union Membership in the Light of Scripture."
94. Ibid.

Economist Bob Goudzwaard goes so far as to question whether a business enterprise, taken as a whole community of persons, can be an object of ownership at all. Normatively understood, a business should be seen as "a work community of living people," in which case it is improper to speak of ownership except in a derivative sense.[95] At most one might be said to own the capital goods, but this does not confer ownership of the work community using those goods, any more than ownership of a church building implies ownership of the church community worshiping therein. Goudzwaard believes that where the business enterprise is properly viewed as a work community, everyone, including management and labor, bears corporate responsibility for its actions. This implies some form of co-responsibility or co-determination with respect to decision-making. Indeed, far from setting the direction of the enterprise, the rights of investors are "fully satisfied" once they have been informed of the handling of their investment.[96]

Goudzwaard's analysis might be seen to imply something along the lines of industrial democracy or worker self-management.[97] Marshal Tito's Yugoslavia pursued worker self-management as a general policy from the 1950s. Based on a somewhat uneasy combination of party autocracy at the top and local participation in the workplace, it did not survive the end of communism and the subsequent breakup of the fractious multinational federation.[98] However, co-determination, or *Mitbestimmung*, has been mandated in the Federal Republic of Germany for all companies of a certain size. A series of laws enacted between 1951 and 1976 require that nearly half of a company's governing board be made up of worker representatives. Originally applying only to the coal and steel sectors of the economy, it was eventually expanded to include all workplaces with more than two thousand employees.[99] English-speaking democracies, even under social democratic governments, have not gone as far in this

---

95. Goudzwaard, *Capitalism and Progress*, 216.

96. Ibid., 216–17.

97. See Webb and Webb, *Industrial Democracy*. Profit-sharing and employee ownership would not adequately satisfy Goudzwaard's critique of the current system, as they are still predicated on the assumption that decision-making authority follows ownership of capital, which in such cases is simply dispersed to more people within the enterprise itself.

98. See Adizes, *Industrial Democracy*, for a mid-stream analysis of the policy.

99. A survey of *Mitbestimmung* up to and including the reforms of 1976 can be found in Fürstenberg, "West German Experience with Industrial Democracy."

direction as Germany and other continental European countries, seemingly content to defend workers' rights within the predominant adversarial collective-bargaining system.

We will not here express a preference for or against industrial democracy, which we believe is only one of a number of possible ways of recognizing the unique contribution of employees to an enterprise. Nevertheless, we do believe that employees bear an authoritative office within the enterprise. The employees themselves may see their own interests limited to ensuring that they are adequately compensated for their labors, that is, given a fair wage, though other considerations, such as workplace safety and the nature of the work itself, may also play a role. In other words, the employees' office may not be one of setting the general direction of the enterprise, and the workers themselves may show no interest in this. Yet that makes their office no less authoritative within its proper sphere. To paraphrase O'Donovan once again, all human authority is simultaneously *authority over* and *authority under*. The authority of workers is under that of management, whose authority is in turn under that of the board of directors. Even if workers are represented on the board, they are still subject ultimately to the board's overall guiding authority. Yet the authority of each of these offices is limited to the context of the enterprise itself, as we noted in chapter 5.

Far from subverting authority, labor unions play a significant role in ensuring that the authoritative offices of the employees are protected within the business enterprise. Given the fallibility of human nature, there is an ongoing temptation for management to view labor as but one more productive factor, along with raw materials and machinery, thereby ignoring the humanity—indeed the God-given *authority*—of workers. This temptation was especially pronounced during the first decades of the industrial revolution, and it is still a reality in much of the two-thirds world, where non-unionized workers labor for far less money than their western counterparts, enabling their transnational corporate employers to produce inexpensive goods for western consumers. Labor unions enable workers to exercise their authority more effectively in a context where they might otherwise be at a structural disadvantage relative to management.

Moreover, where the right to collective bargaining is enshrined in the public law of the state, the collective bargaining agreements between management and labor can be said to possess an authoritative private legal status within the enterprise for both parties to the negotiating process. For either side to violate the agreement would be a serious breach of trust and would itself constitute a subversion of legitimate authority and arguably of the rule of law itself.

Of course, no discussion of the labor movement can be complete without acknowledging that in the real world unions and management alike can abuse their mutual relationship. Each party may act solely out of perceived self-interest at the other's expense. Some workplaces are characterized by a poisoned atmosphere in which managers and workers see each other as real or potential enemies. This class struggle has so often spilled into the political arena that the economic welfare of an entire country becomes hostage. Engelsma and others rightly decry the violence and general lawlessness that has sometimes accompanied strikes. Nevertheless, there are beacons of light within the field of labor relations. One example is the Christian Labour Association of Canada (CLAC), which has operated since 1952 and, apart from the public employees unions, has been one of the more successful unions in that country at a time when the traditional manufacturing unions have been in decline. Founded by Dutch Reformed immigrants raised and educated in Kuyper's neocalvinist revival, the CLAC has deliberately eschewed an adversarial approach, seeking instead to be a force for reconciliation in the workplace. Based on explicitly Christian principles, it nevertheless represents workers of all faiths, with a membership numbering in excess of 50,000 at the beginning of the second decade of the present century. Excoriated by the secular trade unions as a pseudo-union, the CLAC styles itself as "a union with a difference" and "a union that works." From our perspective, the CLAC and similar unions elsewhere undertake to protect the authority of workers within the workplace.[100] In this they play a role similar to that played by different branches and levels of government within a political constitution, in that they serve to keep the authoritative office(s) of management accountable.

Seeking the Commonweal: Two Cheers for the Welfare State

The welfare state developed alongside labor unions in most western countries, with especially social democratic parties using their support base among industrial workers to construct a network of public financial benefits to soften the harsh edges of the marketplace and to even out the

---

100. For a history of the CLAC, see Grootenboer, *In Pursuit of Justice*. The organization's website can be found at http://www.clac.ca/.

boom and bust extremes of the business cycle. Although its origins can be traced to Otto von Bismarck's nineteenth-century German Empire, its international popularity was boosted in large measure by the social and economic dislocations of the Great Depression of the 1930s, with the Scandinavian countries leading the way. After the end of the Second World War virtually all western democracies built welfare states based on the expanding and unprecedented prosperity of the 1950s and '60s. In the United Kingdom a "collectivist consensus" united the Conservative and Labour Parties, until Margaret Thatcher's monetarism reshaped this in the 1980s. Prior to that point, both parties pursued welfare state policies, assuming not simply their rightness, but that they were key to electoral success in postwar Britain. Whatever their other differences, socialists, liberals, and conservatives united behind the welfare state.

In the United States, where socialism never took off as a realistic electoral alternative, it was professed liberals, mostly within the Democratic Party, who championed the programs associated initially with Franklin Roosevelt's New Deal and, a generation later, with Lyndon Johnson's Great Society. Under Roosevelt, not only were trade unions legalized, but his policies saw the establishment of the Social Security Administration, the Tennessee Valley Authority, the Rural Electrification Administration, the Agricultural Adjustment Administration and the National Recovery Administration, all of which were intended to alleviate the effects of the Depression. Many of these, such as Aid to Families with Dependent Children, became nearly permanent fixtures of the federal bureaucratic landscape until the Welfare Reform Act of 1996. North of the border, in Canada, the Conservative government of R. B. Bennett attempted to enact similar policies during the first half of the 1930s, with mixed results. However, it was only during and after the war that successive governments in Ottawa pursued the welfare state in earnest, adopting unemployment insurance, social assistance and universal health care before the federal government began running structural deficits by the early 1980s and the process slowed to a crawl.

Although the welfare state's existence is not especially controversial outside of libertarian circles, it does raise a number of issues meriting deeper reflection than is usually given them. First of all, does the state possess the normative competence to provide a diverse array of services beyond its core functions of making and executing the laws, and judging under the laws? By *normative* we mean more than mere conformity to the positive law of the land, assuming that what we have labeled the pluriformity of authorities imposes intrinsic limits on what various authoritative agents rightfully do in the conduct of their respective offices. In other words, is it just for the positive law to mandate that government look out for the economic well-being of its citizens? Or does it exceed its proper authority in so doing? Related to this is the question whether the state bears a legitimate responsibility for resolving social issues such as poverty, unemployment, homelessness, and disease.

We would respond to these questions with a cautious affirmation that government's divine mandate to do public justice requires that it assume *some*, but certainly not the whole, responsibility for addressing these ills. Normatively speaking, government's authority extends to coordinating justly the various authoritative agents—both communal and individual—within its territorial jurisdiction. Given its intrinsic limits, it cannot claim to control the activities of these agents in totalistic fashion. It properly allows each of them to live out its task according to its own unique calling. At the same time, the state's public character means that it must necessarily concern itself with those phenomena affecting the public realm in which these agents live out their callings. During the nineteenth century it was not uncommon for large urban centers in the western world to experience epidemics of cholera, a water-borne disease still afflicting millions in the two-thirds world. By the twentieth century, when the causes of cholera were better understood, governments undertook to build water and sewage treatment facilities to ensure that drinking water would not be contaminated by human and other wastes. Theoretically these governments could have waited until consumer preference had been expressed in the marketplace, but they wisely decided that improving public health required direct action on their part.

One could make a similar argument with respect to poverty and unemployment, whose causes are not always reducible to personal indolence or private vice but may have a basis in systemic defects in the ordinary economic interactions among people in the marketplace. Government's role can be justified by the reality that widespread poverty will likely prevent authoritative agents from adequately fulfilling their callings. Poverty is not simply a private matter to be addressed on an individual basis only. Where people are hungry and are scrambling to put food on the table or keep a roof over their heads, they will not take the interest in public affairs so needed in a constitutional democracy. They will have neither the time nor the energy to organize the variety of associational groupings needed for a flourishing civil society. A society in which a few wealthy families dominate economic life, with an impoverished majority eking out a living at the bottom, is not a good one to live in. It will not prosper economically, politically, aesthetically, socially, or in myriad other ways, as vertical ties between patron and client prevent the development of the horizontal ties of solidarity necessary for such prosperity. Among the various authoritative agents in society, government is uniquely positioned to coordinate efforts to assist those in need.

Nevertheless, this amounts to only two cheers for the welfare state rather than the conventional three. Libertarians are not altogether wrong to point out that governments are as fully capable of aggravating poverty as of ameliorating it. Indeed governments are more likely to worsen it than to eliminate it outright, an overly ambitious goal lying beyond the reach of any government. In their very efforts to do good, governments may inadvertently cause untold misery. As Sir Bernard Crick puts it, "No state has the capacity to ensure that men are happy; but all states have the capacity to ensure that men are unhappy."[101] This is not to say that governments should do nothing; however they do need to recognize that they cannot do everything. In an ordinary society characterized by a pluriformity of authoritative agents, each of these has a role to play in addressing such social ills as poverty and unemployment. Government efforts to combat unemployment must acknowledge that most jobs will come from the private sector. Something like President Roosevelt's Civilian Conservation Corps may be called for in the short term, but it can only be a temporary measure that must be permitted to expire when the private sector is able once more to accommodate those workers seeking permanent employment. For the most part, governments should be prepared to support, financially if necessary, independent initiatives in the fields of poverty reduction, childcare, education, and healthcare, but equitably and without unduly privileging their own efforts in these areas.

In 1944 Roosevelt proposed a second, economic bill of rights, arguing that the guarantee of political rights in the US Constitution had "proved inadequate to assure us equality in the pursuit of happiness." Among the rights he believed ought to be guaranteed were the "right to a useful and remunerative job in the industries or shops or farms or mines of the nation"; the "right of every family to a decent home; the right to adequate medical care and the opportunity to achieve and enjoy good health; the right to adequate protection from the economic fears of old age, sickness, accident,

---

101. Crick, *In Defence of Politics*, 151.

and unemployment;" and the "right to a good education."[102] Although nothing came of Roosevelt's proposal in the US, similar rights were enshrined four years later in especially articles 22 through 26 of the Universal Declaration of Human Rights (UDHR), which his widow Eleanor played a significant role in developing.[103] Some Canadians have recommended a similar social charter for their country,[104] and one observer has gone so far as to suggest that there may already be a foundation for one in Section 36 of the Constitution Act, 1982.[105] The 1993 Constitution of the Russian Federation claims to protect, not only the full array of personal liberties found in other bills of rights, but a series of social rights similar to those enumerated by Roosevelt and the UDHR.

The key difficulty with subsuming such issues under the category of rights is that it tells us nothing about who is to provide the goods supposedly guaranteed by them, thereby bypassing the issue of authority which is of more than peripheral importance. This is the same problem we met earlier with respect to the Convention on the Rights of the Child (CRC). It is one thing to say that people have a right to a decent home. It is another to indicate which authoritative agent is responsible for providing this and under what conditions. If government itself is regarded as the principal authority for the provision of decent housing, it risks overextending its own resources as well as its competence. This difficulty does not arise with respect to negative rights such as freedom of speech, as government is expected simply to refrain from interfering with their exercise, that is, *to recognize the limits to its own authority*, which it is eminently qualified to do. Positive rights, if they be seen as rights at all, are thus fundamentally different from the negative liberties protected in the US Bill of Rights, the Canadian Charter of Rights and Freedoms, and similar documents, because they call instead for concerted action by multiple authoritative agents. This suggests that the language of rights, as we have noted above, cannot be stretched indefinitely.

The authority of the state should never be supposed to substitute for that of other institutions, when the latter are able to function properly on their own. If the public sector occupies too large a share of a country's resources and if taxes are maintained at too high a level to support it,

---

102. Roosevelt, "State of the Union Message to Congress."

103. Universal Declaration of Human Rights.

104. See, e.g., Ontario Ministry of Intergovernmental Affairs. "A Canadian Social Charter."

105. Kinsella, "Can Canada Afford a Charter of Social and Economic Rights."

other independent initiatives will tend to suffer accordingly. Furthermore, where governments are in the grip of a worldview holding that whatever public funds touch must be secular, that is, "nonreligious," the large public sector will inevitably squeeze out church and para-church ministries undertaking to address the very social ills they may be better equipped than government to deal with. Our society would be spiritually, and not only economically, impoverished if governments were to take over entirely from the Salvation Army, the Jewish Federations of North America, Islamic Relief Worldwide, and local church diaconal ministries.

The Center for Public Justice, a Christian think tank in Washington, DC, took an active role in developing social welfare policy positions in the last decade of the twentieth century and had an influence on the Welfare Reform Act of 1996, formally known as the Personal Responsibility and Work Opportunity Reconciliation Act.[106] Its impact was felt especially in Section 104, "Services Provided By Charitable, Religious, Or Private Organizations." This section provides that, where government disburses funds to openly confessional organizations for public welfare purposes, it must do so on the same basis as it does to nonconfessional organizations. This prohibition of discrimination against faith-based organizations is known as "charitable choice." Such organizations retain their independence from government and their right to maintain their distinctive confessional identities. In particular, they retain the right (read: authority) to limit their hiring to those who agree with the organization's mission and accept its confessional basis. Although those operating within an individualist framework will protest that this amounts to allowing such organizations to discriminate on the basis of religion backed by public funding, those with a better understanding of the pluriformity of authorities will recognize that every organization works within a particular set of purposes with which not everyone will agree. Social darwinists will not be hired by a group dedicated to helping those in need. Nonfeminists will not be brought into a group championing feminist causes. There is nothing amiss in this. The identity of a community implies the authority to determine who does and does not qualify for membership. Government's authority should not be assumed to trump this, except under very exceptional circumstances.[107]

---

106. Public Law 104–93.

107. See "A Guide to Charitable Choice." See also the collection of essays edited by Carlson-Thies and Skillen, *Welfare in America*, for a survey of issues related to the welfare state; and Vanderwoerd, "Is the Newer Deal a Better Deal?"

A variety of authoritative agents bear responsibility for bettering the lot of the poor and needy, including government, the pluriform institutions of civil society, and—we must never forget—the poor themselves.[108] Any scheme that views the poor as little more than passive recipients rather than authoritative agents can never meet the demands of justice. Furthermore, although the notion of a culture of poverty is a contested one, there can be little doubt that, where interpersonal trust outside of extended family is lacking, it will be difficult for people to initiate the sorts of collaborative efforts needed for a successful business enterprise. Investors will hold onto their money if they believe there is a strong chance that the people in whose enterprise they invest will make off with it.[109] This testifies to the cultural aspect of potential economic prosperity. If the legal system makes it difficult for ordinary people to claim ownership of the resources on which they are sitting, this will be a further impediment to the creation of material wealth, as they will not be able to use it for collateral in the formation of a business.[110] If the law does not provide for incorporation of enterprises under conditions of limited liability, would-be entrepreneurs will be unwilling to take the risks necessary to provide economic opportunity for themselves and others. The law too must play a role in encouraging prosperity, even apart from direct provision of goods in the welfare state.

Finally, where governments have come to view marriage, not as an institution, but as a private contract between two consenting adults revocable or alterable at their discretion, it will be difficult to maintain intact marriages and families, the division of which will inevitably tend to make their members financially worse off. This is where the legitimate concerns of social-justice advocates and social conservatives ought to come together. In seeking to better the lot of the disadvantaged, governments must protect marriage and family as genuine authoritative institutions and not as mere private contracts or subunits of the state. Governments may need to provide assistance when families fail, but they should certainly not be pursuing policies that increase the likelihood of such failures. The best welfare state is one in which there is a realistic recognition of the limits of governmental authority, a healthy respect for the pluriformity of authoritative institutions in society, ongoing collaboration among these institutions to meet human needs, and a stable legal system that respects

---

108. See, e.g., Schwartz, *Fighting poverty with virtue*, for a study of reformers in the US who tied personal virtue to escape from poverty.

109. Fukuyama emphasizes the economic role of interpersonal trust in *Trust*.

110. See, e.g., the argument of Soto, *The Mystery of Capital*.

property ownership and the institutions of marriage, family, and even church. In this respect, social justice should be understood, not primarily as a result of the direct provision of goods and services by government, but as the fruit of a concerted and purposeful effort of the institutions of civil society, along with government, to combat poverty and similar ills.

7

Epilogue: Authority and Love

THE PROFESSOR IS IN *his second year of teaching and trying to build up his department's program by meeting socially with his students on a regular basis. He occupies a table in the cafeteria at lunch time and issues an informal invitation for his students to join him. Conversations range from current events, including Mikhail Gorbachev's unprecedented reforms in a moribund Soviet Union, to issues raised in the student-run campus newspaper. On this particular day he shares a meal with a small group of enthusiastic young people, when one young lady repeats to him something he has said in class as though it were gospel truth. Rattled by this sudden and unexpected evidence of his own influence on her, he tries to maintain his composure and continues his end of the conversation as best he can. One by one, the students leave the table to attend class or study until finally the professor himself returns to his office to prepare for the next lecture.*

After going to bed that night, he is unable to sleep. As he lies awake, the words of James 3:1 keep running through his head: "Let not many of you become teachers, my brethren, for you know that we who teach shall be judged with greater strictness." Although he has understood cognitively that teachers have an impact on their students, this episode underscores for him in a profound way the fearful responsibility of a teacher to model truth-seeking—and even love—to those in his care.

The author of I John writes: "Beloved, let us love one another, because love is from God; everyone who loves is born of God and knows God. Whoever does not love does not know God, for God is love" (I John 4:7, NRSV). Although we are not generally accustomed to hearing love and authority used in the same breath, there is more than an incidental connection between the two concepts. We have been arguing here for the centrality of authority in understanding the unique place of human beings in God's creation. Yet, as St. Augustine put it centuries ago, we are motivated in everything we do by what we love. Love is constitutive of our very identity. This love is either properly directed towards the God who has created and redeemed us, or it is misdirected towards something God has created. Echoing Augustine, St. Thomas à Kempis writes that "love is born of God, and only in God, above all he has created, can it find rest."[1]

In the synoptic gospels one of the Pharisees, a man said to be a scribe or lawyer, approaches Jesus and asks him which is the greatest commandment. Jesus responds without hesitation: "You shall love the Lord your God with all your heart, and with all your soul, and with all your mind. This is the great and first commandment. And a second is like it, You shall love your neighbor as yourself. On these two commandments depend all the law and the prophets" (Matt 22:37-40; cf. Mark 12:28-34; Luke 10:25-28). Note the word *all*. The command to love God and neighbor is all-embracing. As it includes the whole of life, nothing is exempt from this command.

This includes the authoritative offices that God has given us as his image. In everything we do, we properly manifest love for God and neighbor, although this love takes different forms depending on the specific office we are exercising. As we have repeatedly noted above, each of us bears multiple offices simultaneously in response to God's call. We should never pretend that our callings are singular in nature. Young people in the classroom are typically trying to discern their calling in life, by which they usually mean their career or livelihood. Yet this is only part of what is meant by calling. In the real world, every one of us assumes a variety of offices each of which carries God-given authority. I am simultaneously husband, father, son, brother, uncle, citizen, church member, teacher, amateur composer and poet, consumer, producer, owner, employee, and so forth. None of these exhausts who I am as created in God's image, yet neither can these offices be separated from that image.

Love is manifested in each of these offices in different ways. For the last century or more, popular music has lopsidedly focused on the romantic love between a man and a woman to the virtual exclusion of other manifestations of love. However, one might notice that few of these

---

1. Thomas à Kempis, *The Imitation of Christ*, 3.5, 91.

songs reference marriage or the offices of husband and wife explicitly.[2] Similarly, although there are many songs about love lost, few make mention of divorce and its impact on the institution of marriage and the communities with which it is so intimately connected.[3] The larger western culture prefers to think of love—especially romantic, sexual love—as free-floating and liberated from the apparent oppressiveness of an institution. Some songs are written about parental love of children and a very few about the love of sons or daughters for parents.[4] Still to be written are songs of nonromantic love in the classroom, in industry, in agriculture, in the market or in the halls of political power. Yet each of these venues is indeed a proper setting for living out the divine command to love God and neighbor.

To do public justice is the primary means of showing love in the political realm. The body politic is not a macro-family, but a jurally-qualified community of government and citizens whose members bear authoritative offices oriented towards the central task of seeking this justice. The term patriotism does not entirely cover this type of love, as the former has more to do with a sentimental attachment to one's homeland than with seeking justice as such. Political loyalty is perhaps the more descriptive term. The focus of patriotism may be either more or less extensive than political loyalty, in accordance with the overlapping identities characterizing real people in real societies. Yet where patriotism may encompass a number of loves, e.g., of the land itself, of its people, of a culture or multiple cultures therein, political loyalty is more immediately connected to the authoritative offices of citizen and ruler.

Much of my own experience is that of an educator in the classroom. Although a teacher may develop genuine affection for his students, the primary way in which he shows love in the classroom is by preparing well for lectures and seminars, informing students of expectations in the syllabus and keeping to them, marking and returning assignments fairly and expeditiously and in general respecting the authoritative office of student by leading those under his care towards the truth. Reciprocally,

---

2. One of the few is Sammy Cahn and Jimmy Van Heusen's 1955 song, *Love and Marriage*, famously recorded by Frank Sinatra for Capitol Records.

3. Hal David and Burt Bacharach's *Mexican Divorce* (1961), recorded by the Drifters for Atlantic Records, falls into this category.

4. Eddie Fisher's *Oh, My Papa* was a hit song in 1954 for the singer, though tellingly its origin was Swiss and not American. Composer Paul Burkhard wrote *O mein Papa* for the 1939 musical play, *Der Schwarze Hecht*.

the student best shows love by fulfilling the assignments, contributing to discussion when called upon to do so, studying for examinations and generally respecting the offices of student held by his peers and of teacher under whose guidance he seeks the truth. In other words, the principal manifestation of love in the classroom is a distinctively pedagogical love, not to be confused with sexual, familial, or other kinds of love. No one is likely to write a song about it, but it is no less significant for that.

God's love for us, created in his image, is more than we can possibly imagine. Although we repeatedly fail in our efforts to live for his glory, God remains faithful to us as no one else could possibly be. His love for us is so great that he assumed flesh in the person of Jesus Christ, who is himself "the image of the invisible God, the first-born of all creation" (Col 1:15). Though all human beings are created in God's image, we who are in Christ bear a special likeness to God through his Son. If redemption restores the good creation, it also restores in us the image of God that was marred by sin. St. Paul famously draws a comparison between the first Adam, created in God's image and fallen into sin, with the second Adam, Jesus Christ, who has defeated sin through his death and resurrection and restored that image to its full glory. Here is Paul, writing to the church at Corinth: "For as in Adam all die, so also in Christ shall all be made alive" (I Cor. 15:22). And to the church at Rome: "If, because of one man's trespass, death reigned through that one man, much more will those who receive the abundance of grace and the free gift of righteousness reign in life through the one man Jesus Christ" (Rom 5:17).

Above all, the image of God, in which we are created and which is renewed in us in Christ, entails a grant of authority, as indicated especially in Psalm 8. Here human beings are granted stewardship over the whole creation. The psalmist runs through an array of God's creatures in heaven, earth, and sea, of which he says: "You have given him dominion over the works of your hands." Humanity has a special relationship with God above all of his creatures. We alone are called to authority over the whole creation. This authority finds its ultimate meaning in our covenantal relationship with God, who is pleased to use it for his glory as he works out his purposes in the world. Our own labors in God's world must be understood to point to the final consummation of creation at the return of Christ, in whom all human offices find their fulfillment. We work as those desiring a better country (Heb 11:16), hopeful that our imperfect efforts might be counted among the wealth of the nations brought before the King of kings in the new heaven and earth (Isa 60:11, Rev 21:24–26).

All human authority derives from God's sovereignty, as Romans 13:1 affirms. This authority is not to be confused with ability—with the mere power to do something. Nor should it be opposed to freedom, which itself has no meaning apart from divinely-instituted authority. Authority is not an arbitrary principle legitimated only through consent, but has a divine origin. Authority is a lofty office given to all human beings, who exercise it in diverse ways according to their respective callings. Only by living in grateful obedience to God's call can we truly know his love for us and hope to fulfill the divine image perfected and redeemed in Christ Jesus our Lord.

Bibliography

Adams, E. Maynard. "Philosophical Grounds of the Present Crisis of Authority." *Southern Journal of Philosophy* 8, nos. 2–3 (1970) 129–42.
Adelman, Frederick, ed. *Authority*. The Hague: Nijhoff, 1974.
Adizes, Ichak. *Industrial Democracy: Yugoslav Style*. New York: Free, 1971.
Adorno, T. W., et al. *The Authoritarian Personality*. New York: Norton, 1950.
Almond, Gabriel, and Sidney Verba. *The Civic Culture: Political Attitudes and Democracy in Five Nations*. Princeton: Princeton University Press, 1963.
———. *The Civic Culture Revisited*. Newbury Park, CA: Sage, 1980.
Althusius, Johannes. *The Politics of Althusius*. Abridged and translated by Frederick S. Carney. Boston: Beacon, 1964.
Arendt, Hannah, "What Is Authority?" In *Between Past and Future*, 91–141. New York: Viking, 1968.
———. *Eichmann in Jerusalem: A Report on the Banality of Evil*. Rev ed. New York: Viking, 1964.
———. *The Human Condition*. Chicago: University of Chicago Press, 1958.
———. *The Life of the Mind*. 2 vols. in one. New York: Harcourt Brace Jovanovich, 1978.
———. *On Revolution*. New York: Viking, 1963.
Aristotle. *Nicomachaean Ethics*.
———. *The Politics*. Translated by Benjamin Jowett. In *The Basic Works of Aristotle*, edited by Richard McKeon, 1113–1316. New York: Random House, 1941.
Austin, John. *Lectures on Jurisprudence, or The Philosophy of Positive Law*. 2 volumes. Ed. R. Campbell. 4th ed. London: John Murray, 1873.
———. *The Province of Jurisprudence Determined*. Ed. W. Rumble. 1832. New ed., Cambridge: Cambridge University Press, 1995.
Austin, Victor Lee. *Up With Authority: Why We Need Authority to Flourish as Human Beings*. London: T. & T. Clark, 2010.
Barth, Karl. *Church Dogmatics*. 4/1: *The Doctrine of Reconciliation*. Edinburgh: T. & T. Clark, 1956.
Bavinck, Herman. *Reformed Dogmatics*. Vol. 2, *God and Creation*. Trans. John Vriend. Grand Rapids: Baker Academic, 2004.
Benne, Kenneth Dean. *A Conception of Authority: An Introductory Study*. New York: Columbia University Teachers College, 1943.
Beran, Harry. *The Consent Theory of Political Obligation*. London: Croon Helm, 1987.
Berger, Peter. *The Heretical Imperative: Contemporary Possibilities of Religious Affirmation*. Garden City, NY: Anchor, 1979.

Berkouwer, G. C. *Man: the Image of God*. Grand Rapids: Eerdmans, 1962.
Berlin, Sir Isaiah. "Two Concepts of Liberty." In *Four Essays on Liberty*, 118–72. Oxford: Oxford University Press, 1969.
Biddle, Francis. *Justice Holmes, Natural Law and the Supreme Court*. New York: Macmillan, 1961.
Blaine Harris, R., ed. *Authority: A Philosophical Analysis*. Tuscaloosa: University of Alabama Press, 1976.
Bousfield, Arthur and Garry Toffoli. "The 'British' Character of Canada." *Monarchy Canada* (April 1996) n.p. http://www.monarchist.ca/mc/britchar.htm.
Brague, Rémi. *The Law of God: The Philosophical History of an Idea*. Chicago: University of Chicago Press, 2007.
Bratt, James D., ed. *Abraham Kuyper: A Centennial Reader*. Carlisle, UK: Paternoster, 1998.
Brunner, Emil. *The Christian Doctrine of Creation and Redemption*. Translated by Olive Wyon. Philadelphia: Westminster, 1952.
———. *Justice and the Social Order*. Translated by Mary Hottinger. New York: Harper & Brothers, 1945.
Buijs, Govert. "'Que les Latins appellent maiestatem': An Exploration into the Theological Background of the Concept of Sovereignty." In *Sovereignty in transition*, edited by Neil Walker, 229–57. Oxford: Hart, 2003.
Burke, Edmund. *Reflections on the Revolution in France*. Harvard Classics. Danbury, CT: Grolier, 1980.
Cai Hua, *A Society without Fathers or Husbands: The Na of China*. Brooklyn: Zone, 2001.
Calvin, John. *Institutes of the Christian Religion*. Edited by John T. McNeill. Translated by Ford Lewis Battles. 2 vols. Library of Christian Classics 20–21. Philadelphia: Westminster, 1960.
Carlson-Thies, Stanley W., and James W. Skillen, eds. *Welfare in America: Christian Perspectives on a Policy in Crisis*. Grand Rapids: Eerdmans, 1996.
"A Catechisme." In *The Book of Common Prayer*, n.p. 1559. http://justus.anglican.org/resources/bcp/1559/Confirmation_1559.htm.
Cebik, L. B. "History's Want of Authority-Some Logical and Historical Speculations." *Southern Journal of Philosophy* 8, nos. 2–3 (1970) 143–56.
Chaplin, Jonathan. "Defining 'Public Justice' in a Pluralistic Society: Probing a Key Neo-Calvinist Insight." *Pro Rege* 32, no. 3 (2004) 1–11.
———. *Herman Dooyeweerd: Christian Philosopher of State and Civil Society*. Notre Dame: University of Notre Dame Press, 2010.
Clark, Burton R. "Faculty Authority." *Bulletin of the American Association of University Professors* 47 (1961) 293–302.
Clouser, Roy A. *The Myth of Religious Neutrality: An Essay on the Hidden Role of Religious Belief in Theories*. Rev. ed. Notre Dame: University of Notre Dame Press, 2005.
Coles, Robert. *The Moral Life of Children*. Boston: Atlantic Monthly, 1986.
Committee on Adolescence. *Power and Authority In Adolescence: The Origins and Resolutions of Intergenerational Conflict*. New York: Group for the Advancement of Psychiatry, 1978.
Cooper, John C. "Crisis of Authority in the Protestant Churches of the U.S." *Southern Journal of Philosophy* 8, nos. 2–3 (1970) 117–20.

Courier, Paul-Louis. *Lettres au rédacteur du Censeur*, Lettre X, 10 mars 1820. *Œuvres*, 62–63. Paris: Firmin didot, 1845. Quoted in Yves R. Simon, *Philosophy of Democratic Government* (Chicago: University of Chicago Press, 1951).

Crick, Bernard. *In Defence of Politics*. 5th ed. London: Continuum, 2000.

"Crisis of Authority." Special issue, *Southern Journal of Philosophy* 8, nos. 2–3 (1970).

De George, Richard T. *The Nature and Limits of Authority*. Lawrence: University Press of Kansas, 1985.

De George, Richard T. "Function and Limits of Epistemic Authority." *Southern Journal of Philosophy* 8, nos. 2–3 (1970) 199–204.

De Maistre, Joseph. *Essay on the Generative Principle of Political Constitutions*. In *The Works of Joseph de Maistre*, edited by Jack Lively, 147–81. New York: Macmillan, 1965.

DeRosa, Marshall L. *The Confederate Constitution of 1861: An Inquiry into American Constitutionalism*. Columbia: University of Missouri Press, 1991.

Dewey, John. "Authority and Social Change." In *The Later Works of John Dewey*, edited by Jo Ann Boydston. 11:130–145. Carbondale: Southern Illinois University, 1987.

Dewey, John, and James H. Tufts. *Ethics*. New York: Holt, 1908.

Diggins, John P., and Mark E. Kann, eds. *The Problem of Authority in America*. Philadelphia: Temple University Press, 1981.

Dooyeweerd, Herman. *In the Twilight of Western Thought*. Nutley, NJ: Craig, 1980.

———. *A New Critique of Theoretical Thought*. 4 vols. Philadelphia: Presbyterian & Reformed, 1953–1958.

———. *The Roots of Western Culture: Pagan, Secular, and Christian Options*. Toronto: Wedge, 1979.

———. *De Wijsbegeerte der Wetsidee*. Amsterdam: H. J. Paris, 1935–36.

Eco, Umberto. *A Theory of Semiotics*. Bloomington: Indiana University Press, 1976.

Éducation, Loisir, et Sport, Québec. Ethics and Religious Culture. N.p. http://www.mels.gouv.qc.ca/fileadmin/site_web/documents/publications/BSM/Aff_religieuses/AvisProgECR_a.pdf.

Engels, Friedrich. "On Authority." In *Marx-Engels Reader*, edited by Robert C. Tucker, 730–33. New York: Norton, 2nd ed., 1978; 1st ed., 1972.

Engelsma, David J. "Labor Union Membership in the Light of Scripture." Pamphlet, n.p. Lansing, IL: Peace Protestant Reformed Church. http://www.prca.org/pamphlets/pamphlet_86.html, last modified 3 December 2004.

Evans, C. Stephen. *Kierkegaard's Ethic of Love*. Oxford: Oxford University Press, 2004.

Farrow, Douglas. "The Audacity of the State." *Touchstone*. 23, no. 1 (2010) n.p. http://www.touchstonemag.com/archives/article.php?id=23-21-028-f.

Filmer, Sir Robert. *Patriarcha*. 1680.

Finnis, John. *Natural Law and Natural Rights*. Oxford: Oxford University Press, 1980.

Flathman, Richard E. *The Practice of Political Authority: Authority and the Authoritative*. Chicago: University of Chicago Press, 1980.

"The Form and Order of Service that is to be performed and the Ceremonies that are to be observed in The Coronation of Her Majesty Queen Elizabeth II in the Abbey Church of St. Peter, Westminster, on Tuesday, the second day of June, 1953." An Anglican Liturgical Library, n.p. http://www.oremus.org/liturgy/coronation/cor1953b.html.

Frank, William A. "Authority as Nurse of Freedom and the Common Good." *Faith & Reason*(1990) n.p. Online: http://www.ewtn.com/library/THEOLOGY/FR90404.HTM.

Friedrich, Carl J. *Tradition and Authority*. London: Macmillan, 1962.

Friedrich, Carl J., ed. *Nomos 1: Authority*. Cambridge, MA: Harvard University Press, 1958.

Foucault, Michel. *Discipline and Punish: The Birth of the Prison*. New York: Pantheon, 1977.

———. *Power/Knowledge: Selected Interviews and Other Writings, 1972–1977*. New York: Pantheon, 1980.

Fukuyama, Francis. *The Great Disruption: Human Nature and the Reconstitution of Social Order*. New York: Free, 1999.

———. Review of *The War Against Authority: From the Crisis of Legitimacy to a New Social Contract*, by Nicholas Kittrie. *Foreign Affairs*, May/June 1996, n.p. http://www.foreignaffairs.org/19960501fabook3909/nicholas-n-kittrie/the-war-against-authority-from-the-crisis-of-legitimacy-to-a-new-social-contract.html.

———. *Trust: The Social Virtues and the Creation of Prosperity*. New York: Simon & Schuster, 1995.

Fürstenberg, Friedrich. "West German Experience with Industrial Democracy." *Annals of the American Academy of Political and Social Science: Industrial Democracy in Comparative Perspective* 431, no. 1 (1977) 44–53.

Glendon, Mary Ann. *Rights Talk: The Impoverishment of Political Discourse*. New York: Free, 1991

Goldman, Emma. *Anarchism and Other Essays*. New York: Dover, 1969.

Goudzwaard, Bob. *Capitalism and Progress: A Diagnosis of Western Society*. Toronto: Wedge, 1979.

Granrose, John T. "The Authority of Conscience." *Southern Journal of Philosophy* 8, nos. 2–3 (1970) 205–13.

Grant, George Parkin. *English Speaking Justice*. New ed. Toronto: House of Anansi, 1985.

Green, Leslie. *The Authority of the State*. Oxford: Oxford University Press, 1989.

Groen van Prinsterer, G. "Unbelief and Revolution." In *Groen van Prinsterer's Lectures on Unbelief and Revolution*, by Harry Van Dyke, n.p. Jordan Station, ON: Wedge, 1989.

Grootenboer, Ed. *In Pursuit of Justice: So Far, So Good: The first 50 years of the Christian Labour Association of Canada, 1952–2002*. Mississauga, ON: Christian Labour Association of Canada, 2005.

"A Guide to Charitable Choice." Center for Public Justice and the Center for Law and Religious Freedom of the Christian Legal Society, 1997, n.p. http://www.cpjustice.org/files/CCGuide_0.pdf.

Gutmann, Amy, and Dennis Thompson. *Democracy and Disagreement: Why Moral Conflict Cannot Be Avoided in Politics, and What Should Be Done About It*. Cambridge, MA: Belknap, 1996.

Hamilton, Edith, and Hutington Cairns, eds. *The Collected Dialogues of Plato, including the Letters*. Bollingen Series 71. Princeton: Princeton University Press, 1961.

Harris, James. "Concept of Authority and Performative Utterances." *Southern Journal of Philosophy* 8, nos. 2–3 (1970) 215–22.

Hart, D. G. *Recovering Mother Kirk: The Case for Liturgy in the Reformed Tradition*. Grand Rapids: Baker, 2003.
Hart, H. L. A. *The Concept of Law*. Oxford: Oxford University Press, 1961.
Havers, G. "Between Athens and Jerusalem: Western otherness in the thought of Leo Strauss and Hannah Arendt." *The European Legacy* 9, no. 1 (2004) 19–29.
Henderson, Dorothy, and Don Muir. "Term Service For Elders." *For Elders*, November/2005 (Presbyterian Church in Canada). No pages. Online: http://web.archive.org/web/20110709025244/http://www.presbyterian.ca/files/webfm/ourresources/education/eldership/for_elders/for_elders_nov05.pdf..
Hobbes, Thomas. *Leviathan, Or, Matter, Form, and Power of a Commonwealth Ecclesiastical and Civil*. Vol. 23 of *Great Books*, 41–283. 1651.
Hogue, Arthur R. *Origins of the Common Law*. Indianapolis: Liberty, 1985. Reprint, Bloomington, Indiana: Indiana University Press, 1966.
Holmes, Oliver Wendell. "The Path of the Law." In *The Essential Holmes*, by Richard Posner, 160–76. Chicago: University of Chicago Press, 1992.
Homans, George Caspar. *The Human Group*. New York: Harcourt Brace Jovanovich, 1950.
Hunt, Sir David, ed. *Footprints in Cyprus: an illustrated history*. London: Trigraph, 1990.
Huntington, Samuel P. *Political Order in Changing Societies*. New Haven: Yale University Press, 1968.
Ignatieff, Michael. *Human Rights as Politics and Idolatry*. Princeton: Princeton University Press, 2001.
———. *The Needs of Strangers: An essay on privacy, solidarity, and the politics of being human*. New York: Viking, 1984.
———. *The Rights Revolution*. Toronto: House of Anansi, 2000.
———. *True Patriot Love: Four Generations in Search of Canada*. Toronto: Viking Canada, 2009.
Jenkins, Iredell. "Authority: Its Nature and Locus." *Southern Journal of Philosophy* 8, nos. 2–3 (1970) 177–90.
Jouvenel, Bertrand de. *Sovereignty: An Inquiry into the Political Good*. Translated by J. F. Huntington. Chicago: University of Chicago Press, 1957.
———. "Authority: The Efficient Imperative." In *Nomos 1: Authority*, edited by Carl J. Friedrich, 159–69. Cambridge, MA: Harvard University Press, 1958.
Kalsbeek, L. *Contours of a Christian Philosophy*. Toronto: Wedge, 1975.
Kant, Immanuel. *Fundamental Principles of the Metaphysics of Morals*. 1785. Translated by W. Hastie. In *Great Books of the Western World*, edited by Robert Maynard Hutchins, 42:251–287. Chicago: Encyclopaedia Britannica, 1952.
———. *Critique of Practical Reason*. 1788. Translated by Thomas Kingsmill Abbott. In *Great Books of the Western World*, edited by Robert Maynard Hutchins, 42:289–361. Chicago: Encyclopaedia Britannica, 1952.
Kaplan, Abraham. "Crisis of Authority." *Southern Journal of Philosophy* 8, nos. 2–3 (1970) 107–16.
Keener, Craig S. *Paul, Women & Wives: Marriage and Women's Ministry in the Letters of Paul*. Peabody, MA: Hendrickson, 1992.
King, Martin Luther, Jr. "Letter from Birmingham Jail." 16 April 1963. African Studies Center, University of Pennsylvania, n.p. http://www.africa.upenn.edu/Articles_Gen/Letter_Birmingham.html.

Kinsella, The Honourable Noël A. "Can Canada Afford a Charter of Social and Economic Rights?—Toward a Canadian Social Charter." A paper prepared for the Chains & Links: Human Rights Activism Conference, Saskatoon, SK, November 1–2, 2007, n.p. http://sen.parl.gc.ca/nkinsella/PDF/Speeches/CanadianSocialCharter-e.pdf.

Kirk, Russell. *The Politics of Prudence*. Bryn Mawr, PA: ISI, 1993.

Kittrie, Nicholas. *The War Against Authority: From the Crisis of Legitimacy to a New Social Contract*. Baltimore: Johns Hopkins University Press, 1995.

Knag, Sigmund. "The Almighty, Impotent State Or, the Crisis of Authority." *Independent Review* 1, no. 3 (1997) 397–412.

Kohlberg, Lawrence. *The Philosophy of Moral Development*. Vol. 1, *Essays on Moral Development*. New York: Harper & Row, 1981.

Koyzis, David T. *Political Visions and Illusions: A Survey and Christian Critique of Contemporary Ideologies*. Downers Grove, IL: InterVarsity, 2003.

———. "We Answer to Another: A Defence of Authority Against Its Recent Discontents." Inaugural Lecture Series, number 15. Ancaster, ON: Redeemer University College, 2003.

Kraynak, Robert. *Christian Faith and Modern Democracy: God and Politics in the Fallen World*. Notre Dame: University of Notre Dame Press, 2001.

Kropotkin, Prince Peter A. "Law and Authority,. In *The Essential Kropotkin: A general selection from the writings of the great Russian anarchist thinker*, edited by Emile Capouya and Keitha Tompkins, 27–43. New York: Liveright, 1975.

Kuic, Vukan. *Yves R. Simon: Real Democracy*. Lanham, MD: Rowman & Littlefield, 1999.

Kuyper, Abraham. *Lectures on Calvinism*. Peabody, MA: Hendrickson, 2008.

Lasch, Christopher. *The Revolt of the Elites and the Betrayal of Democracy*. New York: Norton, 1995.

Laski, Harold. *A Grammar of Politics*. 5th ed. London: Allen & Unwin, 1967.

League of Nations. "Geneva Declaration of the Rights of the Child." 1924. No pages. Online: http://www.un-documents.net/gdrc1924.htm.

Lipset, Seymour Martin. *Continental divide: the values and institutions of the United States and Canada*. New York: Routledge, 1990.

Locke, John. *A Letter Concerning Toleration*. Translated by William Popple. In *Great Books of the Western World*, edited by Robert Maynard Hutchins, 35:1–22. Chicago: Encyclopædia Britannica, 1952.

———. *Two Treatises on Civil Government. Second Treatise: an Essay concerning The True Original, Extent, and End of Civil-Government*. 1690. In *Great Books of the Western World*, edited by Robert Maynard Hutchins, 35:23–81. Chicago: Encyclopædia Britannica, 1952.

Loyola High School. No pages. Online: http://www.loyola.ca/.

Loyola High School v. Courchesnes, Épilogue, 331. Soquij: Intelligence Juridique, n.p. http://www.jugements.qc.ca/php/decision.php?liste=46252591&doc=7FF18D89A2AE5ADB9810CF4B60DAFDFCF774F8F11CE85819B903D21A6CECE9FD&page=1.

Loyola High School v. Courchesnes (2010), Summary of the Judgment. No pages. Online: http://www.mcgill.ca/files/prpp/Loyola_Judgment_English_Summary.pdf.

Luhmann, Niklas. *The Differentiation of Society*. Translated by Stephen Holmes and Charles Larmore. New York: Columbia University Press, 1982.

Machiavelli, Niccolò. *The Prince.* Translated by W. K. Marriott. Edited by Robert Maynard Hutchins. Vol. 23 of *Great Books of the Western World.* Chicago: Encyclopædia Britannica, 1952. Originally published as *Il Principe* (1532).
MacIntyre, Alasdair. *After Virtue.* 3rd ed. Notre Dame: University of Notre Dame Press, 2007.
———. *Three Rival Versions of Moral Enquiry: Encyclopaedia, Genealogy, and Tradition.* Notre Dame: University of Notre Dame Press, 1990.
———. *Whose Justice? Which Rationality?* Notre Dame: University of Notre Dame Press, 1988.
Mannheim, Karl. *Ideology and Utopia: An Introduction to the Sociology of Knowledge.* New York: Harcourt, Brace, 1936.
Mao Zedong. "Problems of War and Strategy." [November 6, 1938.] In *Selected Works,* vol. 2, n.p. Beijing, China: Foreign Languages Press. http://www.marxists.org/reference/archive/mao/selected-works/volume-2/mswv2_12.htm.
Maritain, Jacques. *Man and the State.* Chicago: University of Chicago Press, 1951.
Marx, Karl, and Frederick Engels. *Basic Writings on Politics and Philosophy.* Edited by Lewis S. Feuer. Garden City, NY: Anchor, 1959.
———. *Selected Works in One Volume.* New York: International, 1968.
Mathieu, Christine. *A History and Anthropological Study of the Ancient Kingdoms of the Sino-Tibetan Borderland—Naxi and Mosuo.* Lewiston, NY: Mellen, 2003.
Mayer, John. "Transformation of the Role of Authority in the Modern World." *Southern Journal of Philosophy* 8, nos. 2–3 (1970) 171–76.
McIntire, C. T., ed. *The Legacy of Herman Dooyeweerd.* Lanham, MD: University Press of America, 1985.
Mitcham, Carl, and Jim Grote, eds. *Theology and Technology.* Lanham, MD: University Press of America, 1984.
Middleton, J. Richard. *The Liberating Image: The* Imago Dei *in Genesis 1.* Grand Rapids: Brazos, 2005.
Milgram, Stanley. *Obedience to Authority.* New York: Harper & Row, 1974.
Mill, John Stuart. *On Liberty.* 4th ed. London: Longman, Roberts & Green, 1869.
Miller, Arthur G., Barry E. Collins, and Diana E. Brief. "Perspectives on obedience to authority: the legacy of the Milgram experiments." *Journal of Social Issues* 51 (1995) 1–19.
Molnar, Thomas. *Authority and its Enemies.* New Rochelle, NY: Arlington House, 1976.
Mott, Stephen Charles. *A Christian Perspective on Political Thought.* Oxford: Oxford University Press, 1993.
Muller, Alexander V., ed. *The Spiritual Regulation of Peter the Great.* Seattle and London: University of Washington Press, 1972.
Nemni, Max, and Monique Nemni. *Young Trudeau: Son of Quebec, Father of Canada, 1919–1944.* Translated by William Johnson. Toronto: McClelland & Stewart, 2006.
Neuhaus, Richard John. *The Naked Public Square: Religion and Democracy in America.* Grand Rapids: Eerdmans, 1984.
The New Cassell's German Dictionary. New York: Funk & Wagnalls, 1971.
Nisbet, Robert. *The Twilight of Authority.* New York: Oxford University Press, 1975.
O'Donovan, Joan Lockwood. *Theology of Law and Authority in the English Reformation.* Atlanta: Scholars, 1991.
O'Donovan, Oliver. *The Desire of the Nations: Rediscovering the roots of political theology.* Cambridge: Cambridge University Press, 1996.

———. *Resurrection and Moral Order*. Leicester, UK: InterVarsity, 1986.

———. *The Ways of Judgment*. Grand Rapids: Eerdmans, 2005.

O'Donovan, Oliver, and Joan Lockwood O'Donovan, eds. *From Irenaeus to Grotius: A Sourcebook in Christian Political Thought*. Grand Rapids: Eerdmans, 1999.

Olsen, Glenn W. "John Rawls and the Flight from Authority: The Quest for Equality as an Exercise in Primitivism." *Interpretation* 21, no. 3 (1994) 419–36.

104th Congress. "Personal Responsibility and Work Opportunity Reconciliation Act. Public Law 104-193." August 22, 1996, n.p. http://frwebgate.access.gpo.gov/cgi-bin/getdoc.cgi?dbname=104_cong_public_laws&docid=f:publ193.104.pdf.

O'Neill, John. "Authority, Knowledge and the Body Politic." *Southern Journal of Philosophy* 8, nos. 2–3 (1970) 255–64.

Ontario Ministry of Intergovernmental Affairs. "A Canadian Social Charter: Making Our Shared Values Stronger: A Discussion Paper." Toronto, Ontario Ministry of Intergovernmental Affairs, 1991.

Pareto, Vilfredo. *The Mind and Society: A Treatise on General Sociology*. 4 vols. New York: Harcourt, Brace, 1935. Reprint, New York: Dover, 1963.

———. *Sociological Writings*. Selected and Introduced by Samuel E. Finer. Translated by Derick Mirfin. New York: Praeger, 1966.

Parsons, Talcott. "Authority, Legitimation, and Political Action." In *Nomos 1: Authority*, edited by Carl J. Friedrich, 197–221. Cambridge, MA: Harvard University Press, 1958 (citations are from this edition). Republished in Parsons, *Structure and Process in Modern Societies*, 170–198. Glencoe, IL: Free, 1960.

Passerin d'Entrèves, Alexander. *Natural Law: An Historical Survey*. 1951. Reprint, New York: Harper Torchbooks, 1965.

———. *The Notion of the State: An Introduction to Political Theory*. Oxford: Oxford University Press, 1967.

Pasternak, Boris. *Doctor Zhivago*. London: Collins Sons, 1958.

Pennock, J. Roland, and John W. Chapman. *Anarchism* (Nomos 19). New York: New York University Press, 1978.

Peters, Richard Stanley. *Authority, Responsibility, and Education*. New York: Eriksson-Taplinger, 1960.

Piaget, Jean. *The Moral Judgement of the Child*. Translated by Marjorie Gabain. Harmondsworth, UK: Penguin, 1977. Originally published by Routledge, 1932.

Plachno, Larry. *Sunset Lines: The Story of the Chicago Aurora & Elgin Railroad: 2—History*. Polo, IL: Transportation Trails, 1989.

Plato. *The Republic*. Translated by Paul Shorey. In *Plato: The Collected Dialogues*, edited by Edith Hamilton and Huntington Cairns, 575–844. Princeton: Princeton University Press, 1961.

———. *The Statesman*. Translated by J. B. Skemp. In *Plato: The Collected Dialogues*, edited by Edith Hamilton and Huntington Cairns, 1018–85. Princeton: Princeton University Press, 1961.

———. *The Laws*. Translated by A. E. Taylor. In *Plato: The Collected Dialogues*, edited by Edith Hamilton and Huntington Cairns, 1225–1513. Princeton: Princeton University Press, 1961.

Putnam, Robert. *Making Democracy Work: Civic Traditions in Modern Italy*. Princeton: Princeton University Press, 1993.

Peters, Richard Stanley, and Peter Winch. "Authority." In *Political Philosophy*, edited by Anthony Quinton, 83–111. London: Oxford, 1967. [Exchange between Richard Stanley Peters (pp. 83–96) and Peter Winch (pp. 97–111).]
Rawls, John. *A Theory of Justice*. 2nd ed. Cambridge, MA: Belknap, 1999.
Raz, Joseph, ed. *Authority*. New York: New York University Press, 1990.
Rhodes, Cllifford. *Authority in a Changing Society*. London: Constable, 1969.
Right to Sight. No pages. Online: http://www.righttosight.com/.
Rookmaaker, Hans. *Modern Art and the Death of a Culture*. Downers Grove, IL: InterVarsity, 1970.
Roosevelt, Franklin D. State of the Union Message to Congress. 11 January 1944. American Presidency Project, Document Archive, n.p. Online: http://www.presidency.ucsb.edu/ws/index.php?pid=16518#axzz1YLXM9zxi.
Rothbard, Murray. *For a New Liberty*. New York: Macmillan, 1973.
Rousseau, Jean-Jacques. *On the Social Contract*. Translated by G. D. H. Cole. Edited by Robert Maynard Hutchins. Vol. 38 of *Great Books of the Western World*. Chicago: Encyclopædia Britannica, 1952.
Russell, Bertrand. *Authority and the Individual*. New York: Simon & Schuster, 1949.
———. *Power: A New Social Analysis*. New York: Norton, 1938.
Sabine, George H., and Thomas L. Thorson. *A History of Political Theory*. 4th ed. Hinsdale, IL: Dryden, 1973.
Salisbury, Harrison. *Black Night, White Snow: Russia's Revolutions, 1905–1917*. London: Cassell, 1978.
Schaeffer, Francis A. *Escape from Reason*. Downers Grove, IL: InterVarsity, 1968.
———. *The God Who Is There*. Downers Grove, IL: InterVarsity, 1968.
Schrotenboer, Paul. *Man in God's World (The Biblical Idea of Office)*. Distributed by the Christian Labour Association of Canada, Rexdale, Ontario. Reprinted from the October 1967 Issue of the International Reformed Bulletin.
Schuster, G. *Freedom and Authority in the West*. Notre Dame: University of Notre Dame Press, 1967.
Schwartz, Joel. *Fighting poverty with virtue: moral reform and America's urban poor, 1825–2000*. Bloomington: Indiana University Press, 2000.
Seath, J. D. Annalee. "Canadian Supreme Court Rules against Exemption in Religious Freedom Case." Turtle Bay and Beyond: International Law, Policy, and Institutions, February 22, 2012, n.p. http://www.turtlebayandbeyond.org/2012/family/canadian-supreme-court-rules-against-exemption-in-religious-freedom-case/.
Sennett, Richard. *Authority*. New York: Knopff, 1980.
Shakespeare, William. *King Lear*. Edited by William George Clarke and William Aldis Wright. In *Great Books of the Western World*, edited by Robert Maynard Hutchins, 27:244–83. Chicago: Encyclopaedia Britannica, 1952
Sietsma, Kornelis. *The Idea of Office*. Translated by Henry Vander Goot. St. Catherines, ON: Paideia, 1985.
Sikkel, C. J. *Een waarlijk vrije: levensschets van Dr Kornelis Sietsma (A Truly Free Man: A Sketch of the Life of Dr. Kornelis Sietsma)*. Amsterdam: Kirchner, n.d.
Simon, Yves R. *Freedom and Community*. New York: Fordham University Press, 1968.
———. *A General Theory of Authority*. Notre Dame: University of Notre Dame Press, 1962.
———. *Nature and Functions of Authority*. Milwaukee: Marquette University Press, 1940.

———. *Philosophy of Democratic Government*. Chicago: University of Chicago Press, 1951.

Skillen, James W., and Rockne M. McCarthy, eds. *Political Order and the Plural Structure of Society*. Atlanta: Scholars, 1991.

Skrupskelis, Ignas. "Royce and the Justification of Authority." *Southern Journal of Philosophy* 8, nos. 2–3 (1970) 165–70.

Smedes, Lewis. *Mere Morality: What God Expects from Ordinary People*. Grand Rapids: Eerdmans, 1983.

Smith, James K. A. *Desiring the Kingdom: Worship, Worldview, and Cultural Formation*. Cultural Liturgies 1. Grand Rapids: Baker, 2009.

Soto, Hernando de. *The Mystery of Capital: Why Capitalism Triumphs in the West and Fails Everywhere Else*. New York: Basic, 2000.

Southern Baptist Convention. *The Baptist Faith and Message*. N.p. http://www.sbc.net/bfm/bfm2000.asp#vi.

Strauss, Leo. *What Is Political Philosophy and Other Studies*. Westport, CT: Greenwood, 1959.

Thatcher, Margaret. Interview by Douglas Keay. *Woman's Own* 31 (1987) n.p. http://www.margaretthatcher.org/document/106689.

Thomas à Kempis. *The Imitation of Christ*. Translated by Ronald Knox and Michael Oakley. New York: Sheed and Ward, 1959.

Thomas Aquinas. *On Princely Government*. Translated by J. G. Dawson. In *Aquinas: Selected Political Writings*, edited by A. P. d'Entrèves, 2–83. Oxford: Blackwell, 1948.

"To Be and Not to Seem: My Mother-in-Law, Grand Duchess Olga Alexandrovna, An Interview with Olga Kulikovsky-Romanoff." *Road to Emmaus: A Journal of Orthodox Faith and Culture* 3, no. 4 (2002) 3–33. Online: http://www.roadtoemmaus.net/back_issue_articles/RTE_11/To_Be_and_Not_To_Seem.pdf.

Todd, John Murray, ed. *Problems of Authority*. Baltimore: Helicon, 1962.

United Nations General Assembly Resolution 1386. Declaration of the Rights of the Child. 1959, n.p. http://www.un.org/cyberschoolbus/humanrights/resources/child.asp.

United Nations General Assembly Resolution 44/25. Convention on the Rights of the Child. 1989, n.p. http://www.ohchr.org/en/professionalinterest/pages/crc.aspx.

Universal Declaration of Human Rights, n.p. http://www.un.org/en/documents/udhr/.

Vanderwoerd, Jim R. "Is the Newer Deal a Better Deal? Government Funding of Faith-Based Social Services." *Christian Scholar's Review* 31, no. 3 (2002) 301–18.

Vatican II. *Lumen Gentium, the Dogmatic Constitution on the Church*. 1964, n.p. http://www.vatican.va/archive/hist_councils/ii_vatican_council/documents/vat-ii_const_19641121_lumen-gentium_en.html.

Ware, Timothy (Bishop Kallistos). *The Orthodox Church*. New ed. London: Penguin, 1993.

Wearne, Bruce. "Dooyeweerd and Parsons: Some Initial Dot Points to Consider When Comparing the Philosophical Sociology of Herman Dooyeweerd with the General Theory of Society in Talcott Parsons' structural functionalism." No pages. Online: http://www.isi.salford.ac.uk/dooy/ext/parsons.html.

Webb, Sidney and Beatrice. *Industrial Democracy*. London: Longmans, Green, 1902.

Weber, Max. *Economy and Society: An Outline of Interpretive Sociology*. Edited by Guenther Roth and Claus Wittich. Berkeley: University of California Press, 1978.

Wolff, Robert Paul. *In Defense of Anarchism*. New York: Harper Torchbooks, 1976.
Wolterstorff, Nicholas. *Until Justice and Peace Embrace*. Grand Rapids: Eerdmans, 1983.
———. *Justice: Rights and Wrongs*. Princeton: Princeton University Press, 2008.
Woodcock, George. *Anarchism: a history of libertarian ideas and movements*. Cleveland: Meridian, 1962.

Index

A page number with an 'n' indicates the information is in the notes. An *f* indicates a figure.

ability vs. authority, 23–24
abuse
    of authority, 6, 149–51
    of children, 200–201
    of power, 25
Act of Settlement of 1701 (England), 114
Acton, Lord, 25
Adenauer, Konrad, 35
adolescents, 103
AFL Brotherhood of Telegraphers, Switchmen and Clerks, 210
African National Congress, 49
agentic state, 61, 79–81
agrarian communities, 103
Aleksandrovich, Mikhail, 18
Alighieri, Dante, 133
Almond, Gabriel, 112
Althusius, Johannes, 125, 132, 153, 155, 164–65
Ambtsgedachte (Sietsma), 137
American Civil Liberties Union, 203
American revolt of the American Confederacy (1861–64), 153, 154n33
American Revolution (1775–83), 153, 155, 157
Americans United for Separation of Church and State, 203
anarchism, 9, 26, 71–74
anticipatory analogies, 188
apartheid policies, 49

Aquinas (Thomas)
    autonomy of nature, 128
    image of God, 136
    just war, 153
    laws, types of, 124–25
    natural law, 118
    tyranny, 152
    unjust law, 129
    virtues, 127
Arbeitsdienst, 135
Arendt, Hannah
    as contractarian thinker, 44, 46
    Eichmann trial, 61
    freedom and, 66
    human will, 122
    liberal ideology, 63
    politics and economics, 176–77
    technology and, 56
aristocracy of merit, 101
Aristotle
    citizen, defined, 54
    communities and individuals, 191
    on education of children, 200
    household vs. polity, 176–77
    on justice, 129
    on monarchy, 117
    office as locus of authority, 111
    political pluralism, 178
    slaves by nature, 47
arranged marriage, 16, 106
atheism, 121
Athenian polis, 36

Augustine
  commonwealth defined by, 185
  eternal law and human law, 124
  image of God, 136
  just war, 153
  love, 223
  natural law and human nature, 118
  unjust law, 129
Austin, Victor Lee, 141, 144, 165, 172, 178–84
authoritarianism, 142
authoritative communication, 34–35
authoritative determination, 172
authoritative office
  claims of higher knowledge and, 54
  defined, 3, 8
  differentiation of, 163*f*
  as image of God, 8, 16, 163*f*
  natural ascendancy and, 52–53
  respect and, 140–41
  symbolic elements of, 27
authorities, defined, 199
authority
  abuse of, 6, 149–51
  of authenticity, 170
  defined, 34
  forfeiture of, 149–53, 158–59
  functions of, 171–78, 173*f*
  image of God and, 8, 16, 21–23, 91, 134–40
  images of, 33
  legitimacy of, 36
  limits to, 144–49
  of love, 222–26
  manifestation of, 4
  moral claim of, 37
  origin of, 35, 119–23
  over and under, 140–44, 213
  as performative concept, 180
  power and, 7–8, 17–28, 182–83
  as the principal coordinator, 3
  proper use of, 143–44
  subordination and, 196
  systematic theory of, 142n22
  taxonomy of, 165–71, 166*f*
  theology of, 178–84
  . *See also specific types of authority*

autonomy
  defined, 177–78
  freedom and, 59–71, 83–92
  Kantian anarchism, 71–74
  Kantian liberalism, 74–78
  quest for, 78–82
Ayatollah Ruhollah Khomeini, 158

Bacharach, Burt, 224n3
Bakunin, Mikhail, 71
Balkan Wars (1912–13), 49
Barth, Karl, 129–30, 136
Bavinck, Harman, 136
Beatrix (princess of Netherlands), 135
Becket, Thomas, 202
Belgic Confession, 204
Benedict XVI (pope), 109, 148
beneficence, 97
Bennett, R. B., 215
Bentham, Jeremy, 77
Berger, Peter, 84
Berkouwer, G. C., 136
Berlin, Isaiah, 65, 66
Bill of Rights of 1689 (England), 84
Bill of Rights of 1791 (U.S.), 65, 84, 218
biological superiority, 47–53
birthrate, 86
blind obedience, 34
Bodin, Jean, 13, 164, 197n81
Book of Mormon, 110
boundaries, 145
Bourbon monarchs of France, 120
Bowen, Helen, 29–30
Britain. *See* England
Brown vs. the Board of Education of Topeka, Kansas (1954), 49
Brunner, Emil, 136
Buddha, 70, 110
bureaucracy, 99–102
Burke Edmund, 156
Burkhard, Paul, 224n4
business enterprises, 104

Cahn, Sammy, 224n2
Calvin, John, 125, 136, 144, 152–53, 157, 164–65

Canada
   Charter of Rights and Freedoms, 85, 139, 218
   Constitution Acts, 94, 218
   Monarchist League, 107–8
   Queen's Privy Council, 93–94, 100, 114
   Roman Catholic tradition in, 160–62
Canada Revenue Agency, 42
Canadian National Institute for the Blind (CNIB), 90
Capetian monarchs of France, 119–20
capitalism, 31
Carlson-Thies, Stanley W., 219n107
case studies
   church and state authorities, 201–4
   multiple authoritative offices, 204–9
   parents' and children's authority, 197–201
   workplace authority, 209–14
categorical imperative, 10, 45, 74, 91
Catholic emancipation of 1828 (England), 203
Catholic tradition. *See* Roman Catholic tradition
Center for Public Justice, 219
challenges to authority, 36
Chaplin, Jonathan, 178, 189n73
Charest, Jean, 161
charismatic authority, 14, 51, 109–11, 151
charitable choice, 219
Charter of Rights and Freedoms (Canada), 85, 139, 218
Chiapas, Mexico, revolt (1994), 5
Chicago Aurora & Elgin Railroad, 210, 210n92
children, abuse of, 200–201
children's authority, 197–201
China, Great Cultural Revolution (1976), 157
choice-enhancement state, 119, 198
cholera epidemics, 216
Christian Labour Association of Canada (CLAC), 214

Christian worldview, 81
Chrysostomos (Archbishop, Church of Cyprus), 207
church
   attendance, 86, 86n51
   institutions, 15
   laity in, 205–6
   raison d'etre of the gathered church, 206
   state authorities and, 201–4, 219
   three-fold order of church office, 205
   as voluntary society, 195n78
   . *See also specific religions traditions*
Cicero, 124
citizens and citizenship, 54
civil disobedience, 129
civil religion, 45
Civilian Conservation Corps, (Roosevelt Administration), 217
Clouser, Roy, 21n5, 189n74
coach-driver theory of authority, 44
co-determination, in Germany, 212–13
coercive power, 25, 41, 182–83
collective bargaining agreements, 210, 213–14
collectivism, 191
collectivist consensus, 215
commanding presence, 31
common good, 173–74
common law, 116
Commonwealth of Nations, 98–99
communications, 34–35
communities
   authority and, 4
   boundaries of, 146–47
   coordinative function of, 4
   differentiation within, 103, 105–6
   formations of, 13–16
   identity of, 219
   individuals and, 191–92
   nonstate, 158–59
competence, 170
Concordat of 1801 (France), 203
consent, 51–52
Constantine (King of Greece), 151
Constantinople, 119, 205

Constitution Act of 1867 (Canada), 94
Constitution Act of 1982 (Canada), 218
constitutional governments, 18–19, 93–95, 100–102, 112–13
constitutional monarchies, 193
Continental Congress (American colonies), 153, 155
contractarian thinkers, 42–47, 52, 118
contracts
  pluriformity of authority and, 13
  voluntary, 41–47
Convention on the Rights of the Child of 1989 (CRC), 197, 218
corpus Christi, 146, 183–84
cosmic time, 187–88
Council of Florence (1439), 205
Council of Nicaea (787), 206n89
Courchesne, Michelle, 161
Courier, Paul-Louis, 44
Crick, Bernard, 55–56, 176–79, 217
Critique of the Gotha Programme (Marx), 65n8
Cultural Mandate, 21, 89, 135
culture of poverty, 220
customary laws, 113
cybernetics, 79
Cyprus Republic, 207

Dante, 147
David (King of Israel), 117
David, Hal, 224n3
David Engelsma, 211
de Gaulle, Charles, 35
De George, Richard, 56, 142n22, 165–71
de Jouvenel, Bertrand, 51–52
de Maistre, Joseph, 113
De Monarchia (Dante), 147
Decalogue, 70, 116
Declaration of Independence (U.S.), 42
Declaration of the Rights of Man (France), 171
Declaration of the Rights of the Child of 1924 (Geneva), 198

Declaration of the Rights of the Child of 1959 (UN), 198
deliberative democracy, 56
democracy and democratic theory, 46, 56, 101, 120, 122
denominationalism, 195
derived authority, 11
Derrida, Jacques, 39
despotic régime, 176
differentiation
  of authoritative offices, 163f
  within communities, 103, 105–6
  norm of, 12
  power and, 23
  process of, 12–13, 114
  rights and, 84–85
  in society, 102–9
disincentives, as instrument of power, 38–39
disobedient dependence, 29
diversity, 13–14
divine authority, 81
divine Giver, 98
divine image of God. *See imago Dei*
divine-right, of monarchies, 119–20, 119n44
divorce, 159, 195
Doctor Zhivago (Pasternak), 19
Dooyeweerd, Herman
  creation, 130
  dependence on God, 91
  differentiation of society, 103
  immanent horizon of experience, 13
  nature/grace groundmotive, 127
  pluriformity of authority, 165
  societal pluriformity, 132
  undifferentiated society, 105
Dugré, Gérard, 161
Dutch revolt against Spain (1568–1648), 153, 155, 157

Easton, David, 32–34, 63, 172
ecclesiastical authority, 148, 183, 201–4
economic enterprises, 15
education, of children, 199–200
Eichmann, Adolf, 61
élites, 55–56

Elizabeth II (Queen of England), 93, 98, 114
Ellul, Jacques, 12, 89
employee ownership, 212n97
employees, 209–14
enemy, 171
Engels, Friedrich, 88
Engelsma, David, 211, 214
England
    Act of Settlement, 114
    Bill of Rights, 84
    Catholic emancipation, 203
    "Glorious" Revolution, 153
    government traditions, 95
    Jewish emancipation, 203
    monarchy in, 119–20
    Plantagenets monarchs, 119–20
Epicurus and Epicureans, 40, 118
epistemic authority, 3, 54–57, 169, 170, 181–82
Essay on the Generative Principle of Political Constitutions (de Maistre), 113
eternal law, 124
ethnocentrism, 48
evil, 150
executive authority, 166–69, 201
exemplary authority, 169
expertise, 53–57

family, 105–6, 193
Farrow, Douglas, 87–88
fear, 41
feudalism, 31
Feuerbach, Ludwig, 137
Filmer, Robert, 107
Fisher, Eddie, 224n4
foreign affairs authority, 35–36
forfeiture of authority, 149–53, 158–59
Foucault, Michel, 39
foundational function, 189, 189n74
France
    Bourbon monarchs, 120
    Capetian monarchs, 119–20
    Concordat of, 203
    Declaration of the Rights of Man, 171
    French Law, 203
    Louis XVI, 156–57
    monarchy in, 119–20
    Revolution, 5, 34, 153, 156–57, 162, 186
    Roman Catholic tradition in, 203
    Third Republic, 203
Franco, Francisco, 171
freedom
    allure of, 66–71
    as authority, 83–92, 179–80
    as autonomy, 66–71
    of expression, 208
    inhibition of, 59–63
    personal freedom, 4
French Law (1905), 203
Friedrich, Carl J., 34–37, 51–52, 111, 112, 172
Fukuyama, Francis, 198

gender roles, 107, 107n17
gendered division of labor, 50–51
general will, 44–45, 67, 116
Geneva Declaration of the Rights of the Child (1924), 198
George VI (King of England), 98
Germany
    co-determination, 212–13
    labor laws, 212–13
    Nazis party, 49, 61, 134–35, 138
    Wilhelm II, 98
gifts, 16, 85, 97–98, 109
Giles of Rome, 133
Glendon, Mary Ann, 92
"Glorious" Revolution, England (1688–90), 153
God
    authority and, 119–23
    democratic theory and, 120
    dependence on, 91–92
    disagreement over, 121
    empowerment of, 8–9
    image of. *see imago Dei*
    man creates God in his image, 137
    monarchies and, 119–20
    sovereignty of authority, 123, 131–33, 145
Golden Rule, 70, 101
Gorgias (Plato), 40
Goudzwaard, Bob, 212

Grant, George Parkin, 12, 77
Great Depression (1930's), 215
Great Disruption (Fukuyama), 198
Great Society (Johnson Administration), 215
Great War (1914), 49
Gregory VII (pope), 202
groundmotive, 127
Gulf of Tonkin incident (1964), 25
Gutmann, Amy, 56

harm principle, 87–88
Hauerwas, Stanley, 176, 178–79
Havel, Václav, 12
Hegel, Georg Wilhelm Friedrich, 65, 125
Henry II (King of England), 202
Henry IV (Roman Emperor), 202
Henry VIII (King of England), 50, 71, 98, 164
hereditary monarchy, 71, 107–8, 114, 148, 193, 205
heretical imperative, 84
Herrschaft, 97, 99, 115
hierarchy, 48, 185, 208–9
Hinduism, 126
Hitler, Adolf, 25, 49
Hobbes, Thomas
    authority abuse, 151
    freedom, 66–67
    human will, 13, 116
    individuation, 13
    instruments of power, 38
    laws of nature, 118
    liberty, 64
    political liberalism, 9
    significance of office, 111
    sovereignty, 120, 132
    state of nature, 19, 40, 68
Holmes, Oliver Wendell, 116
Holy Spirit, 109
home-schooling, 104
human community, 147
human law, 124–25
human nature, 118
human rights, 8, 92, 101, 139
human will, 13, 116
humanist idolatry, 92

Huntington, Samuel, 71

Iconoclast Council (754), 206n89
The Idea of Office (Sietsma), 137
identity of a community, 219
idolatry, 13, 92, 133, 185–86
Ignatieff, Michael, 86–87, 92, 101, 198
ignorance, veil of, 75–76
images of authority, 33
imago Dei
    Aquinas on, 136
    Augustine on, 136
    authoritative office as, 8, 16, 163f
    authority and, 8, 16, 21–23, 91, 134–40
    Cultural Mandate and, 21–23
    Kuyper on, 136
    nature of, 115–16, 136–37
    Paul, the apostle on, 136
    Reformed Churches on, 128
immanent horizon of experience, 13
imperative authority, 3, 36, 166–67, 201
incentives, as instrument of power, 38–39
inclusivity, 145–46
individuality, 188
individuals, communities and, 191–92
individuation, 12–13
influence, 25
injustice, 123
innate leadership abilities, 51
institutional communities, 193–97
instrumental approach to authority, 38–42
instrumental limits, 147–48
intercommunal relationships, 192
inter-individual relationships, 192
International Agency for Prevention of Blindness (IAPB), 90
international community, 147
Iranian Revolution (1979), 157–58
Islamic Relief Worldwide, 219

James (King of England), 155
James II (King of England), 154–55

Jefferson, Thomas, 42, 117, 204
Jesus
　charismatic authority, 110
　Golden Rule, 70
　temptation of, 134
Jewish emancipation of 1858 (England), 203
Jewish Federations of North America, 219
Jim Crow laws, 49
John of Paris, 133
John Paul II (pope), 109, 131
Johnson, Administration (Lyndon), 25, 35, 37, 215
Josiah (King of Judea), 117
jural aspect of experience, 129, 207
just war, 153
justice, 39–40, 75–78, 113–14, 124, 129, 224
Justice: Rights and Wrongs (Wolterstorff), 179n45

Kalsbeek, L., 189
Kant, Immanuel
　anarchism, 71–74
　categorical imperative, 10
　deliberative democracy, 56
　freedom as autonomy, 67
　human will, 118, 139
　justice, 129
　liberalism, 74–78
　political liberalism, 9
　positive freedom, 65
　social contracts, 44, 45
Kemal Mustafa, 151
Khomeini, Ruhollah, 158
King, Martin Luther, Jr., 49, 129
kings. *See* monarchy
Kipling, Rudyard, 48
Kirk, Russell, 46
knowledge, 53–57, 102, 181–82
Kohlberg, Lawrence, 10, 68–70
Kraynak, Robert, 90–92
Kropotkin, Peter, 71
Kuyper, Abraham
　common grace, 127
　image of God, 136
　pluriformity of authority, 165
　revolution types, 157
　separation of church and state, 204
　sphere sovereignty, 132, 134, 186
Kyprianou, Spyros, 207

labor
　gendered division of, 50–51
　management and, 209–14
　labor unions, 162, 195, 209–14
laity of church, 205–6
Lasch, Christopher, 55
leadership abilities, 14, 51
League of Nations, 198
legal authority, 71, 99–102
legal tradition, 111–15
legitimacy of authority, 115–19
legitimate authority, 11, 36
Lenin, Vladimir, 18, 35, 110–11, 157
Leo XIII (pope), 125, 131
liberal individualism, 191
liberalism and libertarians, 13, 62, 64, 74–78, 85–88, 119
limits
　to authority, 144–49
　to freedom, 66
Lipset, Seymour Martin, 112–13
Locke, John
　church as voluntary society, 195n78
　On Civil Government, 107
　freedom, 64
　human will, 13
　individuation, 13
　political liberalism, 9
　private property, 151
　social contracts, 41
　voluntary contracts, 42–47
logic, 78
Long Parliament of 1646 (England), 147
Louis XVI (King of France), 156–57
love, authority of, 222–26
Love and Marriage (song), 224n2
Loyola High School v. Courchesne (2010), 160–61
Luther, Martin, 5n4, 164
Lvov, Georgy, 18

Machiavelli, Niccolo, 38, 40
MacIntyre, Alasdair, 113–14, 176
Mackenzie, Shirley, 93–94
Maine (ship), 25
Makarios III (Archbishop, Church of Cyprus), 207
male-centered authority, 50
Mandela, Nelson, 49
manipulation, 25, 33, 42
Manual II (King of Portugal), 98
Mao Zedong, 20, 110, 157
Maritain, Jacques, 123, 131
marriage
    authority within, 142n22
    divorce, 159, 195, 224n3
    exclusivity of, 145–46
    as institutional community, 194–95
    music references to, 224
    as private contract, 220–21
    undifferentiated society, 105–6
Marsilius of Padua, 116
Marx, Karl
    economic power of class, 20, 38–39, 55
    freedom, 65–66, 88
    man creates God in his image, 137
    motive for revolution, 111
    political liberalism and, 9
Marxist philosophy, 39, 97, 111
master-servant relationship, 142n22
matriarchal societies, 105
Matthew (apostle), 143–44
McKinley Administration, 25
Medvedev, Dmitri, 162
Melchizedek (King of Salem), 103
Meribaal, 117
merit
    aristocracy of, 101
    principle of, 53
Mexican Divorce (song), 224n3
Middleton, J. Richard, 22
Milgram, Stanley, 10, 59–61, 78–82, 166
Milgram's experiment, 59–61, 166
military, abuse of authority, 150, 151
Mill, John Stuart, 6, 87, 88

Mitbestimmung (German labor law), 212–13
modal analysis of communities, 186–97, 190f
modal horizon, 186–88
Molnar, Thomas, 196
Monarchist League of Canada, 107–8
monarchy
    appeal to law and, 117
    authority of, 18–19, 22, 98–99
    diving-right of, 119–20, 119n44
    in England, 119–20
    in France, 119–20
    hereditary and, 71, 107–8, 114, 148, 193, 205
    modern-day, 99
    Salic Law and, 50, 96
    tradition and, 95–99
    . *See also specific monarchs by name*
Montesquieu, 64, 120, 164
Monteux, Pierre, 30
moral autonomy, 78–82
moral precepts, 118
moral reasoning, 68–70
moral responsibility, 72
morality, 170
Mormonism, 110
Moses, 8–9, 22, 116, 122
Mother nature, 117
Mountbatten, Lord, 98
Mouskos, Michael, 207
Muhammad, 110
multiple authoritative offices, 160–65, 204–9
Muslims, 110, 119, 121
Mussolini, Benito, 171
My Big Fat Greek Wedding (movie), 49, 104
The Myth of Religious Neutrality (Clouser), 21n5

natural ascendancy, 52
natural communities, 106, 193
natural law, 118, 123–31
natural superiority, 47–53
nature
    defined, 40
    human, 118

laws of, 118
personified or divine, 117
pre-political state of, 43
state of, 19, 40, 64, 68
Nazis party, 49, 61, 134–35, 138
negative vs. positive freedom, 65
nepotism, 53, 99
Neuhaus, Richard John, 121
New Deal (Roosevelt Administration), 215
Nicholas II (Tsar of Russia), 98
Nietzsche, Friedrich, 20, 70, 125
Nikolaevich, Nikolai, 17
Nisbet, Robert, 196
Nixon Administration, 35
nonexecutive authority, 169–70
nonstate communities, 158–59
normative competence, 215–16

O mein Papa (song), 224n4
Obama Administration, 109
O'Donovan, Oliver, 14, 37, 165, 178–84, 213
office
    authoritative. *see* authoritative office
    defined, 137–38
    image of God and, 134–40
    status to, 102–9
    traditional, 111–15
Oh, My Papa (song), 224n4
Olga (Grand Duchess of Russia), 97
Olsen, Glenn W., 77
On Civil Government (Locke), 107
On Liberty (Mill), 6
ontic collectivism, 191
ontological hierarchy, 185
operative authority, 168
oppression, 149–50
oppressive authority, 4–5
organized communities, 106, 193
Orthodox church, 15, 205–6
Ottoman sultanate, 151

Pahlavi, Mohammad Reza, 158
papacy
    election of, 114
    political authority of, 133
    temporal limits of, 148–49
    . *See also specific popes by name*
parental authority, 30, 83, 166–68, 193, 197–201
Parsons, Talcott, 104–5
Pasternak, Boris, 19
paternalistic company, 32
patriarchal societies, 105
patriotism, 224
patronage, 53, 99
Paul (apostle)
    authority, 11, 142
    first and second Adam, 225
    freedom, 67
    government authority, 144
    image of God, 136
    justice, 125
    power of the sword, 38
Peasants' Revolt of 1524–26 (Germany), 5n4
Pentecostalism, 109
perfective function, 174
performative authority, 3, 167
personal authority, 83
personal autonomy, 9
personal freedom, 4
Personal Responsibility and Work Opportunity Reconciliation Act (1996), 219
persuasion, 25, 33–37, 51
persuasive power, 34–37
Pétain, Marshal, 203
Pétain, Philippe, 171
Peter the Great (Russia), 202
Philip II (King of Sapin), 154
physical power, 24
Piaget, Jean, 68–69
Pius XI (pope), 131
Plantagenets monarchs in England, 119–20
plastic horizon, 188
Plato
    doctrine on the forms, 124
    education of children, 200
    justice, 39–40, 129
    monarchy, 117
    office as locus of authority, 111
    polis and the individual, 191

political order, 25, 38
The Republic, 38–40, 48, 53, 177, 191
society as a hierarchy, 48
The Statesman, 39, 53
Plessy vs. Ferguson (1896), 49
pluralist principle, 131
pluriform society, 105
pluriformity of authority
    authoritative office and, 149
    authority in practice, 197–221
    church and state authorities, 201–4, 219
    ecclesial and political authorities, 201–4
    functions of, 171–78, 173f
    individuation and differentiation, 13–15
    labor and management, 209–14
    multiple authoritative offices, 160–65, 204–9
    parental authority and, 32
    parents' and children's authority, 197–201
    sovereignty and, 184–97
    taxonomy of, 165–71
    theology of, 178–84
    welfare state, 214–21
    in the workplace, 209–14
Poland, Solidarity labor union, 162, 195
Polanyi, Michael, 181
police state, 150
political authority, 8, 182, 201–4
political culture, 111–12
political liberalism, 9
political loyalty, 224
political pluralism, 178
political realism, 38
political régime, 176
political revolution, 153–55
political rights, 217–18
politico-legal authority, 168–69
politics, as the authoritative allocation of values, 32
pope. *See* papacy
popular will, 122
positive law, 118

positive vs. negative freedom, 65
possession of powers, 26
poverty, 216–17, 220
power
    abuse of, 25
    authority and, 7–8, 17–28, 182–83
    differentiation and, 23
    disincentives, as instrument of, 38–39
    distribution of, 97
    division of, 64–65
    elements of defining, 7–8
    incentives, as instrument of, 38–39
    instruments of, 38–42
    natural superiority and, 47–53
    separation of, 120
    superior knowledge and, 53–57
    of the sword, 38
    symbolic elements of, 27
    voluntary contracts and, 42–47
    . *See also specific types of power*
power of attorney, 167
Presbyterian Church, 15, 148–49, 205
principle of autonomy, 177
principles of right, 43
Prinsterer, Groen, G., 186
private property, 43, 151
privileges, 101
    . *See also* rights
profit-sharing, 212n97
Programme of the German Workers' Party, 65, 65n8
promises, 41–42
Protestant Reformed Church denomination, 211
Protestant traditions, 86n50, 126–27, 141n1, 184
    . *See also* Roman Catholic tradition; *specific Protestant denominations*
prudence, 175–76
psychological manipulation, 42
psychological power, 20, 28–34
public justice, 198, 216, 224
public safety, 172
public servants, 144
Pullman, George, 31–32
Putin, Vladimir, 162

Putnam, Robert, 112

queens. *See* monarchy
Queen's Privy Council for Canada, 93–94, 100, 114
Quiet Revolution of 1960 (Quebec), 162

racist policies, 49–50
raison d'etre of the gathered church, 206
Rawls, John
  categorical imperative, 10
  compressive doctrines, 121
  deliberative democracy, 56
  justice, 44, 46, 129
  liberalism, 74–78
reason and reasoning, 34–35, 37, 126, 129
Rebel Without a Cause (movie), 103
Reformation, 91, 126, 130, 132
Reformed Churches
  approach to society, 133
  church polity, 15
  Cultural Mandate, 21, 89
  differentiation, 108
  government role supporting faith, 204
  image of God and, 128, 134–35
  on labor unions, 211
  offices in, 205
  on ontological hierarchy, 185
  sin of idolatry, 185
  Synod of Utrecht, 204
The Republic (Plato), 25, 38–40, 48, 53, 177
respect, 140–42
responsible agency, 8
Resurrection and Moral Order (O'Donovan), 179
retirement from office, 148–49
retrocipatory analogy, 188
revolutionaries, 111
revolutionary uprisings, 152–58
  . *See also specific revolutions*
Right to Sight, 90
rights
  human rights, 8, 92, 101

  of individuals, 86–87, 101
  legitimacy of, 90–92
  principles of, 43
  of property, 44
Rights of the Child declaration (Somalia), 198, 198n84
Rights Revolution (Ignatieff), 198
Roman Catholic tradition
  in Canada, 160–62
  on democracy, 171
  in France, 203
  on natural law, 126
  offices in, 205
  papacy of, 114, 133, 148–49
  Second Vatican Council, 206
  on sovereignty, 123
  subsidiarity principle, 131–32, 177, 178
  universality of, 146
  . *See also* Protestant traditions
Roosevelt, Eleanor, 218
Roosevelt Administration (Franklin D.), 71, 100, 215, 217
Rousseau, Jean-Jacques
  authority as socially constructed, 138
  freedom as autonomy, 67
  human will, 13, 116, 118, 122
  individuation, 13
  natural superiority, 47
  political liberalism, 9
  positive freedom, 65
  religious believers and general will, 203
  social contracts, 25, 41, 44–45, 67
routinization of charisma, 111
Russia
  Nicholas II, 98
  Olga (Grand Duchess), 97
  Peter the Great, 202
  Revolution, 17–18, 35, 151, 157
  tsars, 17–18, 35, 97, 187

Salic Law, 50, 96
Salvation Army, 219
Saul (King of Judah), 116
Schaeffer, Francis, 127–28, 130
Schinkelkerk congregation, 134–35

schism (1054), 205
Second Vatican Council (1962–65), 206
secular political authority, 182
segregation, racial, 49–50, 129
self-aggrandizement, 150
self-esteem, 139–40
self-interested domination of authority, 6
self-interested power, 25–26
Sennett, Richard, 27, 28–32, 63, 111
separation of powers, 120
service or servant, 137–38
Shah of Iran (Pahlavi, Mohammad Reza), 158
Siddhartha Gautama, 110
Sietsma, Kornelis, 134–35, 137, 140
Simon, Yves René
    authoritative office, 144
    authority, 4, 62
    authority's function, 165, 171–78
    coach-driver authority, 44
    natural law, 123
    parental authority, 30, 83
sin
    defying authority and, 5
    of idolatry, 185
    natural law and, 127–28, 130
    social authority and, 182
    of willful heteronomy, 73
Skillen, James W., 219n107
slavery, 49, 142n22, 154
slaves by nature, 47
Smith, Adam, 64
Smith, James K. A., 186
Smith, Joseph, 110, 121
social authority, 180–81
social categories, 190f
Social Contract (Rousseau), 25
social contracts, 41, 42–47, 67, 75
social revolution, 154, 155–58
socialist, 71–72
societal relation of authority and subordination, 191
society
    defined, 192
    differentiation of, 102–9
Socrates, 38–40, 53–54, 70, 110

Solidarity labor union (Poland), 162, 195
Solomon (King of Israel), 117
Somalia, Rights of the Child declaration, 198, 198n84
Southern Christian Leadership Conference, 49
sovereignty
    authoritative office and, 164–65
    as belonging to God, 123, 131–33, 145
    source of political authority, 120
    sphere of, 132, 134, 184–97
    spatial or numerical limits, 146–47
sphere sovereignty, 132, 134, 184–97
Stalin, Joseph, 157
state of nature, 19, 40, 64, 68
The Statesman (Plato), 39, 53
Statist totalitarianism, 14
stewardship over whole creation, 163, 225
stoics and stoicism, 117–18, 124
Strauss, Leo, 65, 70, 70n18
Suarez, Francisco, 125
subordinate authority, 3
subordination, 196
subsidiarity principle, 131–32, 177, 178
substantive limits, 147
substitutional functions of authority, 171
superior authority, 3
superiority, 47–53
symbolic elements of power, 27
Synod of the Christian Reformed Church in North America, 204
Synod of Utrecht of the Reformed Churches (Netherlands), 204
systematic theory of authority, 142n22

taxonomy of authority, 165–71, 166f
teachers, responsibility to model truth-seeking, 222
technology, 53, 55–56, 88–92
temporal limits, 148
temptation, 134
Thatcher, Margaret, 192, 215
Third Republic (France), 203

index

Thomas à Kempis, 223
Thomas Aquinas. *See* Aquinas (Thomas)
Thompson, Dennis, 56
threats, 41–42
three-fold order of church office, 205
Tito (Marshal of Yugoslav), 212
Toscanini, Arturo, 30
totalitarianism, 14, 145, 155–56, 162
trade unions, 209
tradition
   in constitutional governments, 93–95
   legal tradition, 111–15
   in society, 103
traditional authority, 95–99
transcendent authority, 12
tribal communities, 189–190n75
trinity. *See* God; Holy Spirit; Jesus
Trudeau, Pierre, 162
tsars, 17–18, 35, 97, 187
tyranny, 45, 145, 150, 152–53

ubiquity of authority, 1–6
Ulyanov, Vladimir Ilyich. *See* Lenin, Vladimir
undifferentiated communities, 189–190n75
unemployment, 217
United Auto Workers, 210
United Nations, 197–98
United States
   constitution, 95, 100, 101, 201, 203
   Continental Congress, 153
   Declaration of Independence, 42
   Vietnam, military action in, 25, 35
Universal Declaration of Human Rights (UDHR), 139, 218
unjust law, 128–29
unthinking compliance, 80
Uzziah (King of Judah), 103

Van Heusen, Jimmy, 224n2
van Prinsterer, Guillaume Groen, 132, 157
veil of ignorance, 75–76
Verba, Sidney, 112
Victoria (Queen of England), 96
Vietnam, U.S. military action in, 25, 35
virtue and virtues, 40, 127, 173
VISION 2020: The Right to Sight, 90
voluntary contracts, 41, 42–47
von Bismarck, Otto, 215
von Hayek, Friedrich, 64
von Mises, Ludwig, 64

Wallace, George, 50
The Ways of Judgment (O'Donovan), 179
Weber, Max
   charismatic authority, 14, 51, 109–11, 151
   legal authority, 71, 99–102
   legitimate authority, 11, 36
   norms of office, 144–45
   traditional authority, 95–99
   traditional office, 111, 138
Welfare in America (Carlson-Thies & Skillen), 219n107
Welfare Reform Act (1996), 215, 219
welfare state, 214–21
Weltanschauung, 98
The White Man's Burden (Rudyard), 48
Wilhelm II (Emperor or Kaiser of Germany), 98
Wilhelmina (Queen of Netherlands), 96, 99, 134–35
will
   general will, 44–45, 67, 116
   human will, 13, 116
   popular will, 122
willful heteronomy, 73
Wolff, Robert Paul, 10, 37, 71–74
Wolters, Albert M., 127, 146n23
Wolterstorff, Nicholas, 179n45
women, position in society, 50–51
workplace authority, 209–14
World Health Organization (WHO), 90

Yoder, John Howard, 178

www.ingramcontent.com/pod-product-compliance
Lightning Source LLC
Chambersburg PA
CBHW050439240426
43661CB00055B/2438